A NATION ON FIRE

America in the Wake of the King Assassination

Clay Risen

WILEY

John Wiley & Sons, Inc.

Published by John Wiley & Sons, Inc., Hoboken, New Jersey
Published simultaneously in Canada

Photo insert credits: DC Public Library; © Washington Post: page 1; Lyndon Johnson Library and Museum: pages 2 top, 4 top, 6 top; Star Collection, DC Public Library; © Washington Post: page 2 bottom; Getty: page 3 top; Corbis: pages 3 bottom, 4 bottom, 7 top, 8 bottom; Lt. James V. Kelly, Baltimore Police Department: pages 5 top, 7 bottom, 8 top; Magnum: page 5 bottom; courtesy of the Washingtoniana Division, DC Public Library: page 6 bottom.

For general information about our other products and services, please contact our Customer Care Department within the United States at (800) 762-2974, outside the United States at (317) 572-3993 or fax (317) 572-4002.

Wiley also publishes its books in a variety of electronic formats. Some content that appears in print may not be available in electronic books. For more information about Wiley products, visit our web site at www.wiley.com.

Library of Congress Cataloging-in-Publication Data:

Risen, Clay.
A nation on fire : America in the wake of the King assassination / Clay Risen.
p.   cm.
Includes bibliographical references and index.
ISBN 978-0-470-17710-5 (cloth)
1. Race riots—United States—History—20th century.   2. King, Martin Luther, Jr., 1929–1968—Assassination.   3. Inner cities—United States—History—20th century.   4. United States—Race relations.   5. African Americans—Social conditions—1964–1975.   6. United States—Social conditions—20th century.   I. Title.
HV6477.R57   2009
973.923—dc22

2008026789

Printed in the United States of America

10   9   8   7   6   5   4   3   2   1

For Joanna

We learn, as the thread plays out, that we belong
Less to what flatters us than to what scars.

—Stanley Kunitz, "The Dark and the Fair"

Contents

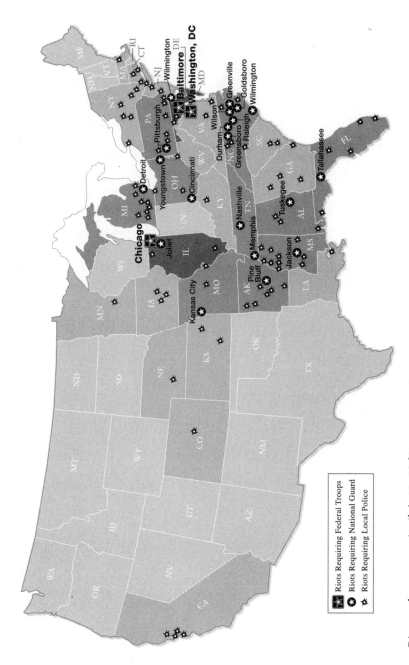

Riots and responses, April 4–11, 1968.

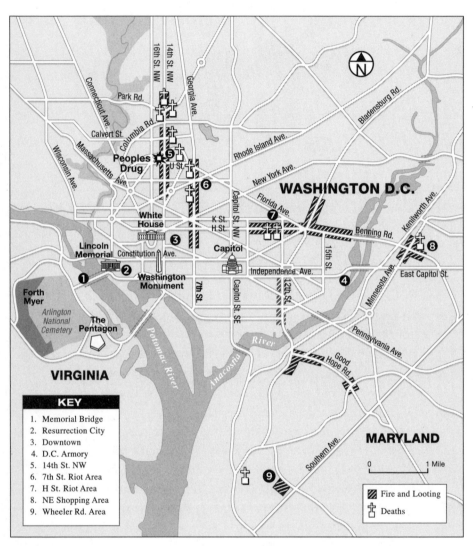

Washington, D.C., April 4–11, 1968.

Acknowledgments

This book emerged from a conversation with my parents about their experiences during the riots. For their inspiration, as well as their encouragement throughout my life, I thank them.

I owe a large debt to my good friends Haywood Moxley and Margaret Renkl. Haywood was my high school English teacher and almost literally taught me to read and write; Margaret is my editor at the *Nashville Scene* and gave me my first journalism gig.

Anyone who writes history knows the importance of librarians and archivists. Too many to name individually, I thank them collectively. I also thank the many people who talked to me for the book, including Ewart Brown, Marshall Brown, Joseph Califano Jr., Ramsey Clark, Paul Devrouax, Peter Edelman, Jim Gaither, Tony Gittens, Adrienne Israel, Lawrence Levinson, Donald Mayhew, Harry McPherson, Steven Ober, George Pelecanos, Stephen Pollack, Leroy Rhode, Isabel Sawhill, Ed Smith, Bob Walton, and Roger Wilkins. Thanks as well to Lieutenant James Kelly of the Baltimore Police Department, who allowed me the use of his stunning collection of riot photographs.

My job as managing editor at *Democracy: A Journal of Ideas* presented both an advantage and a challenge. The intellectual stimulation, not to mention the paycheck, helped get me through my research and writing. But the job also could have been a hindrance. Luckily, the journal's coeditors, Kenneth Baer and Andrei Cherny, as well as our associate editor, Ethan Porter, were more than willing to give me the space and time to complete my research and draft, and later the wise input while I went through revisions. Thank you. I would also like to thank the folks who read portions or entire drafts of my manuscript, including Lee Drutman, Rick Perlstein, Jim Sleeper, Tom Sugrue, and Elbert Ventura. Tom Lindenfeld gets my thanks for setting up many of my early contacts around Washington; ditto to Rachel Hertz and Russ Cobb for putting me up—and putting up with me—during my research adventure at the Johnson archives.

Much thanks as well to my agent, Heather Schroder, who helped conceive my initial proposal and who deserves all the credit for finding it a suitable home. Likewise to my editor, Eric Nelson, who shepherded the book through countless revisions; it was through his keen eye that I was able to see the many holes and weak points in my argument.

My wife, Joanna Osborne, has suffered greatly for this book, perhaps more than even myself. The ever-expanding lake of books and the mountains of research boxes that at times threatened to take over our bedroom; my epic sojourns to libraries; the long hours at my desk; the month I spent at my parents' house writing—through all this, she supported me in every way possible. It is to her that this book is dedicated, and it is to her that I dedicate my life.

PROLOGUE

It was Thursday night, April 4, 1968, and my mother was sitting in the living room of her Alexandria, Virginia, apartment watching a cascade of horrifying images sweep across the television screen. First came the news that Martin Luther King Jr. had been shot and killed in Memphis. Soon after came President Lyndon Johnson, speaking from the White House, pleading with the country to avoid violence in the midst of national mourning. And then, not an hour later, footage of looting and burning along Washington's Fourteenth Street, only a few miles away.

The week leading up to that night had been euphoric. Johnson, by then a despised figure, had pulled out of the presidential race on Sunday, opening the way for Bobby Kennedy's historic trek to fill his slain brother's post. In the same speech that he made public his withdrawal, Johnson had also announced a limited halt to bombing in Vietnam as a gesture toward peace talks. It was a gamble, but three days later the North Vietnamese signaled their interest, the same day they lifted the siege at Khe Sanh.

And then King was dead.

Though she was watching the news unfold from her suburban home, every morning my mother commuted into Washington to her secretary's desk at a brokerage firm on the corner of Connecticut Avenue and K Street, a few blocks northwest of the White House. She grew up in the D.C. suburbs, first Hyattsville on the Maryland side, then McLean in Virginia. But like most other suburbanites in the postwar years, she had a close relationship with the city. Back then, many suburbs were strictly for living. As in cities nationwide, many people still did their working, shopping, and dining in the city. What would soon become the sprawling edge cities of Tyson's Corner and Columbia— and countless other crabgrass towns—were still bucolic crossroads.

And so, despite the riots the previous night, Friday morning my mother joined tens of thousands of other suburbanites on their Friday morning commute. The violence had subsided around midnight; the city was safe until dark, everyone figured, and by then the collective urge to violence might well have passed anyway.

At noon, though, she started hearing whispers around the office. Looting had been reported along Fourteenth Street; some of her colleagues said they'd seen smoke rising over the rooftops. As people gathered in small groups and conferred in hushed tones, a phone rang on a nearby desk. One of my mother's coworkers, a young black woman named Alva (she doesn't remember her last name), answered. On the other end was Alva's mother, who lived in Shaw, the neighborhood at the heart of the disorder.

When she was done, she turned to the rest of the office.

There's a mob headed this way, Alva said. Everyone's gotta get out of here.

My mother's office wasn't the only one to get the message. Out on the street, she found anarchy, rush hour in the middle of the day. No one obeyed traffic lights. Drivers abandoned their cars in the middle of the road. Cars couldn't move because everyone wanted to move. It was the biggest traffic jam in city history.

There was no subway back then, so my mother ran until she found a bus. Most were already full. Eventually she found one with space and squeezed on board. "I can't believe the bus didn't tip over, there were so many people on the bus," she told me years later. After what seemed like a day, they made it to the Key Bridge, spanning the Potomac between Georgetown and Virginia and providing a wide-angle view of the District.

From there, she could look back at the city. Dozens of smoke plumes striated the skyline. Washington was burning.

This all happened long before my parents met. At the time, my father was living seven hundred miles away in a northern Illinois apartment, working at the sprawling Joliet Army Ammunition Plant. A twenty-four-year-old ROTC graduate from Georgia Tech, his bad vision had kept him out of combat, and his engineering background made him useful as a quality-control manager, checking the battle readiness of bullets, shells, and bombs.

Though the Joliet facility was one of the largest munitions factories in the world, life was pretty slow. Most of the employees were private sector, and at times the plant felt more like an appliance manufacturer than a weapons arsenal. After a few months, my father even got to live in his own place off base. On weekends he and his buddies headed to Rush Street, the main drag for Chicago nightlife.

The mood at the plant changed within hours of King's assassination. The gates were locked. Officers living off base were corralled into plant barracks. And when riots broke out in Chicago, the commander ordered all men—my father included—to grab their battle fatigues and rifles. When looting broke out in Joliet, he issued live ammunition. For days, my father and dozens of other servicemen at the plant stood ready to go to war with their fellow citizens.

My parents' stories, which became the impetus for this book, don't tell everything there is to know about the April riots. But they illustrate much of what makes that week so important in American history. Until then, the long, hot summers of ghetto rioting had played out exclusively among blacks, in black neighborhoods, with black victims. But, egged on by the likes of Strom Thurmond on the right and Stokely Carmichael on the left, few—black or white—thought it would stay that way.

When the April riots broke out, my father's commanding officer was hardly the only person in the country to believe that a racial conflagration was at hand. That a race war did not in fact follow takes nothing away from the significance of the moment: 39 people were dead, more than 2,600 were injured, and 21,000 had been arrested. The damages were estimated at $65 million—about $385 million today. Federal troops occupied Washington, Chicago, and Baltimore; National Guardsmen were deployed to more than a dozen other cities. Riots ripped the hearts out of scores of inner-city communities, scaring away residents, merchants, anyone who could afford to flee to the suburbs. There had been riots before—Harlem, Watts, Newark, Detroit—but never so many, in so many places, at the same time. As late as November 1967, a majority of whites told pollsters that a riot could never happen in their hometown. After more than 120 cities erupted in violence five months later, it's a good bet that few people still agreed.

A race war did in fact come to America that day—but it turned out to be a cold war, not a hot one. When the smoke cleared and the sirens ran down, an invisible wall went up between urban and suburban America, every bit as real as the one in Berlin. Many would argue that it's still standing today.

The 1968 riots provided an entrée for conservatives to finally, fully assert law and order as a national political issue. Something that had been brewing for decades at the local level, and that had played a role in the GOP congressional and state-level victories of 1966, became the single most important domestic concern in the 1968 presidential race. Polls repeatedly put racial unrest at a par with, and even above, the Vietnam War. Richard Nixon, who had largely avoided talking about riots and civil rights before April, now made law and order—and the revulsion of white suburbia against the violent images of rioters reacting to King's death—a central theme in his campaign. The riots played a critical role in giving the campaign a bridge to capture the white racial backlash, which it recast as the "Silent Majority": in Nixon speechwriter Ray Price's words, the "rebellion by the quiet Americans—those who pay their taxes, go to their jobs, perform their duties, maintain their homes, send their children to school and college."[1]

Along with the growing appeal of law and order as a political attitude came a rejection of liberal domestic policy, which had dominated national politics since Franklin Roosevelt, and its ameliorationist, integrationist attitude toward the inner-city poor. Conservatives drew a direct line connecting ghetto unrest and liberal social policy, an accusation that also appealed to the pocketbooks of a new generation of middle-class, suburban whites.

And whereas politicians beforehand had often portrayed the ghetto as something to integrate into the rest of society, the riots gave impetus to a new domestic militarism that saw the ghetto as an alien territory within American cities, a cancer that had to be isolated from the rest of the body public. Though Nixon was one of the first to take advantage of the situation, this wasn't an exclusively Republican endeavor: by the early 1970s both parties were competing to out "law and order" the other. In the words of legal theorist Jonathan Simon, in the forty-year wake of the riots, "Americans have built a new civil and political order structured around the problem of violent crime."[2]

In his 1973 State of the Union address, Nixon declared: "A few years ago we constantly heard that urban America was on the brink of collapse. It was one minute to midnight, we were told, and the bells of doom were beginning to toll. One history of America in the 1960s was even given the title *Coming Apart*. Today, America is no longer coming apart"—after which he began to freeze, cut, or eliminate scores of domestic programs.[3] Of course, Nixon's declaration was only true for the millions of Americans now safely ensconced in the suburbs. For those in the inner city, the urban crisis was getting worse. But the ebbing of the "riot era" left a thick air of contempt in American politics toward the inner city, and Nixon and subsequent presidents from both parties relied on that revulsion to drive cuts in small-business loans, funds for inner-city schools, and job training, as well as antibusing campaigns and anticrime legislation.

Despite the wave of urban gentrification of the late 1990s and early 2000s, today the hour of urban crisis continues in dozens of American cities. Blacks in Washington, most strikingly, have not seen a significant increase in income, educational attainment, or job prospects in the forty years since. The urban crisis did not begin the night King was killed. But the long echo of the riots that followed is a critical reason why America abandoned any effort to end it.

It might be surprising, at first, to learn that in the entire library of books on King and his time, not a single work exists that discusses the weeks following his assassination. But it makes sense: King's significance is in his life's work, not his early death. And, as a matter of priorities, telling King's life story, as the country digested the enormous changes the civil rights movement wrought, rightly took precedence in the subsequent forty years. David Garrow, Taylor Branch, and other historians have done the world a service by rendering his life in such thorough detail. King's life is a large enough topic on its own, and these two alone have written more than four thousand pages on it.

But such elision makes less sense when one considers the ever-swelling number of histories on 1968—Mark Kurlansky's *1968*, Jules Witcover's *The Year the Dream Died*, Charles Kaiser's *1968 in America*—and on the 1960s in general—Todd Gitlin's *Years of Hope, Days of Rage*, Maurice Isserman and Michael Kazin's *America Divided*, Milton Viorst's *Fire in the Streets*. While most of them touch on King's death and a few briefly discuss the riots that followed, no single work presents anything more than a superficial, journalistic account of that pivotal week.

These histories do more than skip over that April. Aside from a spate of sociological research in the 1970s, very little work exists on the riots of the 1960s at all. There are a few contemporary accounts of Newark and Detroit and a few histories of Watts, but little else, and nothing significant has appeared in more than a generation. When I mentioned that I was writing a book on the 1968 riots, several people assumed I meant the police riot at the Democratic National Convention in Chicago. When I told them there had been a riot in the Windy City several months before that in which 12 people died and 300 square blocks on the West Side were destroyed, they were shocked—and these included people who were around at the time. Given that over five summers they collectively resulted in 225 dead, 4,000 wounded, and $427 billion in damages (in 2007 dollars), it is striking how little is known about them today.[4] The riots are not just undiscussed today. They have been forgotten.

It's tempting to read a sort of implicit racism into this historical occlusion. The 1960s is, if anything, a decade overexposed in our culture, and yet so much of that exposure focuses on the experiences of white, middle-class Americans. Very little attention is paid to the black experience of the 1960s, outside of glorious set pieces such as the March on Washington or the media frenzy around the Black Panthers. Needless to say, most blacks didn't participate in either, and yet that doesn't make their stories any less noteworthy.

But there is something deeper and more complex going on. The riots seemed to fulfill the worst predictions of white segregationists: that the civil rights movement, its techniques as well as its accomplishments, would lead to violence. Those white Americans who didn't draw such a conclusion for themselves had it forced on them by countless conservative commentators in politics and the media. "We are now witnessing the whirlwind sowed years ago when some preachers and teachers began telling people that each man could be his own judge in his own case," South Carolina senator Strom Thurmond wrote to his constituents in an April 15, 1968, newsletter.[5]

Long before King's death, the fact that so many black communities were falling into disorder seemed to scrub off the moral patina of the civil rights era. As Daniel Patrick Moynihan said after the 1965 Watts riot, urban disorder "threw the civil rights movement entirely off balance. Until then, theirs had been the aggrieved, the just, the righteous cause. In the South an old game had been going on with a new rule, imperfectly understood by whites, that the first side to resort to violence—lost. Now in the North the Negroes had resorted to violence, in a wild destructive explosion that shattered, probably forever, the image of non-violent suffering."[6] Countless polls show a remarkable drop in white support for the civil rights movement after Watts, support that never came back. A May 1965 Harris poll found nationwide white support for civil rights demonstrations at an all-time high of 42 percent; by June 1967, 82 percent said they had an unfavorable opinion of them—and that was before the large-scale Newark and Detroit riots.[7]

Unable to see blacks as anything other than a solid, undifferentiated mass, white observers could hardly avoid drawing a thick red line at August 1965: blacks before Watts were all innocent victims; afterward they were all ungrateful looters. Unable to see the riots within a more complex reading of black history, we are confronted with a seemingly irresolvable paradox. Is it any wonder that in the years since, we have taken the easy way out and erased the riots from our popular memory?

And yet a full accounting of the era demands that we give the riots a more central place in postwar American history. Nor should we be afraid of tarnishing the civil rights movement's legacy. We do it more harm, in fact, by continuing the chronological dichotomy, as if every black in America marched with the SCLC until 1965, when they signed up with the Panthers.[8]

But more importantly, rioting was not primarily a result of civil rights activism, even in its most radical strain. Contrary to Thurmond's ravings on the Senate floor, the ghetto frustrations that led to civil disorder were more a product of long-standing, deep-seated fissures— between blacks and employers, shopkeepers and customers, police and civilians, landlords and tenants—than they were of "rising expectations" or the unintended consequences of civil disobedience.

And yet because we have incorporated the propaganda about radicals instigating violence into our collective memory, we have largely refused to recognize such currents, and in doing so we have ignored the very idea that the ghetto has a history, a character, a life, and a politics of its own. Too many people still think Stokely Carmichael caused the Washington riot. This book will show why they're wrong.

The week following King's death was a signal moment in postwar American history, the violent collision of so many trends, subtle and not so subtle, working their way up through the national psyche: black frustrations, the breakdown of the liberal state, white working-class backlash. They all came to a glaring, ugly head between April 4 and April 11, a week that began with one of the single ugliest events in American history and ended with one of its greatest moments, when Johnson signed the fair housing bill.

King's death was not the end of the story, but the beginning of a new chapter. At the same time, it did not guarantee that things would turn out the way they did; no single event in history ever does. In the days following King's death Bobby Kennedy, almost alone among American politicians, was willing to offer an alternative lesson from King's death, one that pointed toward hope rather than fear and despair. Had Kennedy lived, perhaps we would look back on April 1968 in a different light. History, however, plows on; Kennedy died two months later, and the Republicans marched into the White House.

At the same time, King's death had a decisive effect on the black activist community. In the months leading up to the assassination, Stokely Carmichael, in particular, was moving away from the confused, bombastic media darling he had been since assuming the mantle of unofficial speaker of the black radical community two years earlier. He was making amends with King and developing roots in the Washington activist circles. But King's death sent him over the edge and, eventually, into self-exile in Africa. Carmichael was arguably the only leader charismatic enough to build any semblance of a coherent black activist community after King; without him, the movement spun apart into a thousand pieces.

Had the riots not occurred, domestic liberalism would have still fallen into crisis; the GOP would have still been able to ride a white backlash into lasting political dominance; the nation's ghettos would certainly have continued to deteriorate. But in trying to understand such important trends, it is critical to locate the key moments. The week after King's death was one such moment. The goal of this book is to show, in minute detail, precisely how important it was.

1

King, Johnson, and the Terrible, Glorious Thirty-first Day of March

Dr. Martin Luther King Jr. delivered his last Sunday sermon on March 31, 1968, at Washington's still-uncompleted National Cathedral. Some three thousand people jammed the cavernous sanctuary to hear him; another thousand listened on speakers set up outside and in a room at the nearby St. Albans School.[1]

The sermon, one of the greatest of his career, centered around the upcoming Poor People's Campaign, in which hundreds would camp on the Mall and carry out demonstrations around the capital. They would come from around the country, many by mule train, a host of Americans of all types—black, white, Hispanic, Native American, coming from the South, Appalachia, and the Southwest. For King, this was to be the apotheosis of his lifelong activism: not just civil rights, but human rights, the right to a decent living, the right from fear and want. It was, he said, the least a country as rich as his could do for its downtrodden.

Like Rip Van Winkle, King told his audience, America risked "sleeping through a revolution." His voice booming over the loudspeakers, King said, "There can be no gainsaying of the fact that a great revolution is taking place in the world today. In a sense it is a triple revolution: that is, a technological revolution, with the impact of automation and cybernation; then there is a revolution in weaponry, with the emergence of atomic and nuclear weapons of warfare; then there is a human rights revolution, with the freedom explosion that is taking place all over the world."

Then, dipping into one of his favorite Gospel parables—that of Dives, a wealthy man, and Lazarus, a beggar who sat outside his door—King explained that Dives went to hell not because he was rich but because he refused to help where he could. So, too, he said, would the United States be damned if in its abundance it refused to help those in need, both at home and abroad. "There is nothing new about poverty," he said. "What is new is that we now have the techniques and the resources to get rid of poverty. The real question is whether we have the will."[2]

The question of will was one King had confronted often in recent months. The past few years had not been kind to the civil rights leader. Since his success at Selma and the resulting passage of the Voting Rights Act in 1965, King had been trying to broaden the scope of his movement, both in its reach—out west, up north—and scope—taking on housing discrimination, poverty, and the war. But the public, the media, and the political establishment increasingly saw him in a negative light, a has-been who achieved great victories earlier in the decade but who had no answers for the new issues of the day. Even Walter Fauntroy, his loyal Washington representative, called King a "spent force." That previous fall his literary agent had been unable to find a single magazine to excerpt his latest book.[3]

King had been gradually losing support since 1965, but his real slide in the public's eye began on April 4, 1967, when he delivered a scathing critique of the Vietnam War at New York's Riverside Church. King had never addressed the war publicly before. Why now? Because, he told the overflow crowd of thousands, whenever he went into the streets to try to tamp down riots and urban violence, people asked, "What about Vietnam?" If violence is wrong, why is America overseas killing thousands, to no clear end? "Their questions hit home, and I knew that I could never again raise my voice against the violence of the oppressed in the ghettos without having first spoken clearly to the greatest purveyor of violence in the world today: my own government." [4] The audience erupted in applause.

But King's reception beyond the Upper West Side was not so positive. The speech was almost universally panned. Johnson's staff immediately saw it as a thinly veiled attack on the president. John Roche, Johnson's academic liaison, told the president in a memo that King, "who is inordinately ambitious and quite stupid (a bad combination) . . . is painting himself into a corner with a bunch of losers."[5] King caught flak from Jewish war veterans (who saw his extreme pacifism as an implicit criticism of World War II), the *Washington Post* editorial board, and thousands of letter-writing Americans. Johnson went after King with a vengeance, at one point even ordering the Internal Revenue Service to investigate his tax returns.[6]

The widespread condemnation sent King into a deep funk, one compounded by the massive riots in Newark and Detroit that summer. On Labor Day weekend he gave the keynote speech at a gathering of New Left groups, the Conference for a New Politics, in Chicago; he was shouted down by black radicals crying, "Kill whitey!"[7] As he told two of his advisers, "There were dark days before, but this is the darkest."[8]

King was also in the midst of a personal, intellectual change. He had always seen economic and social justice as necessary counterparts to racial justice, but between 1955 and 1965 his activism had focused on the last of the three. The Watts riots and a summer spent organizing in Chicago made him reassess. In May 1967, he told workers in New York City that the movement needed a second phase, an effort to change not just racial laws, but the unjust allocation of national resources that upheld poverty and economic division. The achievements of the civil rights era were necessary and remarkable, but, he conceded, they did little for lower-class blacks, in the South and elsewhere. If anything, he said in January 1968, "The plight of the Negro poor, the masses of Negroes, has worsened over the last few years."[9]

King soon realized he needed a new project, a way to fuse the successful strategies of his southern civil rights efforts with his new emphasis on poverty and the war. And, over the course of the fall and early winter, he hit on a plan: the Poor People's Campaign.

First conceived of by Robert Kennedy and given shape by activist Marian Wright, the campaign would be a latter-day Bonus Army, bringing hundreds of poor Americans of all races and regions to the capital, where they would camp on the Mall and conduct sit-ins on Capitol Hill. Wright first presented the plan to King at a September 1967

Southern Christian Leadership Conference meeting in rural Virginia, but the bulk of the planning took place during a five-day retreat in Frogmore, South Carolina, that winter.[10] To dramatize the event, which was scheduled for mid-April, participants would converge on the capital by foot and mule train. Once there, they would build Resurrection City, a massive shantytown on the Mall, positioned with the national monuments in the background.

The mere presence of so many poor people in Washington would be disruptive, they realized. Andrew Young, one of King's closest advisers, imagined "a thousand people in need of health and medical attention sitting around District hospitals."[11] Such aggressive posturing made others in the SCLC to blanch; as executive director William Rutherford recounted, "Almost no one on the staff thought that the next priority, the next major movement, should be focused on poor people or the question of poverty in America."[12]

The truth was, no one, not even King, knew what to expect once everyone arrived in the city. It was one thing to organize a march. But what to do with hundreds of desperately poor people, so far from home? How do you feed them? How do you keep them engaged—and calm? King promised to maintain peace, and he worked tirelessly that winter to bring militants such as Stokely Carmichael and H. Rap Brown onto his side.

But he didn't help matters by making predictions—which sounded like veiled threats—about what would happen if no federal action came of the Poor People's Campaign. "We are not coming to Washington to engage in any histrionic action," he said days before he was killed, "nor are we coming to tear up Washington. I don't like to predict violence, but if nothing is done between now and June to raise ghetto hope, I feel this summer will not only be as bad, but worse than last year."[13]

It didn't really matter what King said, though. Fear of the campaign was rampant among the public, the media, and Congress. As one op-ed writer put it in the *Washington Evening Star*, "There is no point in blinding ourselves to the obvious: Martin Luther King's plans for massive demonstrations and civil disobedience in Washington will create conditions that could lead to a tragic riot."[14]

Already agitated by the past summer's riots and afraid of a repeat, or worse, in 1968, the federal government looked at the Poor People's Campaign from inside a bunker. Congress held hearings.

The D.C. Police Department developed extensive antiriot plans. Hotline phones, linked to the police, were installed in Senate offices. And the FBI deployed a massive effort to subvert the entire project, going so far as to plant stories among southern blacks that the SCLC would bring them to Washington and then refuse to take them home.[15] But it didn't work—by March 1968, hundreds were getting ready to move on the capital.

In early 1968, though, events transpired that would fatefully divert King from his planning. On February 12 thousands of city garbage workers went on strike in Memphis, calling for higher wages and better working conditions; pay rates had stagnated for years, and two workers had recently been killed by a malfunctioning garbage compactor.

Memphis is a city of the South, but it is somehow misplaced within it. Though Tennessee had relatively few blacks in 1968, they made up 40 percent of Memphis's citizenry. While the city had a strong, educated black middle class, 58 percent of its black population was poor, 10 percent higher than the national average and four times the rate for the city's whites.[16] And though Tennessee was not a Deep South state, in its culture and politics Memphis was all but an extension of Mississippi—it is said that the Delta begins in the lobby of the Peabody Hotel. And Memphis mixed the worst of northern and southern racism: Legal segregation was firmly established, and where it wasn't, a thick layer of housing and workplace discrimination kept blacks down. Whites wistfully called it Bluff City; many blacks called it an urban plantation.

In the 1960s, Memphis was run by Henry Loeb, a patrician Memphian who in 1967 won 90 percent of the white vote on a platform mixing law and order and urban pride. Loeb's tall, thin frame and upper-class education (Brown) gave him the air of a minor European nobleman, and whites loved him. But he was despised by the city's blacks, who saw him as an obstinate bigot. Predictably, Loeb played precisely that part in the strike, refusing to even recognize the strikers and denying any possibility of negotiations. As he told its leaders at their first meeting, "This is not New York. Nobody can break the law. You are putting my back up against the wall, and I am not going to budge."[17] With the solid backing of the city's white business community, Loeb figured that he could wait out the protesters. With the sanitary workers on strike, the city slowly filled with the aroma of sautéing garbage, made worse by the rising temperatures of an early, muggy spring.

Fortunately for the workers, the strike drew national union support, along with the backing of major civil rights groups. Organizers and supporters flocked to the town, and the strike soon became a national news story. The *New York Times* called it "the current major civil rights confrontation in the nation."[18]

The strike proved irresistible to King. It was, in part, a must-do for the embattled civil rights leader—how could he afford *not* to be involved in the civil rights issue of the year, especially if it were to eclipse his own plans? Plus, it had been almost three years since the Selma–Montgomery march, one of the last unalloyed expressions of nonviolent mass resistance by blacks to receive national attention. But more important was the precise nature of the campaign. Melding civil rights and labor rights, it struck to the core of his evolving message: the need to empower workers and push back against economic injustice. Going against the express wishes of his advisers, who wanted him to focus on the Poor People's Campaign, King decided to visit the city.

His first trip to Memphis came on March 18, when he spoke to an overcapacity crowd of between nine thousand and fifteen thousand at Mason Temple. For the first time in months, thousands had come to hear him, not mock him. King spoke for more than an hour, almost completely extemporaneously. "You are here tonight to demand that Memphis will do something about the conditions that our brothers face as they work day in and day out for the well-being of the total community," he told the cheering audience. Now, he concluded, "the thing for you to do is stay together, and say to everybody in this community that you are going to stick it out to the end until every demand is met, and that you are gonna say, 'We ain't gonna let nobody turn us around.'"[19]

The speech left him drained. "Martin was visually shaken by all this, for this kind of support was unprecedented in the Movement," recalled James Lawson, a Nashville civil rights and labor activist who was helping lead the strike. "No one had ever been able to get these numbers out before."[20] But the reception gave King momentum. He quickly put forth a proposal: he would come back to Memphis and lead a march to support the strikers. Though he immediately drew criticism from whites and even some blacks for inserting himself, uninvited, into a local issue, the strike leaders were overjoyed—King's national prominence, sullied as it was, would give newfound speed to a movement that until then was at a stalemate with the city's power structure. It worked, too: as soon as King announced his plan, white business leaders began to openly question whether Loeb's intransigence was the best strategy.

Early on March 28, thousands began to gather at Clayborn Temple downtown, waiting for King to arrive at 10:00 A.M. But his plane was delayed, and he didn't arrive until 10:30. By then the crowd was growing restless; the air was humid, and it was growing hotter.

They began marching. Signs began appearing in the crowd reading LOEB EAT SHIT. As they reached Main Street, those in front—King, Young, Lawson—began to hear commotion behind them. Several militant groups, along with a klatch of assorted hangers-on, had decided to embarrass King by turning the march into a riot. They were breaking windows, looting, and harassing onlookers.

His aides quickly whisked King away. It didn't take long for the police, already standing by in riot gear, to move in. What followed was several hours of mayhem: police, who had stood by while the strikers turned their city into an open-air garbage dump, wielded their batons and tear gas with glee. Marchers who sought refuge in Clayborn Temple were ordered out, and as they left the building they were beaten by waiting cops. The sole fatality, sixteen-year-old Larry Payne, was shotgunned in the stomach by a cop who claimed he was wielding a knife, though witnesses said the boy had both hands raised. "Instead of King's nonviolent 'dress rehearsal' for the Poor People's Campaign," historian Michael Honey wrote, "the Memphis march left behind a wasteland."[21]

King was hardly to blame, but that was not the way the regional press—goaded by the FBI—spun things. The Bureau sent anonymous missives to its press contacts the next day, elements of which soon appeared in editorials in the *St. Louis Globe-Democrat* and the *Memphis Commercial Appeal.* The St. Louis paper predicted that the Memphis riot was a "prelude to a massive bloodbath" in Washington, while the *Commercial Appeal* labeled King a "hypocrite."[22] But in other cases it didn't take the FBI's prodding—the *New York Times* called on King to

cancel the Poor People's Campaign in Memphis's wake. King headed
back to Washington to give his Sunday sermon. Forlorn, he declared
the Poor People's Campaign "doomed."[23]

It was the evening of March 31, the night before King's final Sunday
sermon, and Lyndon Johnson had gathered his inner circle at the
White House. For weeks the president had been planning a national
address on the war and taxes, and he was having his closest staff members write the final draft. It would, among other things, announce
a unilateral bombing halt over most of North Vietnam, along with a
request for peace negotiations. Though the entire country was planning to watch the address, its precise contents were a secret.

Beset by an increasingly conservative Congress, a debilitating
war abroad, and growing dissent at home, Johnson had been whit-
tled to a nub. The once-proud Texan who towered over his senatorial colleagues now walked stoop-shouldered through Washington.
To make things worse, he was entering a presidential race with low
approval numbers and a pair of intraparty challenges from Senators
Eugene McCarthy and Robert Kennedy. When journalist Theodore
White visited the president in late March, he found him "exhausted.
His eyes, behind the gold-rimmed eyeglasses, were not only nested
in lines and wrinkles, but pouched in sockets blue with a permanent
weariness."[24]

After banging out the portions on Vietnam and a related section
on domestic policy, Johnson's chief counsel and close adviser Harry
McPherson offered to write up a quick wrap-up.

"Don't worry," the president said. "I may have a little ending of my
own." Without telling any of his staff, he then called his old speechwriter Horace Busby, now retired, at his Virginia home and told him
to come in the next morning.[25]

Johnson slept poorly that night. Lady Bird, his wife, recalled that
he tossed and turned, moaning. He was up at seven, against his wife's
urging, to greet their daughter Lynda, who was arriving on a red-eye
flight from California, where she had gone to see her new husband,
Charles Robb, off to Vietnam. Her parents met her at the entrance
to the Diplomatic Reception Room. "She looked like a ghost," Lady
Bird recalled. "She'd had a sedative on the plane, slept a little, not

much—and it was, I think, partly emotion and partly the sedative that made her look so detached, like a wraith from another world."[26] The couple put her to bed, then went back to their own quarters. The president sagged in a chair, his body completely drained. Had he just sent his son-in-law off to die in a pointless war? "There was such pain in his eyes as I had not seen since his mother died," his wife said.[27]

That morning, March 31, the White House buzzed with the activity of two different efforts. Both revolved around that night's speech, but each was exclusive, even secretive, to the other. Johnson had Busby in the Treaty Room going over the end of the speech. Meanwhile, the president's foreign policy team flew around the offices preparing the press and the diplomatic community for the president's bombing halt. Later in the day Johnson, chain-drinking Cokes, huddled in the Yellow Room with national security adviser Walt Rostow, Ambassador-at-Large Averell Harriman, and Soviet ambassador Anatoly Dobrynin, trying to telegraph to the USSR that the unilateral halt was for real.

The mood throughout the White House was tense. "We would meet in the West Hall by twos or threes, or all of us," recalled Lady Bird, "and look at each other helplessly, silent, or exploding with talk."[28]

Several hours before the speech, Johnson phoned McPherson. A fellow Texan, tall, laconic, bespectacled, McPherson had worked with Johnson in his Senate days before being called back to serve as chief counsel. But his real role was less well defined. He was a speechwriter, a domestic policy adviser, and a confidential sounding board.

Brilliant and loyal, McPherson could do anything the president asked, efficiently and quietly. Johnson had even once sent him, along with two black staffers, on a covert fact-finding mission to Harlem, where he interviewed cops, activists, and street preachers on the chances for civil unrest in the ghetto. Johnson devoured the resulting report. But McPherson was more than a lackey. According to Roche, he was one of the few men who could speak openly, even aggressively, with the president, "a guy who used to lay into Johnson, too. I mean he used to really sock it to him."[29]

Johnson asked McPherson what he thought of the speech. "It's pretty good," McPherson said.

"I've got an ending."

"So I've heard."

"What do you think?"

"I'm very sorry, Mr. President."

"Okay," Johnson replied. "So long, pardner."[30]

Otherwise, Johnson kept the conclusion secret until the last minute. Only at the last minute did he have his assistant Larry Temple call around to his cabinet members—he reached all but Secretary of State Dean Rusk—and let them know what was coming.

At 9:00 P.M. Johnson sat in his green leatherback chair in the Oval Office, facing a phalanx of television cameras. His family watched from the back of the room. Johnson exuded a calm rarely seen on his face of late, "a marvelous sort of repose overall," recalled Lady Bird.[31]

"Good evening, my fellow Americans: tonight I want to speak to you of peace in Vietnam and Southeast Asia," he began. "Tonight, I have ordered our aircraft and our naval vessels to make no attacks on North Vietnam, except in the area north of the demilitarized zone where the continuing enemy buildup directly threatens Allied forward positions." He called on the Allies and the North Vietnamese to take the halt as an opening to talks, and accordingly to stop their own attacks and sit down to negotiations.

Then, after making a call for Congress to enact his proposed 10 percent tax surcharge, he changed the subject unexpectedly. "Throughout my entire public career," he said after a pause, "I have followed the personal philosophy that I am a free man, an American, a public servant, and a member of my party, in that order always and only." He had achieved great things, he said, his hands trembling slightly. But he had also become mired in partisanship, at precisely the time when America needed to be united and strong, at home and abroad.

"With America's sons in the fields far away," he said, looking down at his text, "with America's future under challenge right here at home, with our hopes and the world's hopes for peace in the balance every day, I do not believe that I should devote an hour or a day of my time to any personal partisan causes or to any duties other than the awesome duties of this office—the presidency of your country."

He paused again, then lifted his head. "Accordingly, I shall not seek, and I will not accept, the nomination of my party for another term as your president. But let men everywhere know, however, that a strong, a confident, and a vigilant America stands ready tonight to seek an honorable peace—and stands ready tonight to defend an honored cause—whatever the price, whatever the burden, whatever the sacrifice that duty may require. Thank you for listening. Good night and God bless all of you."[32]

Johnson's withdrawal from the race was long in coming. According to his press secretary, George Christian, he had been seriously weighing the decision since October,[33] and he had casually broached the subject with friends even earlier.[34] In January 1968 he had even had Busby, who had left the White House but still helped pen critical speeches, draft a withdrawal statement to slip into the State of the Union address, though he never read it.[35]

Nevertheless, it was clear to observers of the White House inside and out that Johnson was losing the verve that had driven him to early executive success. "Increasingly over the last two years," noted journalist Richard Rovere in the *New Yorker*, "the feeling had been growing that he had already retired, that he had taken himself out of the system, that he had been so seized by the martial spirit that he was no longer functioning as a vote-hungry, consensus-seeking American politician."[36] Nor, concluded the staff, was there much chance of things turning around before 1969. "I didn't see any room for improvement as long as he was in the White House," said McPherson. "And I thought that things were as awful as they could get."[37]

Befitting a man known for his vast internal contradictions, Johnson's reasons for withdrawing were complex and perhaps irreconcilable. Certainly he recognized that even with a great campaign team, he faced significant challenges in both the primaries and the general election. His ratings had plummeted after the Newark and Detroit riots of 1967, so low that at one point all six of his Republican challengers—even Pennsylvania governor William Scranton—were beating him in head-to-head matchups.[38] His health was a major concern; he had suffered a heart attack in 1955, and his doctors and wife feared he would not survive another. Too many Johnson family men had died early, and the president often spoke privately about wanting to spend time with his grandson on his Texas ranch before he died. And his staff was tired, too. "They are good men, but they are beyond asking the hard questions now," McPherson said.[39]

But looming over it all was the question of legacy. From the day in November 1963 when he was sworn in aboard *Air Force One*, Johnson imagined himself a great legislative president, a true successor to Franklin Roosevelt, a man who would leave a record of great accomplishments in his wake and be remembered for them. And while he had achieved much already—Medicare, Medicaid, the War on Poverty, the Elementary and Secondary Education Act, the Civil Rights Act of 1964, and the Voting Rights Act, to name a few of his accomplishments—Johnson still had much he wanted to do, and he feared that his unfinished domestic agenda and the shadow of a continuing war would doom him in history books. And history meant everything to Johnson. As he later told historian Doris Kearns Goodwin, "If the American people don't love me, their descendants will."[40]

Johnson had nevertheless begun 1968 on a fast track. He came out with his legislative guns blazing at his State of the Union address, asking Congress to pass a raft of big-ticket items even as the mood of the nation was souring on Great Society activism. He called for, among many other things, a multinational oceanographic exploration program, expanded international aid, a $2.1 billion job training effort, and six million new low-income homes over the next ten years (though he got the biggest cheers for a proposed anticrime bill). "In January he was still willing to spend whatever capital he had left—and it was dwindling fast—to get his work done without waiting for the war to be over," his domestic policy adviser, Joseph Califano Jr., wrote in his memoirs. "Often, we put so many complex proposals out in a day that reporters were unable to write clearly about them."[41]

But events in Vietnam soon brought Johnson back to earth. Since late 1967, North Vietnamese forces had been laying siege to a Marine base at Khe Sanh, a plateau near the borders with Laos and North Vietnam. It drove Johnson to insomnia; he had the Pentagon build a sand-table model of the Khe Sanh area in the White House basement, and he would pace around it at odd hours, often in his bathrobe in the middle of the night, taking a break to read the latest news dispatches or pore over reconnaissance photos.[42]

Khe Sanh was just a prelude to what began on the evening of January 31, 1968, at the height of the Tet holiday. Tens of thousands of North Vietnamese regulars and Viet Cong guerrillas launched attacks on cities and bases across South Vietnam, locations once believed untouchable by the Communists. They overran the northern city of Hue and held it for twenty-five days. They even stormed the U.S. embassy in Saigon. The offensive surprised General William Westmoreland and the U.S. forces in the country, and it sent a shock wave of disbelief through the White House. "People were far calmer in Saigon than they were in Washington," said General Earle Wheeler, chairman of the Joint Chiefs of Staff.[43]

If Johnson was losing some sleep over Khe Sanh, the Tet Offensive chased away any chance of a good night's rest. He had let himself believe earlier reports that the Viet Cong was demoralized and beaten back. Now he would wander the halls late at night, staring at the portraits of past presidents. Add to this the USS *Pueblo* incident—in which North Korea captured a U.S. naval intelligence ship in the Yellow Sea, imprisoning the crew—and the president had little good to look to on the international scene.

In the short term, Tet actually produced a patriotic boost in support for Johnson's prosecution of the war. But by early March, the public had again soured significantly. On February 27, Walter Cronkite, the nation's most respected television news voice, declared it "more certain than ever that the bloody experience of Vietnam is to end in a stalemate."[44] After watching the broadcast, Johnson said, "That's it. If I've lost Cronkite, I've lost middle America."

Nor did it help that Johnson's blue-ribbon panel investigating the Detroit, Newark, and other recent riots—the National Advisory Commission on Civil Disorders, nicknamed the Kerner Commission after its chair, Illinois governor Otto Kerner—had come out in early March with a devastating indictment of American race relations and an implicit attack on Johnson's social policies. In an introduction written largely by New York mayor John Lindsay, the commission famously announced, "Our nation is moving toward two societies, one black, one white—separate and unequal," and it laid the blame squarely on "white racism": "What white Americans have never fully understood—but what the Negro can never forget—is that white society is deeply implicated in the ghetto. White institutions created it, white institutions maintain it, and white society condones it." Federal efforts had done little to help, and they "often seem self-defeating and contradictory." The country needed to overhaul and massively expand its programs aimed at blacks and the inner-city poor, everything from job training and creation to community relations and police reform. "Only a commitment to national action on an unprecedented scale," its authors announced, "can shape a future compatible with the historic ideals of American society."[45] By some estimates, that meant $26 billion a year, on top of the current social policy bill of $59 billion, a war raging in Vietnam, and a rapidly expanding federal budget deficit.[46]

The due date for the final report had initially been late spring, but the commission felt it sufficiently urgent to move up its release. That, combined with an accidental leak to the *Washington Post*, meant that the report hit the White House unawares.[47] And if Johnson and his staff had been hoping the report would come and go unnoticed, they were sadly disappointed: It sold a hundred thousand copies in three days.

The administration went into crisis mode. Many recommended that Johnson engage with the report and accept it as a positive contribution. They even wrote up a speech, never delivered, in which Johnson would incorporate the commission's ideas into his own new list of policy proposals.[48] "The more I think about it, the more I fear that a cold reception to the Kerner Report is bad policy for us," wrote McPherson in a memo to Califano. "Unless something like this is done—meeting the report squarely and affirmatively, rather than coldly or evasively—I think we will be in trouble."[49] But the president, feeling personally insulted by the reports' conclusions, declined even to meet with the commissioners, and his public statement was limited to a few bland assessments.[50]

Johnson may also have understood the political risks of allying himself with so incendiary a statement. It became instant fodder for law-and-order conservatives. Richard Nixon said it "has put undue emphasis on the idea that we are in effect a racist society," while Ronald Reagan lashed it for failing "to recognize the efforts that have been made by millions of right-thinking people in this country." Even Vice President Hubert Humphrey backed away from supporting it fully. And countless members of Congress, mayors, and police chiefs attacked it for its implication that law enforcement was a cause of, rather than a cure for, riots. Miami police chief Walter Headley Jr. spoke for many nationwide when he said, "They still seem to be using the police as whipping boys. . . . Why shouldn't police departments be stockpiling lethal weapons? Weapons are being stockpiled in Vietnam, and this is a war too."[51]

Beset by critics on both sides of the political spectrum, on issues both foreign and domestic, Johnson's approval rating had evaporated—six weeks after Tet began, he had dropped from 48 percent to 36 percent in overall approval, and from 40 percent to a mere 26 percent on the war itself.[52]

Slowly, he began to realize that the only hope of saving his legacy—and perhaps even the very idea of an activist, liberal government—was for him to sacrifice his political career. It would be a political Hail Mary—withdrawal from the race would remove him from the partisan scene, giving him capital and the maneuverability necessary to pass his legislative agenda and move the war toward a peaceful end. "Abdication," wrote Doris Kearns Goodwin in her biography of Johnson, "was thus the last remaining way to restore control, to turn rout into dignity, collapse into order."[53]

The germ of Johnson's withdrawal statement might have been growing inside him for weeks, but he didn't bring up it up with his advisers (other than Busby) until a March 28 lunch in the White House Flower Garden with domestic policy adviser Joseph Califano and McPherson.[54] With protesters outside the White House gates shouting, "Hey, hey, LBJ! How many kids did you kill today?," Johnson rattled off the reasons for withdrawing.[55] He was worried about his health. He wanted to spend time with his family. Most important, he said, was that his political capital was gone. "I've asked Congress for too much for too long, and they're tired of me," McPherson recalled him saying.[56]

His chief counsel reminded his boss that there was still a lot on his agenda, that there were still many important items that only he could get through. "He said, 'You've got it exactly backwards,'" McPherson said. "'I'm the only one who can't do these things. Bobby, Gene, Nixon, any one of them would get a honeymoon from Congress in their first year. But not me. Cuz I've been, I've asked Congress for too much for too long. And they're tired of me.'"

Before the pair could convince him otherwise, his secretary called him in for an appointment, leaving his two senior advisers sitting in the early spring sunlight, stunned.[57]

Johnson didn't even tell Vice President Hubert Humphrey until the morning of the 31st. After church, he had jumped over to Humphrey's apartment, just a few blocks away (vice presidents didn't take up residence at the Naval Observatory until 1974). Accompanied by presidential adviser Jim Jones, Johnson and Humphrey went into the den, where he handed him the speech. After reading it, Humphrey, who was packing to go to Mexico that night, began crying. This meant he was now the likely establishment candidate, running against senators Eugene McCarthy and Robert Kennedy. Johnson put his right forefinger to his lips. "Don't mention this to anyone until Jim calls you in Mexico tonight," he said. "But you'd better start now planning your campaign for president."[58]

That afternoon the president even sat down with his campaign advisers, including his manager and former North Carolina governor Terry Sanford, to talk about the upcoming Wisconsin primary. It must have been a convincing act. "After spending all day at the White House Terry Sanford left for the airport under the impression that he was the campaign manager," said Roche. "Not only that, I had already put an LBJ '68 bumper sticker on my car and I was wearing an LBJ '68 button. We were left with fifteen thousand of the goddamn things."[59]

When he finished his speech, Johnson quietly stood and hugged Linda and Luci. The pair cried softly. Lady Bird went over and hugged him, too. "Nobly done, darling," she said. Then they all went to the Mansion.[60] The White House was silent. "We were stunned," recalled McPherson.[61]

And then the phones began ringing. First one, then another, then a cavalcade. All night, friends close and estranged alike called with congratulations and approval.[62] In their bedroom, Johnson sat on his bed talking on one line, while Lady Bird stood across the room on another. In between calls he joked and laughed with the close friends and aides who had gathered upstairs.

The White House media exploded in activity, clamoring for a further statement. Lady Bird finally emerged. "We have done a lot," she told reporters. "There's a lot left to do in the remaining months; maybe this is the only way to get it done."[63]

Johnson was already plotting his new agenda. As his wife recalled, "It seemed to me Lyndon was going at an even faster pace than before he made known his decision Sunday."[64] Califano reported that his feelers on Capitol Hill showed a Congress now willing to work with the president on a wide range of issues, foreign and domestic—housing, peace in Vietnam, new civil rights bills, conservation, education, all would be revisited and reinvigorated.

"His demeanor was that of a new man," Busby recalled. "His conversation began to quicken with talk of what could be achieved over the balance of the year. There was fresh excitement and an old bite in his tone as he declared, 'We're going to get this show on the road again.'"[65]

2

April 4

BEFORE THE BULLET

In the early afternoon of Thursday, April 4, President Johnson entered the vast French Gothic chapel of St. Patrick's Cathedral, just across Fifth Avenue from Rockefeller Center in midtown Manhattan. Accompanied by his daughter Luci, Johnson was in the city to mark the inauguration of Terence Cooke as archbishop of New York. Though a lifelong member of the Disciples of Christ, a small Protestant denomination, the president had recently been attending Catholic Mass with increasing regularity. Part of his interest came through the influence of Luci, a religious woman who had converted to Catholicism on her eighteenth birthday, three years earlier. But an equally important part was the solace he found in the services at St. Dominic's, the church he attended back in Washington. Beset by protesters, rioters, a hostile Congress, and the war in Vietnam, Johnson liked to escape to the church in Southwest D.C., to be with his "little monks," as he affectionately called the priests at St. Dominic's, finding comfort in the church's millennia-old rites, if only for a fraction of an hour.[1]

Johnson's New York trip, like many of his decisions in recent days, had been spontaneous and last-minute. Since his withdrawal from the race, he had been moving like Atlas unburdened by his globe. In the late hours after his speech, he decided to attend a conference of radio and TV broadcasters in Chicago the next day. The streets were empty as he rode into town (no one knew he was coming), but he found a packed lobby of well-wishers at his hotel, pouring forth applause and words of congratulations. "I was confident that Lyndon B. Johnson had begun the happiest week of his presidency and, possibly, of his public career," remarked Busby.[2]

It was quite a change for a quite polarizing figure. Before his withdrawal, Johnson was so unpopular that he had been keeping his campaign appearances to military bases and American Legion halls.[3] Now he was loved again. His erstwhile southern Democratic ally J. William Fulbright called it "an act of a very great patriot." Republican Senator Jacob K. Javits likewise said, "In a grave hour of war and national doubt, the president has lifted the office of the presidency to its proper place, far above politics."[4] A Harris poll taken after his announcement showed public approval reversing from 57 percent against to 57 percent in favor of his job as president.[5] And despite the spontaneous nature of his New York trip, the streets leading to the church were lined with hundreds of people, this time not heckling, but cheering.

As he and Luci walked down the aisle toward the front pews of St. Patrick's, the five thousand attendees rose, turned to him, and began clapping. It was, Johnson noted proudly in his memoirs, only the second time a standing ovation had occurred in the church, the first after an appearance by Pope Paul VI.[6]

Just after 1:00 P.M. Archbishop Cooke, his round glasses framing his equally round face, mounted the white marble pulpit. He must have made several late-stage changes to his sermon, because a large section of it was dedicated to his honored guest, who listened with his hands clasped and his legs crossed. "Let us pray with all our hearts that God will inspire our president," Cooke intoned. "Mr. President, our hearts, our hopes, our continued prayers go with you."

Cooke touched on the other reason Johnson was in such high spirits that morning. On April 3, Hanoi had responded positively to Johnson's call for talks, sending shock waves through the international community. Peace, after so many years of pointless fighting, might well be at hand.[7]

"In the last few days," Cooke said, "we have all admired his heroic efforts in the search for peace in Vietnam. We ask God to bless his efforts with success. May God inspire not only our president, but also other leaders and the leaders of all nations of the world to find a way to peace."[8]

As Johnson strode back up the aisle after the service, he paused to speak with Jackie Kennedy, the widow of his former boss and sister-in-law of one of his most bitter political rivals. Then, true to his new-found verve, he paid an unannounced visit to the United Nations, where he met with U.S. ambassador Arthur Goldberg and Secretary-General U Thant about the prospects for peace in Vietnam.[9] He finally left JFK airport at 5:30, joking the whole flight back with the accompanying press corps—the same people he had so recently blamed for everything from Communist victories in Vietnam to his own political downturn at home. He even took time to check on his grandson, Lyn, who was sleeping in the back of the plane. "The world that day seemed to me a pretty good place," Johnson later wrote.[10]

April 4 found a very different mood in Memphis. With King returning from Washington to lead a new march, the city girded for the worst. After Watts, Newark, and Detroit, no one expected the emotions raised by a day of rioting to simply disappear. If anything, they figured, the worst was yet to come. An anonymous flyer appeared on Memphis streets on April 3, saying, "MARTIN LUTHER KING has proven himself to be a yellow Uncle Tom," with the author promising to make the city "famous the World over—something that your two bit carnival never could, and you will Burn Baby Burn."[11]

The state legislature gave Loeb emergency powers to impose curfews and even prohibit people from being in public without a permit. The state also passed an antiriot law so strict that if a riot ever developed from a demonstration, the demonstration planners could be arrested—a not-so-subtle warning to King and his associates. Loeb enacted a 7:00 P.M. to 5:00 A.M. curfew, to last five nights. Four thousand National Guardsmen, carrying live ammunition and accompanied by a squadron of armored personnel carriers, descended on the city over the weekend.

Low-level violence met them: over the next several days, National Guard jeep and foot patrols were harassed by bottle throwers, while arson incidents rose precipitously. The Memphis police responded with the same brutality with which they had put down the March 28 riot. They stopped blacks in the streets and harassed them, sometimes beating them and then taking them downtown. At the height of a violent era, there was little surprise at Loeb's tactics. As a later investigation by the Southern Regional Council concluded, "There can be little doubt that Mayor Loeb and the city fathers of Memphis were faithfully reflecting the temper of whites in their city. By many indications they were reflecting, as well, the mood of the nation."[12] Though the National Guard withdrew on April 2, everyone got the message: The city was ready, willing, and able to turn itself into a police state at the first sign of violence.

The quasi-military reaction in Memphis was hardly unique. Along with the mounting white backlash and the rising appeal of law and order as a political touchstone during the late 1960s was a turn, especially at the local level, to the militarization of law enforcement in the ghetto, especially after the Watts riot of 1965, when police departments began to see the ghetto not just as a dangerous place, but also as the front lines of a war zone. The solution was to militarize the police.

One of the central promoters of taking a war footing on the domestic front was the LAPD's front-line commander during Watts, Daryl Gates. "The streets of America's cities had become a foreign territory," he wrote in his memoirs.[13] Gates, a model of the new, college-educated professional cop, soon introduced a new paradigm for urban policing: Special Weapons and Tactics, or SWAT. Officers, highly trained in sharpshooting, home invasion, and other quasi-military skills, would be organized into military-style platoons, trained in secret at the marine base at Camp Pendleton. As Gates emphatically concluded one chapter in his memoir, "At times, *assault* is not a dirty word."[14] Gates became an instant celebrity in the law-enforcement community. The manual he wrote for countering riots appeared in precincts nationwide, and he traveled the states giving lectures on the latest in urban combat techniques.

But if Gates succeeded, it was only because the country was so eager for a voice like his to appear. By late 1965, Barney Fife had made way for Harry Callahan. Advertisers in magazines such as *Police Chief* pitched police shields, armor-piercing bulletproof vests, tear-gas guns, and "Pepper Fog," a CS-gas-delivering hand grenade. More exotic tools— sound "curdlers," a superslick substance called "liquid banana peel," and even rockets designed to deliver gas at long distances—became hot items at law-enforcement conferences. Helicopters, pioneered by the LAPD, soon became standard equipment and regular sights in the nighttime skies over American inner cities, their spotlights poking into backyards and alleys. Surplus military equipment, increasingly available thanks to Vietnam War spending, ended up in local police departments: gas masks, armored cars and trucks, and high-powered rifles.[15]

"Gatesism" coincided with a new willingness in the federal government to extend economic and technical assistance to local law enforcement. In September 1965 Johnson signed the Law Enforcement Assistance Act, the main function of which was the creation of the Office of Law Enforcement Assistance (OLEA), which gave federal grants to local and state police. A September Harris poll showed 61 percent of Americans were concerned about their personal safety, up from 53 percent in August.[16] The OLEA was Johnson's response, the core of his "War on Crime." As he said during the bill's signing, "I will not be satisfied until every woman and child in this Nation can walk any street, enjoy any park, drive on any highway, and live in any community at any time of the day or night without fear of being harmed."[17] The OLEA wasn't perfect, but through extensive grant programs it established a precedent for federal involvement in local law enforcement and a framework through which federal resources could flow to cities.

The military also became increasingly focused on inner-city violence, positioning stockpiled gas masks, ammunition, and other equipment near potential riot cities; training police officers and National Guard units; and planning for occupation in the event that a president decided to send in troops. After the Detroit riot of 1967, Pentagon planners undertook a major overhaul of its domestic operations, including the creation of thick guidebooks on major American cities for commanding officers. Updated regularly by army surveillance teams, the books contained detailed data on everything from local civil rights leaders to the location of liquor stores.[18]

Nor was government the only sphere of antiriot activity; the private sector made it a cottage industry in the mid- to late 1960s. The defense industry was, of course, happy to see yet another market open for its weapons and equipment, while government contractors bid heavily for projects overseeing summer camps for inner-city youth,

established with the intention of getting potential rioters out of the
city for the summer.

Taken together, such efforts at the local and federal levels were the
beginnings of a change in the way the country viewed inner-city life.
Under the old, liberal conception, the ghetto was something to be
ameliorated, if not eliminated, its residents being the victims of discrimination and the perils of poverty. But as the 1960s progressed and
the number of riots mounted, this attitude was slowly replaced by an
aggressive, militarized posture that saw the ghetto as something alien
and dangerous, something foreign that could not be removed, but only
isolated and controlled. After Watts, Los Angeles mayor Sam Yorty
warned of a coming era of "urban guerrilla warfare," and the idea of
general armed conflict emerging from the ghetto quickly became com-
monplace. In early 1968, journalist Garry Wills published an account
of traveling the country, meeting with police officers, riot-control
experts, and community leaders. He called the book *The Second Civil
War: Arming for Armageddon*.[19] With all this in mind, in early April
many people—from civilians to police officers to Pentagon planners—
were watching King's return to Memphis, wondering if Bluff City
would be ground zero for Wills's racial cataclysm.

None of King's associates had wanted him to return to Memphis.
He had been the object of death threats since he had begun his civil
rights work thirteen years before, but something about the specific-
ity of recent threats, the tension in Memphis, and the overall tone
of the country gave his new plans an ominous cast. American Airlines,
the carrier he was to take through Atlanta, received a bomb threat on
April 1: "Your airlines brought KING to Memphis, and when he comes
again a bomb will go off and he will be assassinated." Other threats
warned of plots to kill him during the march, many intercepted by the
FBI, army intelligence, and the local police. None of these was passed
on to King, but there was no mistaking the risk he was taking.[20]

"I asked him not to go to Memphis a second time," recalled Roger
Wilkins, the head of the Justice Department's Community Relations
Service (CRS). "But he said, 'I promised them.'"[21]

The strike needed him, King told his associates. He had made a
mistake, and the striking workers had suffered. What went wrong,

he realized, was not that he had spread himself too thin, but that he hadn't spread himself enough. He had simply walked into Memphis, not understanding the posture of the community. This time he would work closely with the militants. He would give speeches and sermons to seed the community with a nonviolent ethos. The SCLC would run nonviolent training seminars in the days leading up to the next march. And he would make sure there were enough well-trained marshals to keep the crowd in check.

King arrived at the Memphis airport a little after 10:30 A.M. on April 3. A quick press conference allowed him to reaffirm plans for the march, scheduled for Monday, April 8. Thousands would be coming from across the country, he said. King and his entourage then went to the Lorraine Motel, where they spent the afternoon meeting with local leaders, including some of the militants thought responsible for the violence on March 28. Lodged just down the hall was James Laue, a representative from the CRS, who was working with the SCLC staff on the Poor People's Campaign.[22]

That evening at Mason Temple, with thunder and lightning outside, King gave his last sermon. The building was packed, the air sticky and hot. King had tried to beg off from the speech—he was tired, and suffering from a sore throat—but he finally gave in. After a lengthy introduction from his right-hand man, Ralph Abernathy, he rose to the podium.[23]

"I'm delighted to see each of you here tonight in spite of a storm warning," he said. "You reveal that you are determined to go on now. Something is happening in Memphis, something is happening in our world."

The audience was right with him, responding to his cadences with "Yeah, all right" and "Keep on." No National Cathedral or Riverside Church for him; he was best in front of a responsive, verbal Baptist audience.

Times were hard, he said, but there has been no time in human history so full of promise as the present. "The nation is sick, trouble is in the land, confusion is all around," he said. "But I know, somehow, that only when it is dark enough can you see the stars." To reach them, however, "We've got to stay together. We've got to stay together and maintain unity." And that was why he had come back. Because only by standing with the sanitation workers could he demonstrate the importance of solidarity, not only to working-class blacks but also to all Americans.

He then went into the specifics of the strike. An injunction had been filed against the march, and he was fighting it. Meanwhile, he was calling for a boycott against products made by Memphis companies with unfair hiring practices. He called on his audience to bank with black-owned savings-and-loan companies and to buy insurance from only black-owned companies—what he termed a "bank-in."

Finally, he spoke of the Good Samaritan, who had stopped along the dangerous Jericho Road to help a Levite who had been robbed and beaten. "The Jericho Road is a dangerous road," he said. But the Samaritan stopped to help even as others had passed on by. "The question is not, 'If I stop to help this man in need, what will happen to me?' The question is, 'If I do not stop to help the sanitation workers, what will happen to them?" By now the audience was on its feet, applauding and shouting "amen!"

Was King saying he was the Good Samaritan? No—only one of many. Everyone in the audience, he said, must be good Samaritans. "We've got some difficult days ahead. But it really doesn't matter with me now, because I've been to the mountaintop. And I don't mind. Like anybody, I would like to live a long life—longevity has its place."

His voice began to rise. "Yeah!" shouted the audience.

"I've seen the Promised Land. I may not get there with you. But I want you to know tonight that we, as a people, will get to the Promised Land. And so I'm happy tonight; I'm not worried about anything"—his voice now at a fever pitch—"I'm not fearing any man. Mine eyes have seen the glory of the coming of the Lord!"[24]

King half-collapsed; the audience erupted. His eyes welled up in tears as the cavernous temple echoed with shouts and applause.

King stayed up all night eating, meeting with colleagues, and enjoying the company of his brother, A.D., who arrived at about 1:00 A.M. After an early-morning strategy session, they all went to bed, exhausted but excited. More meetings followed that afternoon, as did a pillow fight in King's room.

At about 6:00 P.M., King, Abernathy, A.D., and a few others began getting ready for dinner at a friend's house, after which they would head to yet another rally. King, tucking in his shirt, wandered outside his room. He leaned over the railing, chatting with Jesse Jackson, who had just arrived with Ben Branch, a singer from Chicago. Branch sang a great version of the hymn "Precious Lord," and King asked him if he'd sing it that night. "Play it real pretty."[25]

Unknown to King and company, scattered around the Lorraine was a web of local and federal law-enforcement officers. Some were there to protect him; others, like those manning a secret observation post in a nearby fire station, were monitoring him. The 111th Military Intelligence Group, based out of Fort McPherson, Georgia, had been keeping tabs on King and the SCLC for signs of an impending riot. Police cruisers patrolled area streets. They knew well the flurry of death threats against King, but their concern was less for his safety than for what his death might mean for an already tense city.

Somehow, through this web slipped James Earl Ray. A drifter, he had arrived in town from Birmingham, where he had bought a Remington 30.06 rifle, fitted with a telescopic sight. Under the name Eric Galt, earlier that day he had rented a room for a week at a flophouse a few hundred feet from the Lorraine. The room didn't afford a clear view of the motel, though, so after a little while he moved down the hall to a bathroom. There, through a pair of binoculars, he spent the afternoon watching the SCLC crew coming and going. A few minutes after 6:00 P.M., he picked up his gun.[26]

3

April 4

THE NEWS ARRIVES

Attorney General Ramsey Clark entered the large domed room adjacent to his office a little after 6 P.M. eastern time. Arranged around the room's long conference table were fifteen members of his core staff, primarily the assistant attorneys general who helped him oversee the federal government's wide-ranging law-enforcement and legal operations, everything from counterintelligence to counterfeiting. Seated nearby was his deputy, Warren Christopher, a well-regarded California lawyer hired because of his experience investigating the Watts riot.[1] His arrival in 1967 had sent a clear signal that civil disorder was now the Justice Department's number-one priority.

Clark, tall and taciturn but with a youthful face, had grown up in the shadow of Lyndon Johnson. His father, Tom Clark, was a Supreme Court justice and an old friend of the Johnson family back in Texas. His uncle had been Johnson's Senate campaign manager. It was Johnson who pulled Clark up through the ranks at Justice, from assistant attorney general to deputy and then, in March 1967, to the top post. Rumor had it that Johnson had given Ramsey the head office in exchange for his father's retirement from the Court, thus making room for Thurgood Marshall's historic nomination.

But the younger Clark had proven a little too liberal for the Johnson White House. He was a firm supporter of law enforcement—many police chiefs loved him—but he resisted calls in Congress to crack down on black militants and antiwar demonstrators, earning him the nickname "Ramsey the Marshmallow" around the White House water cooler. Johnson came to privately regret his choice; as he once told Califano, "If I had ever known that he didn't measure up to his daddy, I'd never have made him attorney general."[2]

The focus of the meeting that night was the anticrime bill currently snaking its way through Congress. The bill included wiretapping provisions and looser rules on admitting confessions, as well as a block-grant structure for federal aid to police departments that denied the attorney general a say in how the money was spent. Clark strongly opposed all three planks, but he was in a tough spot: Johnson had endorsed crime control legislation in his 1968 State of the Union address, drawing the biggest applause of the night.

The phone in Clark's office rang a few minutes after seven. His secretary forwarded the call to the conference room. It was James Laue of the CRS, in Memphis.[3] Laue told him about King.

"How bad is it?" Clark demanded. His assistants listened in horror.

Pretty bad, Laue said. It was hard to tell if he'd live.

"Anybody see anything?" Clark demanded.

No.

Clark told Laue to stay on the scene and let them know as soon as he heard anything. He hung up, told his staff what had happened, and went through a side door to his office. He scribbled a statement that he would read to Johnson: "7:10 P.M. Eight minutes ago Dr. King was shot. Gaping hole in right side of jaw. One shot from a distance of 50–60 yards back of Main Street. Lorraine Hotel & Motel. Laue—Room 308."

Then he called the president.[4]

Johnson had arrived at the White House just thirty minutes before, carrying his sleeping grandson up the South Lawn from the still-whirring helicopter. At the moment King was shot, he was in the Oval Office meeting with Averell Harriman, discussing the upcoming peace talks with North Vietnam. Clark got through to presidential aide Tom Johnson at 7:25, who then took a slip of paper to the president. It read simply, "Mr. President, Martin Luther King has been shot."[5]

Clark then put in calls to the FBI, Vice President Humphrey, and Tennessee governor Buford Ellington, a close Johnson ally. Long on record against deploying troops too quickly in civil disorders, Clark cautioned Ellington about moving the National Guard back into Memphis preemptively. If a riot wasn't actually under way, an over-anxious occupation could likely set one off, he told the governor.

With nothing to do until further news arrived, Johnson stayed at his desk in the Oval Office. He met with Carl Sanders, a former governor of Georgia, and Robert Woodruff, chair of Coca-Cola; then with Llewellyn Thompson, U.S. ambassador to the Soviet Union. All the while he had his trademark three televisions on in the background, each tuned to one of the networks.

By now, all three were reporting on King's shooting. Strangely, Johnson still planned to keep his evening schedule: At eight he and Lady Bird were slated to attend a Democratic fund-raising dinner at the new Hilton on Connecticut Avenue, and later that evening he was to leave on *Air Force One* for Hawaii, where he would meet with General Westmoreland.[6]

Meanwhile, things were moving fast in Memphis. King had been hit in the jaw at a downward angle, so that the bullet passed through his jugular vein and spinal cord. The force pushed him away from the railing and onto his back. A woman shouted, "Oh, lord, they shot Martin!" An ambulance arrived a few minutes later, and Laue himself helped lift King onto a stretcher.

The ambulance rushed King to St. Joseph's Hospital. Police heli-copters were already in flight over the city, ostensibly looking for the shooter but also on watch for signs of incipient disorder. Abernathy and another SCLC minister, Bernard Lee, went with the ambulance, and they stood outside the operating room as doctors went to work, trying to save King. But there was little they could do: King's spinal cord had been severed. Even if he did live, he would be incapacitated, perhaps unable to ever regain consciousness. "It would be a mercy of God if he did pass," one of the attending doctors told the pair. And then, at 7:05 P.M., he did.[7]

The news of his death reached Johnson via his press secretary, George Christian, at 8:20 Eastern Time.[8] Johnson immediately can-celed his appearance at the dinner, and he ordered Christian to book time on the networks. He wanted to address the nation as soon as possible. Then he canceled the Hawaii trip, too. "A jumble of anxious thoughts ran through my mind," the president later recalled. "What does it mean? Was it the act of one man or a group? Was the assassin black or white? Would the shooting bring more violence, more catastrophe, and more extremism?"

As surely as this was the end of something, it was the start of something, too. But what?

By then Califano had come in, and the two went to the White House barbershop to get the president cleaned up.[9] From there he called Coretta Scott King in Atlanta. Mrs. King had been out shopping with her daughter, Yolanda, when she heard the initial news from Jesse Jackson. She immediately scheduled a flight to Memphis for that evening. Atlanta mayor Ivan Allen Jr., a liberal Democrat and a close friend of the Kings, drove her to the airport, complete with police escort. But news of her husband's death met her there, and she decided to postpone the flight until the morning.

She took the president's call back at home, on one of the three phone lines she had installed at the home to handle the flood of condolence calls coming in that evening.[10] She thanked him for calling, but said there was nothing he could do for her that evening.

The president went on TV at nine, speaking from the same West Lobby podium where, just twenty-four hours earlier, he had triumphantly announced the news of Hanoi's agreement to peace talks.[11]

"America is shocked and saddened by the brutal slaying tonight of Dr. Martin Luther King," he began. "I pray that his family can find comfort in the memory of all he tried to do for the land he loved so well." But Johnson's immediate concern was peace. "I know that every American of goodwill joins me in mourning the death of this outstanding leader and in praying for peace and understanding throughout this land. We can achieve nothing by lawlessness and divisiveness among the American people. It is only by joining together and only by working together that we can continue to move toward equality and fulfillment for all of our people."

But he was unclear on what his next step would be, saying only that he had canceled his evening plans and postponed "my trip to Hawaii until tomorrow." With that, he went off the air.[12]

As almost the exact same moment, Vice President Humphrey was delivering his own impromptu address to the three thousand Democratic donors and politicians gathered at the Hilton for a $250-a-plate fund-raiser. A week before, Humphrey had been a sideshow. Now, with Johnson out of the race, he was the establishment candidate. Though Johnson had said publicly, and reiterated to him privately, that he would stay out of the primary fight, Humphrey was looking forward to sharing the dais that night with a leader suddenly back in national favor. Instead, shortly after nine, he found himself writing a statement for reporters, then taking the podium to address the audience.

"I am sure some of you know that a great tragedy has taken place tonight," he reported. "A renowned leader of civil rights has been shot down. Martin Luther King was shot and killed in Memphis." Many did not, in fact, know. Gasps ran through the enormous ballroom.

Then Senator Edmund Muskie of Maine, the chair of the Democratic Senatorial Campaign Committee and the man running the event, took over to report that Johnson had canceled his appearance, and that in turn the evening itself would draw to a close. "Events catch up with us these days before we can react, and now they have caught up with us again," Muskie said. "And so, it does not seem to us to be appropriate to continue an evening of partisanship and festivity."[13]

A chaplain gave a short prayer, and with that the dinner was over. People in the audience turned to each other, stunned. Some hurried to leave. Others wandered in and out of the hall in a daze. Some cried. Others wondered how soon the city would fall into riots. One attendee asked a reporter whether King was really dead.

Not everyone was sad, though. For those who had always been openly hostile to racial progress, this was no big tragedy; for some it was even good news. One guest told Mary McGrory, who was covering the event for the *Washington Evening Star*, "Of course, I'm from the South, and I'm glad."[14]

Not far from the Hilton, Stokely Carmichael sat listening impatiently to the news coming over the radio at SCLC headquarters, located on U Street just west of Fourteenth. Carmichael—young, telegenic, radical—had been making inroads as a militant community activist in D.C. that winter. A Trinidad native who had grown up in New York and attended nearby Howard University, he had risen quickly through the ranks of the student civil rights movement to become the head of the Student Nonviolent Coordinating Committee (SNCC) in 1966.

Almost immediately, his name and tall, handsome figure became synonymous with the radicalization of the movement, which in turn became inextricable from the now-regular violence erupting in urban ghettos each summer. Obsessed with his bombastic rhetoric, newspapers reported on his every move, as if his mere presence in a city meant a riot was soon to follow.

Carmichael, who made camouflage jackets and dark sunglasses de rigueur for black radicals, fed off the attention. He gave scores of interviews, vamping for the cameras and tossing off incendiary bons mots about white America and the coming black revolution. When pushed by reporters or stuck behind a campus lectern, he was all too happy to dish out zingers about blacks arming themselves, killing cops, and launching a guerrilla war. At a black college in Alabama, he told students, "To hell with the laws of the United States. . . . If a white man tries to walk over you, kill him. One match and you can retaliate. Burn, baby, burn!"[15] Not for nothing did his critics in the movement dub him "Cokely Starmichael."

In his more subdued moments, though, he could sound rational, even reasonable about the need for blacks to empower themselves, and he talked up black power as the logical next step in the civil rights movement. In his 1967 manifesto *Black Power*, he said the eponymous term was merely "a call for black people in this country to unite, to recognize their heritage, to build a sense of community. It is a call for black people to define their own goals, to lead their own organizations." But while the book sold well, it baffled audiences. "This book is disappointing, first of all because it makes so few concrete proposals for action, and these seem hardly revolutionary in nature," wrote Christopher Lasch in the *New York Review of Books*.[16]

Like Malcolm X before him, Carmichael's thinking was at once more complex and less shocking than his rhetoric let on. Indeed, many people who came to his speeches, once they cut through the talk of guns and honkies, found him less inspiring than they'd expected. As James Jones, a professor at the traditionally black Texas South University, reported to a 1967 congressional hearing, "Once our students were exposed to him, it was anticlimactic. It was like going to a jazz concert: Having been amused otherwise, they went away without any deep reaction."[17] Where was the overthrow of capitalism? Where was the call to the barricades? How could rebellion be so boring? Could Carmichael be less radical than he let on?

Carmichael probably didn't know himself—he was, after all, only twenty-seven in 1968. In any case, there was no united radical sentiment in the black community, even though frustrations and ideologies swirled through the city streets. At best, historian Claiborne Carson wrote in his magisterial history of SNCC, Carmichael's "attitudes coincided with the unarticulated feelings of many other blacks, especially in northern urban centers." He reflected, rather than led, those inchoate sentiments. "Carmichael was an innovator who could not control nor fully understand the social forces he had set in motion."[18]

This may explain in part the self-imposed exile Carmichael undertook in late 1967. Just over a year after his predecessor, John Lewis, was drummed out of SNCC, Carmichael split with the organization himself and went on a world tour, visiting Europe, Africa, and North Vietnam. The *New York Times* assiduously tracked and reported on his every stop, while in Congress politicians called for him to be tried for treason and, at the very least, for violating passport restrictions. The trip did not gain him many fans internationally. The British government denounced him, as did Nelson Mandela's African National Congress, which accused him of "meaningless and arrogant demagoguery."[19] On his return in December 1967, Carmichael was stripped of his passport. The FBI, which already had a thick file on him, began an intense surveillance program, with his every move tracked, written up, and filed.

But like the hajj of Malcolm X, Carmichael's world tour seemed to, if not exactly mellow him, in some ways mature him. The new Stokely wasn't launching blanket attacks on black moderates and whites. He stopped talking about riots and violence. He began talking more about political unity and grass-roots organizing. "Suspicions that Carmichael would serve as a pied piper to Washington's black militants proved premature," wrote *U.S. News & World Report* in early 1968.[20]

By mid-January Carmichael was busy founding a new organization, the Black United Front (BUF), an umbrella group for the city's black organizations, from the staid NAACP to SNCC, from Baptists to marxists. Washington activists had a lot of potential, but they needed coordination. As he later wrote in his memoir *Ready for Revolution*, "Sure, there were a lot of groups, but no real programs. Local community organizations had different programs, different emphases, connections, commitments, capabilities, and leadership. Nothing that collectively addressed the overall interests and issues of black folk."[21]

The BUF dove into local politics, announcing its opposition to the planned Capital Beltway and its support for community-run schools. It was a creative endeavor, not a revolutionary one. As the *Washington Post* wrote, "Carmichael, whose reputation has been that of a fiery revolutionary, has shown an extremely conciliatory style in bringing together a coalition of Civil Rights activists and spokesmen of every cast." Carmichael even met with King, a man he had rudely dismissed in the past, and promised his peaceful support for the Poor People's Campaign. "Dr. King is a black man," he told the press in February 1968. "He is flesh of my flesh and blood of my blood. We have worked with Dr. King in the past and we will continue to work with Brother King."[22]

Carmichael was still close with many of the D.C. SNCC people, and when he wasn't touring the country giving speeches on college campuses—his primary source of income—he could be found hanging out at their new headquarters, near what was fast becoming the heart of the local black activist world, the intersection of Washington's Fourteenth and U streets. SCLC had its D.C. headquarters there, too (another of Carmichael's favorite hangouts). The NAACP and the New School for Afro-American Thought were just down the street. Pride, Inc., Marion Barry's new community-organizing outfit, was two blocks away, at Sixteenth and U.

The intersection was a lively locus of black Washington, and not just the activists. It had once been the center of the community's cultural world, the black Broadway of the District. By 1968, though, it had gone downhill; as *Washington Post* journalist Ben Gilbert wrote, "This was a spot to pick up a woman, purchase narcotics, make a deal."[23] And Carmichael was setting himself up as the neighborhood power broker, the insurgent head of the black community and its mediator with the white power structure.

It wasn't all peaceful progress. On April 2, just two days before King's murder, a security guard at the Peoples Drug on the northwest corner of Fourteenth and U, just to the right of the SCLC offices, had caught a black teenager shoplifting. He took him to the back room. The boy's friends started spreading a rumor that the guard was beating him, and a crowd gathered.

When the guard emerged, a fight broke out, and someone slashed the guard's lip with a razor. Two boys doused a nearby tree with lighter fluid and set it on fire, bringing the fire department to the scene. The police arrived and calmed things down, only to have them heat back up once they left. Suddenly, just as it looked like the crowd might pitch over into a riot, Carmichael appeared. Pointing at the guard and the white store manager, he said, "I done warned you, now you've had it." He slashed a finger across his throat. "We don't want white managers around this store." Then he turned to the cheering crowd. Chill out, he told them. This isn't the way to get things done. Now go home. And, like that, they did.[24] Carmichael, it was becoming clear, could bring peace, and not just agitation, to the black community.

Two nights later, as word of King's shooting spread through the neighborhood, Carmichael burst into the SCLC headquarters. Several office workers milled about, all black save for an elderly white couple and two young volunteers. Who shot him? Carmichael demanded. No one knew. The radio was on, and they were trying to listen. Carmichael sat in a chair and propped up his feet on a pair of desks.

He fidgeted. He got up, then sat down. He grabbed a nearby phone and made a call. "Well, if we must die, we better die fighting back," he told the person on the other end. "Now that they've taken Dr. King off . . . it's time to end this nonviolence bullshit."[25] He slammed down the receiver and turned his attention back to the radio. He bounced his long legs. Nothing new. Finally, Carmichael got up. "I'm not going to wait for the final verdict," he said. "I'm going to get my guys." Then he left. The SCLC staffers turned to each other, silently asking what he meant, and what was in store that night.

Was Carmichael going to fulfill his long-standing promise to bring violent revolution to the streets? Or was the man who just stormed out the new Carmichael, committed to radical, nonviolent action? Would he cause a riot—or stop one?

As Carmichael was leaving SCLC headquarters, Robert Kennedy's plane was touching down in Indianapolis. The New York senator had entered the race on March 16, just days after Eugene McCarthy had nearly beaten Johnson in New Hampshire. Though he had earned a less-than-enthusiastic following among civil rights leaders during his tenure as attorney general, Kennedy had since taken a new, progressive tack on social justice. He opposed the war and supported social programs, even as he attacked the administration's domestic efforts as hastily constructed and shortsighted.

Like King, Kennedy didn't want simply more of the same government programs. He wanted a whole new way of looking at the relationship between government and the public. Not just social welfare, but social justice. The links between the two were more than just intellectual affinity: Kennedy, like King, had been calling for a "Marshall Plan" for America's cities, and the Poor People's Campaign, King's final crusade, was originally Kennedy's idea, passed to the SCLC through activist Marian Wright, who was engaged to Peter Edelman, Kennedy's policy director.[26]

Kennedy had been in Washington the day before to meet with Johnson. The two had a long-standing, very public mutual contempt. But recently Johnson had been hinting to his inner circle that he might favor a Kennedy win in November. Kennedy, he figured, was a fighting liberal who could stand up to the encroaching conservatives—unlike his own vice president, whom he thought was too thin-skinned, or McCarthy, whom he found too intellectual and moralistic for Washington politics. And, indeed, when Johnson and Kennedy sat down that morning at the White House, the president told his former rival that he would abstain from endorsing anyone in the primary—a victory for the senator, who could have reasonably expected the newly empowered president to throw his support behind Humphrey, his heir apparent.[27]

On the afternoon of April 3, Kennedy held a rally in a vacant lot in Washington's Columbia Heights neighborhood, off Fourteenth Street and about a half-mile north of U Street. The D.C. primary was May 7, and in a tight race he needed every win he could get, even tiny Washington. In a scene that was becoming typical of Kennedy rallies, several hundred people, mostly black, showed up well before the candidate, jostling for a good view. Kennedy arrived late, waving from the backseat of a convertible with his wife, Ethel. He signed autographs as he struggled to get to the platform, which was mounted on the back of a truck. Two women fainted. A car backed over a police officer's foot. Little children screamed. Boys climbed a nearby lattice window to get a better view. And the crowd, numbering more than a thousand, cheered.

"I think that our campaign is making some progress," Kennedy said sardonically. "Yes!" shouted the crowd. He didn't deliver his full remarks; he didn't have time, and the people were too excited for dry policy talk. Instead, he spent a few minutes talking about the need to rebuild the city—"We must act, in all these areas, to make the nation's capital a place of pride"—before giving up to the noise of the crowd and, descending the platform, going to sign more autographs.[28] "No one seemed interested in what he was saying," reported the *Washington Afro-American*. "They wanted to touch him."[29]

A day later, Kennedy was in Indiana. The state was the next big primary, and he needed the win to prove he was a viable candidate in the Midwest. Appearing at Ball State University in Muncie, he ran through his agenda for new federal programs to alleviate poverty and social injustice. Soon a question emerged from a student: Can you really say these programs will work? Don't they put too much faith in the white establishment?

Yes I can, Kennedy replied. "The vast majority of white people are decent and want to do the right thing."[30]

Barely an hour after speaking those words, press aide Pierre Salinger delivered the word that a white man had shot King. It came just as Kennedy was about to board a plane to Indianapolis, where he would attend a rally at the Broadway Christian Center, in the city's black section, and then several evening events. Salinger told him to postpone the appearances. But Kennedy wanted to wait and see.

When they landed in Indianapolis, they learned King was dead. "Oh, God, when is this violence going to stop?" Kennedy wailed.[31] He canceled his schedule that evening, save for the rally. He sent Ethel on to the hotel. Then he got in the waiting limo and told the driver to head out.

As campaign aide Fred Dutton, who rode in the car with him, recalled, "He had planned a fairly standard stump talk. But he sat alone in the backseat, gazing out the window into the dark." The ride took about twenty-five minutes. At one point, Kennedy asked Dutton, "What do you think I should say?"[32]

The evening was cold, windy, and slightly raining. But as usual Kennedy proved enough of a draw to bring out hundreds. And, despite waiting for an hour, the predominantly black crowd was in a good mood. Red, white, and blue bunting hung around the parking lot and the speakers' platform. A spotlight zigzagged across the clouds. But when he arrived, Kennedy mounted the back of a flatbed truck instead. In his black overcoat, his face thin and anguished, he walked straight to the microphone.

He ran his left hand over his head. "I have some bad news for you," he said, "for all our fellow citizens, and people who love peace all over the world." Some people cheered—maybe they couldn't hear him, maybe they were just caught up in the moment. "Martin Luther King was shot and killed tonight." Screams ran through the crowd.

Kennedy went on, speaking without notes:

> In this difficult day, in this difficult time for the United States, it is perhaps well to ask what kind of a nation we are and what direction we want to move in. For those of you who are black—considering the evidence there evidently is that there were white people who were responsible—you can be filled with bitterness, with hatred, and a desire for revenge. We can move in that direction as a country, in great polarization—black people amongst black, white people amongst white, filled with hatred toward one another. Or we can make an effort, and Martin Luther King did, to understand and to comprehend, and to replace that violence, that stain of bloodshed that has spread across our land, with an effort to understand with compassion and love.

Reporters and advisers pushed in around him. One journalist stuck a tape recorder over his left shoulder.

Then Kennedy spoke about something he had never before addressed in public: the death of his brother John. "For those of you who are black and are tempted to be filled with hatred and distrust at the injustice of such an act, against all white people, I can only say that I feel in my own heart the same kind of feeling. I had a member of my family killed, but he was killed by a white man. But we have to make an effort in the United States, we have to make an effort to understand, to go beyond these rather difficult times. My favorite poet was Aeschylus. He wrote: 'In our sleep, pain which cannot forget falls drop by drop upon the heart until, in our own despair, against our will, comes wisdom through the awful grace of God.'"

But could that wisdom comfort a nation the same way it had comforted Kennedy? He believed it could. "What we need in the United States is not division; what we need in the United States is not hatred; what we need in the United States is not violence or lawlessness; but love and wisdom, and compassion toward one another, and a feeling of justice toward those who still suffer within our country, whether they be white or they be black." This was precisely what Kennedy had been saying throughout his short campaign, but never did it have more meaning than on that night.

Kennedy knew there would be violence, even as he begged the audience to remain peaceful. "We will have difficult times in the future. It is not the end of violence; it is not the end of lawlessness; it is not the end of disorder. But," he said, "the vast majority of white people and the vast majority of black people in this country want to live together, want to improve the quality of our life, and want justice for all human beings who abide in our land. Let us dedicate ourselves to what the Greeks wrote so many years ago: to tame the savageness of man and make gentle the life of this world. Let us dedicate ourselves to that, and say a prayer for our country and for our people."[33]

And with that, Kennedy got down off the truck. He asked the organizers to close the rally and tear down the bunting. Then he went back to his hotel.

At 2:00 A.M. he called Mrs. King. "I'll help in any way I can," he said.

"I'm planning to go to Memphis in the morning to bring back Martin's body."

"Let me fly you there," he offered. "I'll get a plane down."

Mrs. King thanked him. Kennedy also offered to hook up more phone lines to the house, to handle the impending wave of consolation calls. "It was something I hadn't thought about," she said later. "He said, 'I'll get that done tonight.' I said, 'How fantastic! Tonight!' I'd never heard of such a thing. But, of course, the telephone men came in that same evening and put the phones in, and they stayed in for several weeks."[34]

John Lewis, the former SNCC leader and future Georgia congressman, had been working for Kennedy's campaign, and he urged the candidate to keep an appointment he had set up that evening with a group of local black militants. Kennedy agreed, but by this time he was long overdue.

The men weren't happy. "Our leader is dead tonight, and when we need you we can't find you," one of them said as soon as he sat down. All you establishment people are the same, the man told him. You'd rather be grandstanding than working out real solutions.

But Kennedy would have none of it. "Yes, you lost a friend. I lost a brother. I know how you feel," he said. "You talk about the establishment. I have to laugh. Big business is trying to defeat me because they think I am a friend of the Negro."

The militants paused. Maybe Kennedy was right. They backed off, and turned to the scheduled agenda. What was Kennedy's platform really about? What did he think about the big issues facing the ghetto? Apparently Kennedy passed—when the meeting ended, they shook hands, and the candidate walked away with their endorsement.[35]

It is impossible to know whether Kennedy's words on that flatbed truck in Indianapolis prevented a riot from breaking out in the city. But Indianapolis, virtually alone among the nation's major cities, did avoid even the mildest of violence in the following days. It is hard to image that things would have been as peaceful had a white presidential candidate not given the city's black community the news, delivered in a way to draw them toward unity in mourning rather that division in hatred. As two radicals who had attended the rally to stir up violence later told researchers, "We went there for trouble, [but] after he spoke we couldn't get nowhere."[36]

The immediate question, though, was whether Kennedy's message would move quickly enough beyond Indianapolis to prevent violence elsewhere.

4

April 4

U and Fourteenth

At the White House, Johnson was settling into crisis mode. With riots now an annual event, the president had become a master in the clutch, a vital skill given that the past three years could seem, in retrospect, like one long chain of domestic and international emergencies. He had even structured his core domestic staff—Califano, McPherson, Larry Levinson, James Gaither, and a handful of others—in a loose, almost casual fashion, so that in a pinch they could fall into whatever roles needed to be filled: speechwriting, military liaison, civil rights outreach, congressional fixer.[1]

Now Johnson needed all those skills. After his TV appearance, he went back to the Oval Office, where he dove into a flurry of calls. He touched base with Governor Ellington, who told him that despite Clark's admonition, he was sending the Guard into Memphis. He called mayors, civil rights leaders, and still more governors. He told black leaders to get out in the streets, to meet with people and express their sorrow. He told the politicians to be careful about using force.

But he soon grew dismayed. "I'm not getting through," he told his aides. "They're holed up like generals in a dugout getting ready to watch a war."[2]

Busby, who had come in from Virginia to help with speechwriting, watched as his old friend once again took on the weight of a national meltdown. "The exuberance of the week seemed to be draining from his long face as I watched him behind the desk," he later wrote.[3]

Johnson set Califano, McPherson, and their assistants to work telephoning the nation's leading black figures. The president was calling a meeting at the White House the next day, and he wanted all the civil rights leaders to be there: Roy Wilkins of the NAACP; Whitney Young of the Urban League; Gary, Indiana, mayor Richard Hatcher; Thurgood Marshall of the Supreme Court; and almost a dozen others. Martin Luther King Sr., a prominent Atlanta preacher, was too ill to come. "The president asked me to say that his prayers are with you," one of Johnson's aides told him over the phone. "Oh, no," replied the ailing patriarch. "My prayers are with the president."[4]

Meanwhile, Califano was on and off the phone with Clark, over at Justice, who was getting regular updates from the FBI, U.S. district attorneys, and police departments around the country. Memphis police director Frank Holloman sent a report that read, "Matters getting critical—they're shooting at police cars. We have general looting." Looters were reportedly even firing at police helicopters.[5] Memphis, it seemed, was falling into chaos (or so Holloman reported; very little violence actually erupted in Memphis).

A little after 10:00 P.M., Johnson went to the White House Residence for dinner, stopping along the way at a secretary's office to try on a new pair of Sebago loafers. He liked them. At dinner with Secretary of Defense Clark Clifford, adviser Arthur Krim, and several members of his family, he told Califano and Busby to stay overnight.

"Dinner was a strange, quiet meal," Mrs. Johnson remembered. "We had been pummeled by such an avalanche of emotions the last four days that we couldn't feel anymore, and here we were, poised on the edge of another abyss, the bottom of which we could in no way see."[6] In between playing with Lyn, who climbed into and out of his grandfather's lap, Johnson finally got to put something in his stomach. But most of the others—Clifford, Krim, Busby—didn't eat.[7]

From the SCLC offices, Carmichael, in a bright green sweater and yellow-tinted sunglasses, went across the street to SNCC. There he found Lester McKinnie, who had recently replaced Marion Barry as the moribund organization's Washington head; C. Sumner Stone, former editor of the *Washington Afro-American*; and more than a dozen other staffers.[8]

Like the people at the SCLC, they were listening to the radio. The dial was tuned to local DJ Bob Terry of WOL, D.C.'s most popular soul station. "This is no time to hate," Terry was saying, his usually raucous voice coming across smooth and quiet. "Hate won't get you anywhere. And let me tell you something, white man. Tomorrow, before you get back in that car and go out to the suburban house, you better say something nice to that black man on the job beside you. You'd better stop hating, too."[9]

Carmichael conferred with McKinnie and Stone in a back office. After a few minutes, McKinnie came out and told the room that they were considering calling a "black strike." But, he said, they wanted to wait and take "some time to react to this great tragedy." Caution, he said, was the watchword.

Suddenly Carmichael was beside him. "They took our leader off," he said, cutting off McKinnie. "So, out of respect, we're gonna ask all these stores to close down until Martin Luther King is laid to rest." And with that he headed out, with all but McKinnie and Stone behind him.[10]

Seconds later Carmichael burst through the front door of Peoples, just steps away from SNCC. Some twenty young men trailed in his wake. A small crowd had gathered at the front of the store, watching the news from Memphis on television. Carmichael brushed past them; he was looking for the manager, G. M. Simirtzakis.

"We're going to close this store!" he shouted. "Because when Kennedy was shot the businesses were closed, and they are going to be closed now that King's dead."

He went to the back, straight into the manager's office. Behind him, his "guys" snatched items off the shelves, careful not to let their boss see. A few minutes later Carmichael came striding back to the front of the store, Simirtzakis in tow. "Look, I hear you," the manager pleaded. "I'm going to close the store."

Carmichael turned to the crowd. "Everybody out! Everybody out!"[11]

From Peoples, Carmichael and his crew headed south. At a Safeway supermarket, he rapped on the windows, but it had already closed. Methodically he proceeded down the west side of Fourteenth, stopping at each open store and ordering it closed. After a block he crossed the street, headed north, and did the same with the stores on that side. No one refused. It was 8:45.

The crowd behind Carmichael grew as he headed east on U Street. It was no longer just his "guys." Adults, teenagers, even little kids— anyone and everyone who was out in the streets already, seeking solace and news in the balmy night. Some joined Carmichael to help, some just to watch.

Others were looking for trouble. At the Republic Theater, a large and popular movie house at Thirteenth and U, Carmichael sent several men in to stop the show and hustle moviegoers out the door. He had others do the same at the Lincoln, on the next block. As he was barking orders, a stocky fifteen-year-old boy, dressed in dungarees and a sailor's cap, punched his first through the front window of the Republic, reached into the concession stand, and grabbed some popcorn. As the boy shoved the popcorn into his mouth, Carmichael turned and yelled, "We don't want any damaging! We just want the stores to close."[12]

But even as Carmichael was trying to control the crowd, others were trying to incite it. Floyd McKissick, the outgoing chair of the increasingly radical Congress on Racial Equality (CORE), told a reporter on the scene, "The next Negro to advocate nonviolence should be torn to bits by the black people."[13] The D.C. NAACP chapter released a statement that read, "No one can be blamed for the consequences that might occur. There is a lot of unrest in this area right now. A lot of the leaders are not coming out tonight because they are afraid of becoming irrational themselves."[14]

At some point, while Carmichael was crossing the street ahead of his now substantial crowd, he ran into Walter Fauntroy, a prominent local minister and the SCLC representative in the capital. Fauntroy was the closest thing the black community had to a power broker: he knew most of Congress and had a direct line to the president. Long after King and Johnson had stopped speaking to one another, Fauntroy continued to play liaison between the civil rights movement and the president. If anyone represented King's memory in D.C. at that moment, it was this man.

Fauntroy had been on the phone with the White House all evening, reporting on the scene in black Washington. Now he was out in the streets, trying to calm the public himself. "This is not the way to do it, Stokely," he told Carmichael, his short, stocky frame standing a full head shorter than the lanky Carmichael's. "Let's not get anyone hurt. Let's cool it."

We're not looking to start anything, Walter, Carmichael said. "All we're asking them to do is to close the stores."[15]

Fauntroy looked at the bubbling crowd behind Carmichael. What could he do? Carmichael sounded reasonable, but who knew what this self-styled revolutionary would do next? Who knew what the city—and the country—would do next?

In any case, this was no place to make a stand. Fauntroy said okay and retreated. He had other fires to put out that evening.

It began to rain lightly, but Carmichael pressed on, and people kept gathering. Like King in Memphis six days prior, a violent energy was building behind him. Kids marched in the streets, singing "beep beep—black power!" A man ran to a city bus and punched through the front glass before he was pulled away. A large-posteriored woman bumped into the plate-glass window of Belmont TV and Appliance Store, shattering it. SNCC workers ran over quickly to prevent would-be looters from getting inside.[16]

At one point, some in the crowd saw a white man beside a car, taking pictures. They pushed him to the ground, then kicked him. "Kill him!" someone shouted. "Get the film!" shouted another. The man groped for his camera, ripped out the film, and threw it. The crowd backed off. Someone reached out from the mob and helped him to his feet—an undercover police officer, it turned out—and shepherded him down the street.[17]

Carmichael had gone back to Fourteenth, then headed north, uphill toward the Columbia Heights neighborhood, a major shopping thoroughfare for black Washington. By now the crowd filled the four-lane street, from one side to the other and a block deep. Several kids started punching the plate-glass window at Peoples. Suddenly someone threw a brick through it. "Let's kill 'em!" people shouted. "Burn this town down!" "Kill those honkies!"

Carmichael turned on his heels. "You really ready to go out and kill?" he yelled to the crowd.

"They killed our leader!" someone shouted back.

"You won't get one this way," Carmichael said. "How you gonna win? What you got? They've got guns, tanks—what you got? You got a gun?"

The crowd was silent.

"Well, I do," and he reached into his back waistband and pulled out a small-caliber pistol. "If you don't have a gun, go home. We're not ready. Let's wait until tomorrow. Just cool it. Go home, go home, go home."[18]

But most people already were home. And besides, who wanted to leave all this excitement?

Just then, two black security guards pulled up in front of Peoples, right as it was closing. They got out of their car and froze. More than a thousand angry locals milled around them. One by one they turned to the guards. Anger jolted through the crowd, anger at the system, at the authorities, at the man. For the time being, two unarmed black rent-a-cops would have to do. The crowd pressed in.

Just then Carmichael, holding his gun in the air, broke through and grabbed the pair. He pushed them back in their car and signaled for some nearby SNCC workers to make space for them. "Now get out of here!"[19]

The crowd backed off, and the mood seemed to cool down several degrees. People stood silent. For a moment it looked like Carmichael might have stopped the riot after all.

The nation's capital wasn't the only place teetering on the edge of violence that night. Memphis remained surprisingly calm, but in the middle of the state, four thousand Tennessee National Guardsmen deployed in northern Nashville after reports of vandalism and looting began pouring into police headquarters. Farther east, in Raleigh, North Carolina, a march near predominantly black Shaw University descended into a window-smashing spree, and police sealed off the area. Cops used tear gas in Jackson, Mississippi, after a mob started breaking car windows and set a reporter's car on fire. Molotov cocktails ignited a furniture store in Houston. Hartford, Connecticut, and Tallahassee, Florida, experienced minor riots, while police battled with youths throwing bottles and rocks in two separate sections of Newark.[20]

But with Memphis intact, the real concern that night shifted to New York. Ever since Watts the media, the public, and the city and federal governments had assumed that the Big Apple was in for a major conflagration—"the mother of confrontations between black youths and the police force," as *New York* magazine later characterized it.[21]

And almost as soon as the news of King's death hit the airwaves, Harlem residents were out in the streets. Music store owners pointed speakers out their front doors, playing recordings of King's speeches. Like the crowds in Washington, most people were looking for comfort, conversation, and more news. But others were expressing their anger in more direct ways, harassing motorists and roughing up pedestrians.

In midtown Manhattan, Mayor John Lindsay was at the Alvin Theater, sitting through the first act of a new Broadway musical, *The Education of H*y*m*a*n K*a*p*l*a*n*, starring his friend Tom Bosley. Lindsay was a liberal Republican, one of the most liberal in national politics. It was he who had pushed the Kerner Commission to blame "white racism" for the riots, and it was he who had urged its members to call for massive new federal spending efforts.

First elected in 1965, Lindsay had spent most of the previous summer dealing with minor and not-so-minor outbreaks of violence around northern Manhattan and Brooklyn, a few of which would have been classified as full-scale riots in other cities. A July 1967 disturbance involving several hundred people in East Harlem resulted in the looting of twenty-five stores and three deaths. But Lindsay ruled this merely an "antipolice demonstration," while the gasoline-filled bottles with flaming wicks were not Molotov cocktails but "unidentified objects."[22] He was determined not to have riots in New York, even if he had to alter the very meaning of the term.

If Lindsay was wary of admitting the frequency of riots to the press, however, he was more than willing to recognize their existence to himself and his staff. He may have come across as an out-of-touch, Ivy League–educated dandy to some, but he possessed an acute sense of how the city worked, particularly its lower-income areas. During the summer of 1967, he poured money into summer jobs and activity programs to keep kids occupied and out of trouble. Then he created a city task force to maintain constant communication with ghetto leaders. And these leaders weren't the ministers, businessmen, and other middle-class blacks that whites typically assumed "led" the ghetto, either. Lindsay opened lines of communication with militants, gang leaders, and youth organizers, the people who truly understood and spoke for the concerns of Harlem, Bedford-Stuyvesant, and East New York. Lindsay didn't try to co-opt them, nor did he try to win them over to "his" side. "They could be pro-police, they could be anti-police.

They could hate John Lindsay. But these were people whom we could call on if something happened," recalled mayoral aide Sid Davidoff.[23]

What Lindsay understood was that there were natural divisions between truly violent radicals and Harlem's run-of-the-mill gang leaders and activists; the former were often from out of town with few real ties in the community, while the latter, regardless of their legal standing, were usually local dudes who had an investment in community stability. And he counted on that investment to keep the peace. (It may be apocryphal, but a popular story going around Harlem had it that when H. Rap Brown came to town talking about violent revolution, a drug dealer and his crew jumped him, saying, "If you ever come back here talking that sort of shit, we'll kill you."[24]) These were the real ghetto peacekeepers, and Lindsay treated them almost as a shadow government. In turn, he earned their grudging respect. That might be a bad way to run a city, but Lindsay felt it was his only hope for avoiding mass destruction.

At about 8:30, during the song "Spring in the City," a plainclothes detective came to the mayor's seat and handed him a note about King. Lindsay immediately went to the lobby and called the police commissioner's office. No violence yet, they said. But things are getting hairy in Harlem. Lindsay got into a waiting sedan and sped uptown to Gracie Mansion, the mayoral residence on the far Upper East Side, not far from Harlem.[25]

Along the way, he talked over options with David Garth, his press aide. Lindsay wanted to get to Harlem immediately. That's a really bad idea, Garth said. But Lindsay persisted. "Somebody just has to go up there," he said. "Somebody white just has to face that emotion and say that we're sorry."

From the mansion, which he declared his emergency headquarters, Lindsay began calling neighborhood leaders. He set up four secretaries on shifts, manning a phone bank—if one of his contacts had to get in touch with him, he wanted to talk to them immediately. He also had Barry Gottehrer, another close aide, activate the task force, which would get gang leaders and other influential Harlemites out on the street calling for calm. The news coming in was gloomy; Harlem was "really uptight; bad," Lindsay was told. Police and fire units were on the way. Soon, so was Lindsay, riding in an unmarked black Plymouth.

The mayor first went to the 25th Police Precinct in central Harlem, where he got a briefing on the situation. Then, with Garth at the wheel, he went to the center of the neighborhood, at 8th Avenue and 125th Street. Hundreds of people were milling about, young and old. "There was a mob that was so large that it went across 125th Street from storefront to storefront," Garth recalled. "My life is over," he said to himself.

Suddenly Lindsay got out of the car—and walked toward the crowd. Garth stared in shock.

But this wasn't Lindsay's first stroll through Harlem, and people recognized him immediately. "That's the mayor," said one kid. What's the latest on King? they asked. How could this happen? Others complained about the heavy police presence, despite the absence of any real violence. Why was there a barricade on 125th? someone asked. Lindsay turned to a nearby officer. "Better keep them moving, don't you think, officer?" And so the barriers came down. Lindsay told the crowd how much he regretted King's death. He told them how important it was for the city to now make real progress in alleviating poverty and discrimination. "He had no written speech. No prepared remarks. He just held up his hand and said, 'this is a terrible thing.' He just calmed people," recalled Garth. "And then this gigantic wave started marching down 125th Street, and somehow Lindsay was leading it."[26]

Though tensions appeared to drop, they didn't dissolve completely—one boy in the procession said, to no one in particular, "Man, there's gonna be white blood in the streets tonight." As Lindsay moved on, scattered looting took place in his wake. But the peace held.

Lindsay walked over to Frank's, a popular 125th Street restaurant, where he met with labor leader Joe Overton and a few other Harlem notables. As he left, forty minutes later, a local tough, who called himself Bobby, fell in behind the mayor. "Don't worry," the bulky black kid told Lindsay. "Nobody can get to you while Bobby's here."

At Convent Avenue and 125th Street, Lindsay and company encountered three hundred students marching from the City University of New York, several blocks north. He called on them to stop. There was plenty of time for memorial demonstrations during daylight hours. As Lindsay later recalled, "I kept moving, but finally I was hemmed in from all sides. Occasionally, I could hear my name shouted, and at other times I could hear men and women weeping or moaning. . . . We edged to a clearing in the crowd, where another group of men moved close—also men I knew. The group began arguing about which was the better route for me to take."[27]

Bobby's presence next to the mayor was a problem, too. Why did he get to play bodyguard? Members of a rival gang demanded that they be allowed to provide the mayor protection instead. A shouting match erupted, with Lindsay in the middle, suddenly helpless to calm things down. Just as things were getting nasty, Manhattan Borough president Percy Sutton, who had been quietly tailing the mayor, pulled up in his car and yelled for Lindsay and Bobby to jump in. They did, gladly. Without their object of competition, the rival crowds eased back, and the streets stayed peaceful.

Harlem wasn't out of the woods yet, so to speak, but everyone agreed that Lindsay had made a huge difference by showing up at a time when many mayors across the country were hiding out in bunkerlike emergency operations centers. Jimmy Breslin, the city's leading columnist, wrote, "He looked straight at the people on the streets and he told them he was sick and he was sorry about Martin Luther King. And the poor he spoke to who are so much more real than the rest of us, understood the truth of John Lindsay. And there was no riot in New York."[28] Garth later called him "the most courageous man I've ever seen." Even historian Vincent Cannato, who wrote an excellent but highly critical biography of Lindsay, admitted that "in some ways, Lindsay's reaction to the King riots represented a high point in his administration."[29]

The mayor got back to Gracie Mansion at 11:30. There he found an entire wing of the house buzzing with people: mayor's office, police, fire, emergency services. His children had to double up in a spare bedroom to make space for weary staffers in need of a few minutes' sleep.

That night five thousand cops and firemen were deployed in and around Harlem and in scattered parts of Brooklyn. There had been minor damage, twelve arrests—ten in Harlem, two in Brooklyn—and even a few fires. But nothing concentrated, and nothing sustained.[30] At 1:00 A.M. Lindsay hopped back in the city Plymouth and visited Harlem again. Things had died down significantly; glass and debris littered some of the streets, but nothing uncontrollable.

Lindsay ordered the sanitation department out in force, so that the streets would be clean come daylight—better not to remind people of what had just happened. He went back to the mansion once more, this time to sleep. The mayor was in bed by three.

But where Lindsay succeeded, Carmichael failed. Even as he was holding the line in front of Peoples, several young men were inside the pharmacy ransacking it, overturning display cases, stealing whatever they could grab. A few SNCC workers saw what was going on and rushed in to stop them. But the urge to riot had caught. Like the proverbial finger in the dike, the SNCC workers' intervention just sent the looters across the street to other stores. Within minutes, as if a switch had been flipped, everyone was looting.

A man with a two-by-four went down a row of shops on Fourteenth, smashing windows; as he did, a troop of teenagers poured into the stores. Liquor stores, five-and-dimes, pawnshops, all came under attack. A young woman walked along the street carrying a cooking pot, singing to herself, "Got me something, got me something."[31]

Carmichael saw what was happening, and he realized the night was lost. Even more, he realized he would get blamed. And indeed he was. As soon as the news of King's shooting broke, all the local and national news outlets with staffers to spare flooded the Fourteenth and U neighborhood. The *Washington Post* and the *Washington Evening Star* were there, as was the *New York Times*. TV stations had their camera crews were deployed. And predictably, each reporter told a slightly different story about what happened that night. The *Post* reported that Carmichael was simply ordering stores to close, and that at the first sign of violence he told people to go home. The *Times* reporters, on the other hand, told their editors that Carmichael had brandished a pistol and ordered the crowd to "go home and get your guns."[32] An extensive FBI investigation later concluded that the *Times* version was incorrect.[33] But, not surprisingly, that's the story many other outlets went with, and which in turn many later accounts have latched onto. Carmichael, in any case, didn't stick around—he fled the scene and wasn't heard from the rest of the night.

The first report of violence, that looters had broken into a U Street appliance store and were carting out televisions and radios, came in to the police at 10:15.[34] Within minutes cops in white riot helmets began arriving on the scene. But as one officer later told Senator Robert

Byrd in an interview, "We were outnumbered. It must have been hundreds to one, children of all ages, women, everybody, just like a holiday. They thought everything was for free down there. They were running and grabbing, holding up dresses to see if they fitted them."[35]

The police made some arrests, but they were trying to stop a river with a bailing bucket—a few rioters shuffling into a police van didn't make a difference against thousands. Several cops threw gas grenades. "But some of the officers didn't have gas masks, so we were hurting the officers," the cop reported to Byrd. At about 11:15, an officer shot and wounded a suspect at Fourteenth and Irving, several blocks from U Street. An ambulance was dispatched to pick them up.[36]

Public safety chief Patrick Murphy, a tough-minded New Yorker who had been on the job for less than six months, was just getting into police headquarters, having learned of the shooting at home. He and police chief John Layton conferred and immediately decided to call in the midnight shift early. But that still meant only a few hundred more cops would be on the scene, and who knew where else the city could blow up that night? As Murphy told a reporter that night, "We're giving it the light touch . . . there are no great numbers of men available."[37]

Meanwhile, panicked calls were coming in from officers at the scene. "Won't someone please tell us what to do?" one officer pleaded over the radio. "Surrounded by a mob of about fifty people. What do we do? They are rioting. Do we arrest them?"[38] No one had the answer. The disorder on the streets was matched by the disorder among the police.

The lack of law enforcement seemed to goad on the rioters. "It was like musical chairs," an anonymous looter later told an interviewer from Howard University. "First of all, the kids would run in and grab clothes and the cops would pull up, and every time the cops would pull up they would have their lights flashing and their sirens would blast and they would talk over their loudspeaker—whatever it was— and tell the kids to disperse." The police would stay for a few minutes, then leave without making an arrest. Those looters who hadn't moved on to another store would quickly filter back, and the ransacking would continue.[39]

Layton and Murphy, who had rushed to Fourteenth and U themselves, decided to seal off the street from U Street northward. But as a later city government investigation concluded, this proved "extremely difficult," since the officers quickly came under intense "verbal abuse and were the targets of some thrown bottles."[40] And by then the looting had spread north by several blocks, so that its epicenter was now half a mile up Fourteenth, at the intersection with Park Road. There, half a block away from the parking lot where Bobby Kennedy had spoken just over twenty-four hours before, hundreds of people, then thousands, were tearing into shops of all kinds—alongside liquor stores and pawnshops, they sacked jewelry stores, clothing boutiques, salons, and hardware outlets.

Once the looters moved out, the arsonists moved in. Eighteen separate fires erupted along Sixteenth Street that night. At 11:50, Fire Chief Henry Galotta instituted "Plan F," something never before done in city history. The city had thirty-two engine companies, each with a truck and an apparatus, but Plan F split the two vehicles into separate units, doubling the number of fires they could tackle—but also increasing the risk of a fire getting out of control.[41]

D.C. mayor Walter Washington was monitoring the situation from his home at Fourth and T streets, just ten blocks due east from the center of the riot. A reserved, bespoke Howard Law graduate, Washington had been installed by Johnson less than a year before, and his face bore permanently the ironic bemusement of someone tasked with the impossible—in his case, building the country's first black-run city government, in a town dominated by a rich white minority and a racist congressional oversight committee, all during a time of social and economic tumult. When Washington delivered his first city budget to Congress, Representative John McMillan, the southern Democrat who headed the Committee on the District of Columbia, had a truckload of watermelons sent to the mayor's office.[42]

Alongside him in front of the Washington family TV were two of his closest advisers, Julian Dugas, his director of the Department of Licenses and Inspections, and D.C. corporation counsel Charles Duncan. Seated nearby, quietly taking notes, was *Washington Star* reporter Paul Delaney.[43]

Suddenly Washington stood up and said he wanted to see things firsthand. Mrs. Washington said it was a bad idea, but the four men—Washington, Dugas, Duncan, and Delaney—along with Duncan's wife, were already out the door. They piled into Duncan's brand-new gray Pontiac Tempest and slowly began rolling toward Fourteenth Street.

Light rain splattered the windshield. Maybe it'll slow down the rioting, said Dugas. Washington didn't reply. Nearing the intersection, they could see broken windows and, by now, an occasional fire. Every once in a while, a cop.

At Fourteenth they turned right, heading uphill. Suddenly hundreds of people were pouring past the car in both directions, oblivious to the police and unaware that the mayor was looking right at them. "It looked as though they were shopping," Delaney later wrote.

They mayor just shook his head. Kids were running through the streets with loot. Others dashed into and out of stores. "Well," Washington finally said, "I guess this is our recreation program for the summer." No one laughed. They pulled onto a side street, and as they did, the headlights lit on two teenage girls, each with armfuls of clothing. "Look at that stuff, will you!" Washington exclaimed, his first hint of emotion all evening. "Just look at that stuff!"

Finally a cop pulled them over. After they identified themselves, he told them to get out of the area. Despite the carnival atmosphere, not everyone was harmless. A few hours earlier, the cops had pulled over four white men in a Chevrolet, one bleeding profusely. The men said they'd gotten lost trying to cut through the city, and when they stopped to ask for directions at a gas station, a gang of black kids had started beating one of them, a man named George Fletcher. Then they stabbed him in the head. Fletcher was rushed to Fairfax City Hospital in suburban Virginia, where he died.[44]

Duncan headed toward Sixteenth, a traditional border between wealthy and poor Washington. There, Delaney recalled, it was like they had "entered another world. The people at the bus stops, the couples walking hand in hand, seemingly oblivious to what was happening two blocks away."[45] The car headed down the hill to the Third District headquarters, just west of Sixteenth on a leafy residential street.

As Washington and his fellow passengers came through the door of the police building, they passed a white man who had been brought in for public drunkenness. "Nigger bastards trying to wreck my town," he muttered.[46]

After dinner at the White House, the Johnsons went to their bedroom. But the president couldn't sleep, and soon he was up again, making phone calls in his bathrobe, getting reports on the situation uptown. At 11:30 a heavy rain hit Washington, and the rioting mercifully petered out. Two hundred store windows had been smashed, and 150 stores looted. Eighteen fires had been set. And the police had arrested 200 people, 50 of them children.[47]

After midnight Mayor Washington called to say his police finally had control of the streets, that the fires were under control, and that he had ordered out the sanitation department to clean up as much of the damage as possible before daybreak. The real concern, he reported, was the next night, when the news of King's death would be fully absorbed and the militants would have had time to rile up the locals.[48]

Johnson and Lady Bird then talked to Atlanta mayor Allen, a close personal friend and the head of King's hometown. Rioting there, everyone suspected, could be brutal. But the city was so far completely calm, Allen reported. Finally, just after 2:00 A.M., at Clark's insistent suggestion, Johnson sent his attorney general to Memphis to head the Justice Department team overseeing the manhunt for King's assassin.[49] Clark would leave at daybreak.

Johnson returned to bed, and this time he slept.

5

April 5

MIDNIGHT INTERLUDE

The news of King's shooting reached the Army Operations Center, deep inside the Pentagon, at 7:30, and before his death was even confirmed, the center was coming online. Operating twenty-four hours a day, the AOC was the nerve center for all domestic military operations. If the Soviets invaded, this enormous room—the size of a naval dry dock—was where the United States would run its counterattack.

Brigadier General Harris Hollis, who ran AOC operations, called Memphis and ordered the Tennessee National Guard to keep him personally updated. By 10:30, when news of disturbances at Fourteenth and U streets first started rolling in, Hollis—who by then had been joined by his deputy and Undersecretary of the Army David McGiffert—had placed a company of the Third Infantry Regiment, located at nearby Fort Myer in suburban Virginia, on a thirty-minute alert, ordered two battalions of the Eighty-second Airborne at Fort Bragg, North Carolina, on a six-hour alert, and gotten in touch with the air force to put the necessary transportation resources in order. Within minutes, fifteen C-130 Hercules transport planes were getting ready at Pope Air Force Base, near Fort Bragg, to ferry troops to Washington in the event the White House ordered the city occupied.[1]

Then they waited.

Originally intended to manage a potential war on U.S. soil, during the 1960s the AOC was taking on a different, additional job: overseeing the Pentagon's riot-control efforts. The army's postwar role in domestic disturbances had evolved in two stages. Until 1963 it had been a largely ad hoc endeavor. Troops went into Little Rock to impose school desegregation and into Oxford, Mississippi, to oversee James Meredith's registration at Ole Miss. But in both cases the mission plans had developed as the crises unfolded. And while both had gone off successfully, there was concern that poor oversight could someday lead to a disaster (in Oxford, National Guard troops had clashed with prosegregation protesters). If the army was going to play a role in riot control, it wanted a much better idea of what it had to do. At the same time, the army, wary of operating domestically, also wanted to establish a structure that might reduce its own deployment, and that meant better training for National Guard units, better intelligence sharing, better equipment transfer, and closer coordination with the Department of Justice.[2]

In September 1963, soon after a near-deployment to Birmingham, the army promulgated its first operations plan for domestic disturbances, code-named Steep Hill. It earmarked twenty-one thousand soldiers in seven brigades for riot duty, with required annual training; it also established protocols for moving them around the country. Any operation was to be run out of the AOC.[3] Until 1967, though, the task had primarily involved monitoring and support, watching what was going on, and sending supplies to National Guard units when they went into Watts and elsewhere. Occasionally it meant gearing up for possible deployment.

Then, in July 1967, President Johnson deployed the Eighty-second Airborne to Detroit after horrible rioting broke out there, so bad that even the Michigan National Guard proved unable to contain it. In the aftermath, the AOC's job changed dramatically. The need for federal troops to occupy portions of American cities was no longer a frightening possibility, but a sad fact. For some, it was worse than sad—it was potentially apocalyptic. Writing in an army journal, one officer predicted U.S. cities could witness "scenes of destruction approaching those of Stalingrad in World War II. . . . In the next decade at least one major metropolitan area could be faced with guerrilla warfare requiring sizable United States army elements."[4]

While the Detroit operation went off well, it revealed stark shortcomings in the army's capabilities. One concern was time. Once alerted, it took several hours to gather troops, get enough planes together to move them, decide where to move them to, then unload and organize them once they arrived. And that was before the soldiers even went into action.

In addition, the Michigan National Guard, which the army had hoped could contain the violence, proved dangerously inadequate. The Guardsmen were trigger-happy and scared, willing to open fire on the slightest noise, which they took to be snipers but was more often than not ricochets from their own rifles—in one instance peppering an apartment with .50-caliber machine-gun fire that badly wounded a woman and killed her four-year-old niece. As of July 28, several days after the Eighty-second Airborne arrived, the Guard had fired 155,576 rounds to the regular army's 202. The Guard killed between 7 and 9 people, while the regulars killed 1 and the police at least 20.[5]

Nor were there clear lines of communication or command among the local and state police, the National Guard, and the army. Technically, the federalized Guardsmen were under the command of General John Throckmorton, the commander of the Eighty-second Airborne. But the reality of the situation was much less clear-cut. Guard commanders resented having federal commanders from outside the state telling them how to manage "their" riot, especially when the new commanders insisted that Guardsmen remove their ammunition from their guns.[6] Throckmorton worried that, if pushed, they would resist orders.

After the riot, Cyrus Vance, a former deputy secretary of defense who had served as Johnson's on-the-ground liaison in Detroit, wrote a report containing the lessons he believed the federal government needed to learn from the event. That report, the "Vance Book," quickly became the bible to riot planners around the country, especially inside the Department of the Army.

That fall Secretary of Defense Robert McNamara tasked Undersecretary McGiffert with upgrading the Pentagon before the next long, hot summer. He and an interagency task force examined every aspect of the military's counterriot operations: intelligence, transportation, training, and command and control. Eighteen brigades were designated for civil-disorder deployment. As early as August 1967, McGiffert directed the commanders of each of these units to reconnoiter the cities under their watch and liaise with local officials, from the mayor to the police chief to the state National Guard adjutant general.

The army then drew up universal plans for units deployed to areas of civil disturbance, outlining chains of command, lines of communication, and arrest procedures. According to an army report, "These omnibus plans were highly flexible and applicable to all potential areas of civil disturbance in the United States."[7] Then, building off these general plans, each commander put together specially tailored planning "packets"—thick, regularly updated notebooks that documented each city in detail. They covered the locations and contact information for vulnerable retail outlets such as liquor and gun stores; the location of critical infrastructure such as bridges, dams, water sanitation plants, and electrical facilities; the demographic and economic layout of the city; and background information on local militants, community activists, and business leaders. The plans were so detailed that every company knew in advance which precinct it would deploy to, and which police officers it would work with once there.

When the packets were finished, the army required commanders down to the company level to make regular forays, in mufti, into their designated cities to meet with their precinct liaisons and get tours of their territory. Meanwhile, McGiffert directed each of the nation's homeland armies to place one company on six-hour alert, one battalion on twelve-hour alert, and an entire brigade on twenty-four-hour alert. He also established six regional task force headquarters at army bases around the country, so that civil disturbance deployments could be managed from close up. These new plans, replacing Steep Hill, were code-named Garden Plot.[8]

By April 1968, the U.S. Army was as ready to invade its own cities as it was to invade most foreign countries.

But it was one thing to have a plan in place; it was another to have troops ready to execute it. So McGiffert established the Senior Officers' Civil Disturbance Orientation Course, known as SEADOC, at the U.S. Army Military Police School at Fort Gordon, Georgia. The course was aimed at army officers, but it was open to all levels of government: other military branches, the FBI, the National Guard, and, eventually, even local police departments. The army issued a revised civil disturbance training manual, which it used in conjunction with a new requirement than all troops based in the continental United States complete at least thirty-two hours of counter-riot training (officers had to complete forty-eight hours). The course even included practice in a mock-up slum, "Riotsville," in which students had to restore order to a "mob" made up of army MPs dressed as looters.

Finally, back at the AOC, McGiffert had commanders draw up extensive logistical plans for every contingency they could imagine. If a riot broke out in Oakland, for example, he wanted to know which units would go there, what they would take, who would take them there, and how they would be supplied once they arrived. The plans even contained orders for how commanders should approach their missions (for example, "Commanders were to so employ their forces to avoid appearing as an invading, alien force. Rather, they were to present themselves as part of a force whose purpose was to restore order with a minimum loss of life and property and with due respect for the great number of citizens whose involvement was purely accidental"; "When shooting is necessary, shots will be aimed to wound rather than to kill"[9]).

All of this was made possible by an extensive army domestic intelligence network. Located in the D.C. suburbs at Fort Holabird, Maryland, the Continental U.S. Intelligence Branch, part of the U.S. Army Intelligence Command (USAINTC), oversaw some one thousand agents around the country whose job was to monitor "indicators of imminent violence," including the "presence or participation in local activities by militant agitators," the "increase in efforts of extremist, integrationist, and segregationist groups to instigate violence, e.g., increase in number of handbills, pamphlets, and posters urging acts of violence," and "reports and rumors of planned violence, presence of known instigators of violence."[10]

At first, this information was collected passively, with federal, state, and local law enforcement agencies feeding data into a vast computer database stored in a locked mesh-wire cage at Fort Holabird. But as the army's planning efforts grew more complex, its domestic intelligence operations expanded accordingly. Active intelligence collection was only supposed to occur once a disorder was deemed imminent. But soon enough, the army was spying on dissent activities of all kinds, all in the name of riot prevention. As a later secret report concluded, the program "was perhaps most deficient in that it did not limit the degree to which Army Intelligence field elements were to monitor civilian affairs"—in other words, no one defined what constituted an "imminent" risk of disorder, and so the operation naturally metastasized.[11]

The scope of organizations "of interest" widened continuously; at one point the NAACP and even the Daughters of the American Revolution were under surveillance. Army spies infiltrated antiwar groups as well; forty-five agents spied on and even took part in the March on the Pentagon in the fall of 1967, some riding on the buses that ferried protesters from New York. And despite an explicit ban on domestic activity, the Army Security Agency, which ran the service's electronic intelligence operations, prepared to jam and engage in "deceptive transmitting" of false information across organizers' radios. Though this was never implemented, the army did receive support from the National Security Agency, which monitored a lengthy watch list of individuals involved in the march and other dissident activities.[12]

Washington, as the nation's capital, came under particularly close attention. As one August 1967 memo regarding the 116th Military Intelligence Group, based at Fort McNair in Southwest Washington, noted, "Their intelligence gathering efforts include the use of roving patrols in radio equipped, unmarked automobiles."[13] Agents registered as students at U.S. colleges, passed themselves off as activists in civil rights organizations, and even disguised themselves as reporters while filming protests. When a few commanders raised their eyebrows at the legality of such extensive operations, they were ignored; after all, a top-secret report concluded, "There is no statutory prohibition on Army [counterintelligence] operation collection activities within [the continental United States]."[14] This was only true in the narrowest sense, but it was taken as truth by an army aggressively expanding its domestic operations.

The Army Intelligence Command pulled out all the stops during the fall and winter of 1967–1968. As part of his reform efforts, McGiffert had ordered a report drawn up recommending ways to improve army intelligence-gathering. The obvious answer was drastic expansion. As the report, which was implemented in early 1968, concluded, "Continuous counterintelligence investigations are required to obtain factual information on the participation of subversive personalities, groups or organizations and their influence on urban populations to cause civil disturbances."[15] In other words, the only way to prevent rioting was for the army to turn into an American Stasi.

Soon reports on every activist meeting, every minor crime, every rumor that the army came across were vacuumed into its vast intelligence apparatus. The information was then processed and sorted into personal files, of which, at the height of the operation, there were almost twenty thousand. Relevant information was then included in daily and weekly reports, which went out to the various continental U.S. commanders, as well as to the FBI, CIA, DIA, Selective Service, Passport Agency, even state and local law-enforcement agencies.[16]

Needless to say, this posed a grave civil liberties threat. But it is indicative of the times that no one considered this a concern. With a war in Asia already putting America on edge, civil disorder seemed a threat not just to urban peace but also to the very survival of the nation. A top-secret intelligence report issued days before King's assassination concluded, "Racially oriented civil disturbances can be expected to continue with increasing intensity in urban areas in the United States during 1968. . . . Although hard evidence of any actual or planned communist conspiracy to dominate and control racial and anti-war protest movements is not now available, the threat of such conspiracy is sufficiently strong as to cause immediate concern and necessitate constant observation."[17] As William Yarborough, the blustery general known as "the Big Y" who ran the Fort Holabird effort, later told a reporter, "What some people don't remember was the terror that all this struck into the hearts of the people that thought the empire was coming apart at the seams."[18] America was fast becoming a "dossier state," with government records on even the most quotidian details of its citizens' lives, all in the name of social order.

By 10:00 P.M. on April 4, reports of massive rioting were coming in to the AOC from around the country, some unconfirmed, some unconfirmable. A mob was said to be massing in downtown Chicago. Students were gathering near Fisk University in Nashville. The governor of North Carolina had deployed 142 National Guardsmen to Greensboro and another 169 to Raleigh to counter local violence. Hollis ordered the Sixth Armored Calvary Regiment, based at Fort Mead, halfway between Washington and Baltimore, to put a company on one-hour alert. At midnight, the Intelligence Command reported disturbances in New Haven, Connecticut, and Monticello, New York, along with Memphis, New York City, and Washington; by 12:50 they had added Jackson, Mississippi, Charlotte, North Carolina, Huntsville, Alabama, and half a dozen other cities.[19]

But Washington was critical: with New York apparently under control, all eyes were focused on preventing a Detroit-sized conflagration in the nation's capital. No one wanted to imagine the newspaper headlines that would follow U.S. troops having to violently suppress rioting a few blocks from the White House. Nevertheless, the army designated two brigades to deploy to each of the top-priority Garden Plot cities. The army also sent out undercover units from the 116th Military Intelligence Group, which circled through Washington, interviewing police and firemen and reporting back on the extent of the violence.[20]

At 3:15 A.M., just eight hours after King's assassination, the AOC held its first emergency staff meeting. Things were looking up, at least for the moment. The rain had tamped down the rioting, and the fire department had all the major fires under control. There had been only one death. Along with the AOC staff, the conference included a staffer from the Department of Justice; Robert Jordan, the army's general counsel; General Ralph Haines, the commander of the Military District of Washington, who would likely lead any occupation of the city by army troops; and D.C. safety commissioner Murphy.[21]

Coffee poured forth like water. Murphy had been dashing around the city for hours and would pass the night without sleep, while many of the others had been rousted from their beds after midnight. The city, they decided, was safe for now; the real concern, Murphy said, was Friday night.

Murphy, whose otherwise bright, boyish face was marred by ever-present bags under his eyes, was under pressure to get this one right. A liberal reformer and retired police inspector out of New York, he had been called from the OLEA by Walter Washington to oversee the city's police, fire, and emergency operations. It was a politically treacherous situation; the current police chief, Layton, was beloved by his officers but hated by community groups, who saw him as an antireformer and a symbol of the institutional racism of a department that was 80 percent white but patrolled a city that was more than

60 percent black. Not wanting to cause too much tension by axing Layton, Washington created the post of "public safety commissioner" and gave it to Murphy, who took over in December 1967.

Though a lifelong cop, Murphy was highly critical of the job police departments across the country had been doing in the inner city, particularly when it came to civil disorders. As he later wrote in his memoirs, "In three major American cities [Los Angeles, Detroit, Newark], police had demonstrated an unexpected depth of incompetence, insensitivity, and lack of preparedness in dealing with these civil disorders; and, despite all this, there was unfortunately no indication that the bottom of the barrel had been plumbed."[22]

He didn't feel good about 1968, either; surveying the state of riot-control preparedness, he concluded, "It was as if hundreds of different fingers were on guns pointed directly at the nation's cranium—with every single one of those fingers inclined toward panic."[23] It was he who, while still at the Department of Justice, had suggested to Attorney General Clark that he organize a series of conferences for police chiefs on how to manage riots without resorting to violent suppression. "We were less interested, for instance, in maximizing the fatality-effectiveness of a department's arsenal of submachine guns that [sic] in minimizing a department's potential contribution, to heightened racial tension, and its occasional proclivity toward pointless exercises in brutality and other forms of macho-policing," he wrote.[24] In other words, he was as liberal, if not more liberal than, Clark, and his appointment as Washington's top cop meant that the city would become a much-watched laboratory for police reforms and new "enlightened" approaches to riot control.

Murphy moved into his office in the District Building in downtown Washington and immediately ran into problems. Layton proved obstinate on even the most basic, commonsense reforms, such as banning the use of the word "boy" by officers when speaking with adult black men. Veteran officers resented his plans to emphasize protection of life over the protection of property. But Murphy was a skilled tactician; knowing he had the personal support of not just the mayor but also the attorney general and the president, he moved several black officers into leadership positions, then elevated one of his allies, Jerry Wilson, to assistant chief for field operations. He recognized that the fear of riots drove the rank and file's opposition of restrained operations during a disorder, and so Murphy ran his force through extensive riot drills to give them confidence.

Still, what he characterized as the "redneck" sentiment on the force persisted. One night in early 1968, some D.C. officers who lived in suburban Maryland, just off duty, got drunk behind the Sixth Precinct house. On their way home they drove past the residence of James Nabrit, president of the traditionally black Howard University, and took potshots at the house's brick walls with their service revolvers. A private security guard chased them and got their license plate number.

Layton quickly intercepted the news but didn't tell Murphy. However, the news leaked to the media the next day, and when Washington's office called demanding an explanation, Murphy said he didn't know what they were talking about. It wasn't until that night, when a black DJ called for an interview, that he realized what had happened. "I felt like a complete fool," he recalled.[25]

For some reason, he didn't can Layton. More than likely, he couldn't. Layton was backed by the rank and file, as well as the Washington business community and, perhaps most importantly, the southern Democrats in Congress who ran the D.C. subcommittees in the House and Senate. But while he let Layton stay, Murphy knew the two would, sooner rather than later, come to a head, personally and intellectually.

A major riot would certainly do it. "Washington's April riot was to become a twofold test: of Murphy's ability to control his men and of the restrained tactics that D.C. civilians had sold to the military and the police," the *Washington Post*'s Ben Gilbert wrote.[26] As Murphy left the Pentagon in the still-dark hours of April 5, he must have realized that collision was close at hand. And not just between the two men: the coming days would be the collision of two worldviews on law enforcement, the ghetto, race relations, even American society itself.

Murphy drove back into the city through darkened streets, some eerily serene, others full of debris from the night's riots. Police officers stood watch on the occasional corner. Outside the White House gates sat the luggage of the press corps that had been lined up to fly with the president to Hawaii. The bags were to have been loaded into a truck and driven to Andrews Air Force Base, where they would be stowed on *Air Force One*.

But with the trip canceled and other pressing issues at hand, they had been forgotten by their owners and White House staffers.

Inside the West Wing, Johnson's team was busy rounding up civil rights leaders for an 11:00 A.M. meeting, after which they would accompany him to a noon service at the National Cathedral. It was no easy task—the invitees were spread around the country, tending to their own priorities. Several had to beg off. Martin Luther King Sr. was too ill, as was A. Philip Randolph, the aging former head of the Brotherhood of Sleeping Car Porters. Cleveland mayor Carl Stokes, the first black man to run a major U.S. city, said he was too concerned about disorder at home to risk a trip to Washington. Charles Evers, who took over the Mississippi NAACP chapter after his brother Medgar's 1963 assassination, said he didn't want to leave Jackson for the same reason.

But the rest of the civil rights establishment agreed to show up: Wilkins, Young, Marshall, Fauntroy, Washington, Rev. Leon Sullivan, Democratic National Committee vice chairman Louis Martin, Washington NAACP chapter head Clarence Mitchell Jr. and his son, Maryland state representative Clarence Mitchell III, National Council of Negro Women president Dorothy Height, HUD secretary Robert Weaver, Judge Leon Higgenbotham, and Gary, Indiana, mayor Richard Hatcher. By chance, Bayard Rustin, who was about to board a plane to Memphis, was able to divert his flight through Washington and just make the meeting.[27]

One person not on the list was Floyd McKissick, the charismatically militant leader of CORE. Not that they hadn't tried to invite him. When Jim Gaither, one of Califano's assistants, called him early that morning, McKissick demanded to know whether Stokely Carmichael, H. Rap Brown, Lester McKinnie, and other black militants were invited. Gaither refused to tell him. MicKissick hung up. As Gaither then wrote in a memo to Johnson, "It seems apparent that McKissick will not come and that he may well denounce the meeting, saying that he had been invited but refused."[28] In that case, the whole event—which was really less about the substance and more about the image of the president sitting down with black leaders—could backfire. But there was no time to reconsider.

Johnson woke at about 7:00 A.M. and immediately started working the phones from his bedroom. He called around to the nation's big-city mayors, getting a read on the national situation. "Don't wait till dark to holler for help," he told them. One midwest mayor reported that as far as he could tell, the crisis had passed. "I hope you're right," the president said, "but we shall see what we shall see."[29] He talked over the military situation with Secretary Clifford. He chatted with Abe Fortas, his trusted adviser and now Supreme Court justice. And, still in his pajamas, he went over the plans for the civil rights meeting with Califano and McPherson—what he would say, and what he would ask of his guests.

Johnson's relationship with King was one of the most complex and inexplicable of his presidency. As journalist Nick Kotz demonstrates in his account of Johnson and King, *Judgment Days*, until 1967 the two men had a solid working relationship, if not always a cooperative one. "The alliance between Johnson and King was critical in turning opportunity into a realized American dream," Kotz writes. "Without both Johnson and King, the civil rights revolution might have ended with fewer accomplishments and even greater trauma."[30]

Johnson was much more committed to civil rights than many historians have allowed; his often coarse language in private, leaked out over the years, has distracted from his record of path-breaking accomplishments. He saw himself as nothing less than a latter-day Abraham Lincoln. In 1965, with the Civil Rights Act passed and the Voting Rights Act on its way, Johnson committed himself to a bill ending housing segregation. At the time, this wasn't progressive—it was radical. Even many moderate liberals didn't support it, as it would control what people could do with their private property. But Johnson's dream for an integrated America trumped such civil liberties concerns. "We've got to end this God-damn discrimination against Negroes," he told Califano while the two were at the Johnson ranch. "Until people—whether they're purple, brown, yellow, red, green, or whatever—live together, they'll never know that they have the same hopes for their children, the same fears, troubles, woes, ambitions."[31]

Johnson's view was not wholly enlightened, however. As an ardent New Dealer, he saw the solution as strictly government-centered, with legislative victories on rights and social programs gradually, then more quickly, uplifting black America. And he often betrayed a distrust of blacks as a group. His was still the white man's burden. Whatever role King played was subsidiary, rallying blacks to support legislation and the Democratic Party while also keeping in check urban unrest.

For his part, King saw legislation as a necessary but insufficient step toward racial equality. Voting and civil rights guarantees were only the beginning. The achievements of the civil rights era were necessary and remarkable, but, he conceded, they did little for lower-class blacks, in the South and elsewhere. Real change, he believed, was not just a matter of uplifting blacks; it was also a matter of effecting changes at the root of American society to bring about true social and economic justice. Only then could racial equality be achieved. Government programs could merely alleviate the effects of social, economic, and racial injustice until then.[32]

Despite repeated one-on-one talks, Johnson never fully warmed to King. The SCLC leader was more cerebral and introverted than the pragmatic, outgoing men Johnson was used to dealing with in the movement, such as Roy Wilkins and Whitney Young, men who understood and had patience for the game of politics. "I think from Johnson's standpoint, they were much more regular guys," recalled Attorney General Clark. "There was something a little austere about King. He didn't have the earthiness in his personality that is so wonderful in many African-American leaders. They speak from the pain they've suffered. Dr. King was more intellectual. He'd been middle-class, even upper middle-class for blacks."[33]

It is also hard to underestimate the impact that FBI director J. Edgar Hoover had on Johnson's impressions of King. Hoover and Johnson had an equally complex relationship: for decades the two lived practically next door to each other in Washington's tony Spring Valley neighborhood, and they carried on the sort of incidental, quotidian friendship, often obscured by public prominence, that can nonetheless indelibly mark political history. A lifelong bachelor and workaholic, Hoover glommed onto the Johnsons as an almost surrogate family. He often came over for casual dinners. He once gave them a dog as a gift. And he visited Lady Bird in the hospital at the birth of both of their daughters.[34]

Hoover was useful to Johnson professionally as well. During the 1964 Democratic National Convention in Atlantic City, where Mississippi civil rights activists were challenged by the segregationist Democratic delegation for the floor, Johnson had the FBI wiretap the activists' rooms. In turn, Hoover, an avowed enemy of King and the civil rights movement, fed the president reams of information defaming both, including an infamous recording of King purportedly cheating on his wife. Whether Johnson believed the tape is unclear. But Hoover's smear campaign seemed to work: more than once after hearing the tape Johnson referred to King as a "sex-mad preacher."[35]

Hoover also relentlessly tagged King as a Communist sympathizer, at the very least a Communist patsy. He was helped in this effort by Johnson's appointments secretary, Marvin Watson, who was the unofficial conduit between the FBI and the White House. Hoover would gin up scurrilous reports and send them to Johnson via Watson. The secretary was a true believer: in his memoirs, written more than thirty years later, he still insisted that civil rights and antiwar "protests were materially aided and abetted by foreign governments and their agents whose true objective was to weaken the United States."

Moving the reports was a smooth process unencumbered by the critical eyes of Hoover's nominal boss, Clark. As Watson later wrote, "I came to trust and rely on [FBI deputy director Cartha] DeLoach as though he were a member of the White House staff. My relationship with DeLoach resulted in far closer coordination between the President and the FBI than was enjoyed by any other agency in government."[36] By April 1968, such reports, whether Johnson fully believed them or not, could only have complicated his feelings toward the slain preacher.

That said, Johnson's real fear on the race-relations front was not communism, nor was it King's purported philandering. It was that rioting would erode the already fast-shrinking support among the public and in Congress for his civil rights agenda. Unrest, he believed, was the inevitable result of the opening up of opportunities for blacks. "When someone is kept as a slave, there is a minimum of trouble," he told a group of reporters. "As suppressed people begin to rise from prejudice and discrimination, there [are] naturally going to be more problems."[37]

What was not inevitable, though, was black militancy, which he saw as a catalyst for turning frustration into violence. Of course, he failed to realize that militancy was both a long-standing posture in the black community and a part-and-parcel result of the civil rights revolution; it was not a cause of the riots per se, but a coequal result of newly empowered blacks, particularly of the younger generation, running up against the stubborn walls of racism. But his fundamental analysis was sound: black radicalism was in fact alienating white America, even liberals.

Nor could Johnson understand why militant leaders would reject him so fully and brazenly. In June 1966 SNCC boycotted a major civil rights conference at the White House, "To Fulfill These Rights," because of what they saw as a hypocritical gap between the Great Society promises and the realities of a permanent war footing in Southeast Asia. When King highlighted the same gap in his Riverside Church speech, Johnson decided that his erstwhile ally had finally crossed over to the militant side. The fact that both the Urban League and the NAACP, among other establishment civil rights groups, denounced King's speech—the NAACP called it "a tragic mistake"— only made Johnson feel more confident in his reaction.[38]

To the president, King was worse than mistaken. Like almost everyone who disagreed with his foreign policy, he was a borderline traitor. By 1967 the president was at the depths of his malaise over Vietnam and the course of the country; embattled and embittered, he lashed out at even constructive criticism in Congress and the press. He deployed his aides to foment anti-King sentiment in the press, and he gave a green light to Hoover to ramp up his own subversive efforts.

Over the next year—it was, in fact, exactly one year between the Riverside speech and the assassination—King became the target of renewed FBI and military surveillance, planted editorials, and scurrilous public attacks. Had Clark not been attorney general, it's a good bet that King could have even been subject to aggressive legal maneuvers— accusing him of tax fraud, libel, and the like, tactics that had often landed him in jail in the Jim Crow South.

Johnson likely saw the Poor People's Campaign as a near-apocalyptic confrontation between him and King. On the surface he was circumspect; when asked about the campaign by a reporter on March 30, just after the Memphis rioting, he said coolly, "I would hope, if there is a march, that it will be in keeping with the law, that the law will be obeyed, that the individual rights of all will be respected, and that no violence will flow from it."[39] Inside the White House, though, Johnson and his staff were looking at the upcoming "occupation" with trepidation. "We have permitted the Stokely Carmichaels, the Rap Browns, and the Martin Luther Kings to cloak themselves in an aura of respectability to which they are not entitled," said Johnson aide Larry Temple in a note to the president. "When Martin Luther King talks about violating the law by obstructing the flow of traffic in Washington or stopping operations of the government, he is talking about criminal disobedience. 'Civil disobedience' is a complete misnomer. There is no such thing. . . . As the time nears for Dr. King's April activities, I hope the President will publicly unmask this type of conduct for what it really is."[40]

The president obviously did not get to make such an unmasking. It must have struck Johnson as ironic that the man who had been his chief ally, then chief enemy, on an issue as dear to him as civil rights, had left the American scene so soon after he had announced his own departure. King, of course, was gone completely, while Johnson was still president, albeit a lame duck. Which meant that regardless of how he felt about King, on the morning of April 5, it was he who had to deal with the aftermath of the assassination.

6

April 5

"ANY MAN'S DEATH DIMINISHES ME"

P resident Johnson entered the Cabinet Room a few minutes after 11:00 A.M. Seated at the long table were the assembled civil rights leaders and a bipartisan selection of congressional and administration leaders: Senator Thomas Kuchel and Representative William McCulloch, both Republicans; Senate majority leader Mike Mansfield and House Speaker John McCormack, both Democrats; Clifford; Califano; Christian; Undersecretary of State (and former attorney general) Nicholas Katzenbach; Acting Attorney General Christopher (Clark was in Memphis); and Assistant Attorney General Stephen Pollak, who oversaw the Civil Rights Division at the Department of Justice.[1]

Louis Martin, from the DNC, was conspicuously absent, despite a personal invitation from Johnson to move into the White House and help run the president's response efforts. Martin was one of the party's most powerful black figures and a vital link between the Democratic leadership and the black community.[2] It was Martin who had suggested to Johnson that he name Walter Washington as the capital's first mayor. And he had saved the president from humiliation on numerous occasions: when word came that SNCC activists participating in the 1966

"To Fulfill These Rights" conference were planning to disrupt the closing dinner, Martin called a contact at Howard University and asked them to send a coterie of young women to serve as hostesses. "That'll make those SNCC boys think twice about raising hell," he said. And it worked: As McPherson put it, "The dinner was as restrained as a Chamber of Commerce convention."[3]

Johnson could certainly use Martin's political acumen now. But as his staff later learned to their horror, at the moment, Martin was being detained by White House security. An avid golfer, the previous afternoon he had packed his clubs in his car trunk, planning to hit the links after work on Friday. In the rush of the previous evening's events (Thursday had also been his daughter's wedding), he hadn't thought to unpack them. When he pulled up to the White House gates, the guard found the clubs while searching his car. Assuming that he must have looted them, they took him inside for questioning.[4]

The meeting was significant beyond the fact that so many civil rights leaders had gathered so quickly in the wake of King's death. In recent years, the movement had been splintering. While any number of splinters can be counted, the primary fissure emerged between the establishment, biracial, and nonviolent leaders—King, the NAACP, the Urban League, the black business community, and the majority of black religious leaders—and the more militant organizations—primarily SNCC and CORE, which had once been strongly biracial but which had recently expelled almost all their white members.

The split wasn't necessarily new. As the NAACP was gathering strength in the early twentieth century, Marcus Garvey was preaching a separationist militancy and agitating for a return to Africa. As Martin Luther King was leading nonviolent boycotts and marches in Alabama, Malcolm X and the Black Muslims were telling crowds gathered on 125th Street in Harlem about the evils of the white race. Nor was nonviolence ever the dominant posture of black agitation. Ralph Bunche reported in a 1940 memo to Gunnar Myrdal, "There are Negroes, too, who, fed up with frustration of their life here, see no hope and express an angry desire 'to shoot their way out of it.' I have on many occasions heard Negroes exclaim, 'Just give us machine guns and we'll blow the lid off the whole damn business.'"[5]

But the split of the 1960s was different, because so much of it came from within the establishment itself. SNCC and CORE, after all, were once considered part of the Big Six establishment civil rights groups. But beginning with the lunch-counter sit-ins of 1960, young blacks, primarily college students and recent college graduates, began to take a more militant approach to civil rights; rather than simply marching, they wanted to create spectacles that overtly invited white retaliation. SNCC's members clashed repeatedly with the NAACP, both rhetorically and tactically. They were averse to compromise, and they welcomed the thought of a nationwide white backlash, if only because it would more nakedly expose the hypocrisy of the white liberal establishment.

But as SNCC radicalized, it shrank in size and influence. By 1967 it was practically bankrupt. Donors, largely wealthy white liberals, were less willing to give to an organization that, by that point, explicitly excluded whites and that took an increasingly militant, obscurantist approach to the civil rights movement. In 1964 SNCC had three hundred permanent staffers; by fall 1967, it had about twenty-five, including part-timers. Many of them were under indictment for draft refusal. Most weren't getting paid. Their antiwhite radicalism had cost them dearly; the organization's moderate backers fled in disgust, while the new supporters it did attract were hardly equal compensation— Upper West Side radical chic may have made for great satire material, but Leonard Bernstein's living room churned out less cash than many assumed.[6] "Help, help, we're sinking fast," read one SNCC mailer. Rather than fading away in the public's eye, however, SNCC merged with the broader landscape of black militancy evolving in the northern ghettos. The riots of the 1960s gave the street-corner speakers and basement Marxists a new currency, both in the ghetto and in the media. Groups such as the Black Panthers and the Revolutionary Action Movement never totaled more than a few thousand members, but the press (and the government) showered them with such attention that they seemed much larger and more powerful than they really were. One would think, reading the *New York Times*, that with a few phone calls the Black Panthers could launch riots in twenty cities. As the Urban League's Whitney Young said of Carmichael, "His following right now amounts to about fifty Negroes and about five thousand white reporters."[7] It takes nothing away from legitimate black frustrations in the

1960s to point out that the vast majority were wary of, if not outright hostile to, the black militants who seemed to be tearing apart the civil rights movement from within.

Nevertheless, if few actively signed on to the post-1965 SNCC agenda, it did express a growing frustration among many nonsouthern blacks with the course of both the establishment organizations and the SCLC-led southern movement. Put simply, they were victims of their own success. So much was achieved between the Montgomery bus boycott of 1955 and the signing of the Voting Rights Act of 1965 that the leaders were taken unawares when confronted with the question "What next?" As both Johnson and King recognized, legal changes, particularly changes targeted at a particular region, were only the first step in a long battle to raise African Americans to true equality in America. It meant interventions in the housing and job markets; it meant massive government programs in education, health, job training, and housing; and it meant, most elusively, a change in the way America writ large approached its black population.

But this sort of challenge also meant the inclusion of all the players, and not just the ones Johnson liked. The exclusion of SNCC, CORE, and everyone else deemed unacceptably radical that morning may have made for better photos and a more manageable discussion. But it also meant that at the crucial moment after King's death, when tragedy had made possible the ingathering of so many of the movement's leadership, political showmanship had triumphed over the opportunity for vital, if difficult, dialogue.

Johnson sat down at the center of the Cabinet Room table and greeted the men solemnly. Justice Marshall sat on his right and Mitchell Jr. on his left; Wilkins, Humphrey, and Young sat across from him. King, the president began, "held deep convictions about the great issues of the day. Some of them did not agree with mine. But on the issue of human dignity, there was no difference between us."[8] Everyone nodded in agreement.

"It was intended to be a healing meeting," recalled Christopher, "a meeting that sought to reassure through this group the Negroes and other minorities of the country that this should not be a cause for violence or a loss of hope."[9] It was, Christopher wrote in his memoirs,

"Lyndon Johnson at his best," but a dark mood nevertheless hung over the room: "They were communicating what I suspected everyone in the room already knew: no one could do much of anything to head off the destruction that was about to come."[10] Christopher had already been in touch with McGiffert, at the Pentagon, telling him to be ready to deploy troops to Washington and other cities as soon as possible.

Staff photographers took pictures, and the president filled everyone in on the latest news regarding the investigation in Memphis. Then Johnson dove into his real concern: violence. He explained how close the country was to widespread unrest, and how important it was to avoid an outbreak. He read them a telegram from King's father. "Please know that I join in your plea to American citizens to desist from violence and permit the cause of nonviolence for which my son died not be in vain."[11]

Johnson looked up from the page. "If I were a kid in Harlem, I know what I'd be thinking right now," he said. "I'd be thinking that the whites have declared open season on my people, and they're going to pick us off one by one unless I get a gun and pick them off first."[12]

Mentioning Stokely Carmichael by name, Johnson said that militants were already out there fomenting disorder. That couldn't be allowed to happen. He told them that he was asking John Gardner of the Urban Coalition, a national antipoverty nonprofit, to organize black leaders in various cities to speak out against violence. He asked them to do the same. "He was basically saying, I can understand the grief, but you guys have a responsibility. You've got to cool it," recalled Califano.[13]

For Rustin, at least, the meeting was effective. Johnson promised "that he would put all the forces of government to work to find out who it was who had done this heinous act, and that in the meantime he wanted us to reassure the community that these things would be done," he later said. "I think it was exactly what he should have done, and although things didn't seem very cool, the very fact that we were there I think helped."[14]

It was an ironic turn for Johnson: just weeks before he had publicly belittled the recommendations of the Kerner Commission, which had argued that only several hundred billions in additional social spending could avert further unrest. Now he was essentially promising to do just that.

Then Johnson asked for input. What did they want to see him do? Almost unanimously, the gathered leaders told him they wanted to see real action on poverty, as well as a renewed effort on civil rights issues. "I hope this moral leadership will be matched by practical leadership soon," said Fauntroy.[15]

Halfway through the meeting, an aide called Califano out into the hall. He returned a moment later and went directly to the president. Whispering in his ear, he told Johnson that McKissick had showed up after all, and he had brought along Roy Innis, a chemist and the incoming head of CORE. Innis's militancy made McKissick look like a scoutmaster. Previously the head of the New York CORE chapter, Innis had fought aggressively and vocally for community-controlled schools, which many liberals felt amounted to black self-segregation. (In a measure of his quick temper, years later Innis attacked Rev. Al Sharpton on the *Morton Downey Jr. Show*, pushing Sharpton over in his chair; he also got in a fight with white supremacists on *Geraldo*.[16]) McKissick alone might have held his tongue in front of the accumulated civil rights leadership arrayed around the cabinet table. For Innis, it would be an open invitation to disruption—especially if he came along to the service at the National Cathedral.

Johnson ordered Califano to tell Martin, who had quietly sneaked in a few minutes prior, to deal with it. As Martin later told an interviewer, it would "be a perfect occasion for a real headline to have a formal ceremony with the President of the United States memorializing King and have Roy Innis blast everybody! As a matter of fact, I was afraid McKissick was going to do it. But I was even more afraid of Roy."[17]

Martin went down to the west basement gate of the White House, where the two men were waiting. He told them they could only let one of the men up. But the two would have none of it, and they ordered Martin to go back and get permission for them to join the meeting. Martin returned to the Cabinet Room, this time to Wilkins's side.

"I've got a problem," Martin said in a low voice. "Innis is acting up, and I don't know what the problem is. I don't want to mess this thing up because you fellows are supposed to go with the president over to the service at the Cathedral."

But Wilkins was no help. "Well, keep him out of here. We don't want any confusion."

Martin, thinking fast, went back to the basement. Why was Roy here? he asked McKissick. "We sent this invitation to you. You did not indicate to anybody that you were bringing anybody else. The Secret Service doesn't know anything about it," he said.

But McKissick still refused. "I'm not going to the meeting without Roy Innis."

Martin parried. "Floyd," he said, "suppose every guest insisted on bringing an associate. How could we have a meeting?"

The three went back and forth for several minutes. "I was really sparring for time," Martin said later, "because I wanted the [buses going to the National Cathedral] to vanish before we got back outside. So after ten minutes of fake argument, I said, 'Look, let me check on the meeting.'" By the time he got up to the Cabinet Room, the buses had already left. He went back and told the men as much in his most sympathetic voice. McKissick was livid. He'd call a press conference, he declared. He would denounce them all.

Martin tried to reason with them, but it didn't matter. He'd kept them away from the meeting, and Johnson got what he wanted—a productive meeting with civil rights leaders, to which McKissick was invited but refused to attend.[18] But in doing Johnson's bidding, Martin had also cut short the possibility of real conversation between the White House and two people who, disruptive as they were, understood the anger and frustration of the country's blacks. The exclusion of McKissick and Innis didn't cause the riots, and their inclusion in the meeting wouldn't have prevented them. But the way Johnson and Martin summarily dismissed the input of these and other strident black leaders is indicative of the moment: just when such disparate voices needed to be talking together, they were pushing away from each other. And in their wake, violence was almost inevitable.

While Johnson was meeting with the establishment civil rights leaders at the White House, Carmichael and his SNCC allies were giving a counter-press conference uptown, at the New School for Afro-American Thought. The conference had been scheduled before King's death, originally to discuss the upcoming trial of SNCC chairman H. Rap Brown in Richmond. Few journalists were scheduled to show up then, or even knew of the event. But by Friday morning the rumor that Carmichael had caused the riots had become conventional wisdom, and a brazen public appearance proved a powerful draw.

Dozens of reporters, cameramen, and photographers showed up at the tiny building, trying to crowd themselves in around a small table. As they entered, SNCC workers forced them through a body-search line, piling up lighters and pocketknives beside them. Eventually only twenty got in; others crowded outside, waiting to talk to their colleagues when they emerged.[19]

First, McKinnie, the new SNCC D.C. coordinator, laid out the ground rules. "This press conference will be for only five minutes and as soon as the press conference is over you gentlemen will not leave anything in here," he directed them. "Your films, your cigarette butts, you take them with you." Then he introduced Carmichael.

Though clearly distraught, this was also Carmichael's zone—they didn't call him "Starmichael" for nothing. Wearing a sweater and plastic-frame sunglasses, he launched into a bitter lecture, though one delivered in a smooth, soft voice.

"I think white America made its biggest mistake when she killed Dr. King last night because when she killed Dr. King last night, she killed all reasonable hope," he said. "When she killed Dr. King last night, she killed the one man of our race that this country's older generations, the militants and the revolutionaries and the masses of black people would still listen to. Even though sometimes he did not agree with them, they would still listen to him."[20]

It was different, he said, when the U.S. government deported Marcus Garvey, or when "they got rid of" Malcolm X. Both men were radicals, and given to talk of violence and upheaval. But King was different. King had been preaching love, "the one man who was trying to teach our people to have love, compassion and mercy for what white people had done."

Now, he said, the gloves were off. "The rebellions that have been occurring around these cities and this country is just light stuff to what is about to happen. We have to retaliate for the deaths of our leaders. The execution will not be in the courtrooms. They're going to be in the streets of the United States of America." Was this a threat, or just a prediction? Carmichael left the question unanswered. He merely said, "White America will live to cry since she killed Dr. King last night. It would have been better if she killed Rap Brown and/or Stokely Carmichael." Then he took questions.

What about liberal whites, who loved King? asked one reporter. "The honky, from honky Lyndon Johnson to honky Bobby Kennedy, will not co-opt Dr. King," he replied testily. "Bobby Kennedy pulled that trigger just as well as anybody else."

What about the Poor People's Campaign? Will you still support it? "Whatever the Southern Christian Leadership Conference asks for today we will give to them—except our tears."

What about the black people who could die following your orders? What do you say to them? "That they take as many white people with them as possible." No one laughed.

"Mr. Carmichael, are you declaring war on white America?" someone asked. "White America has declared war on black people," he said. "The only way to survive is to get some guns."

Yet another reporter stood and asked, "Stokely, what do you see this leading to? A bloodbath in which nobody wins?"

Carmichael stared at him. "First, my name is Mr. Carmichael. And secondly, black people will survive the bloodbath. Last question."

"Do you fear for your life?"

"The hell with my life!" Carmichael shouted. "You should fear for yours. I know I'm going to die. I know I'm leaving."

The room erupted in applause from McKinnie and the SNCC volunteers.

The reporters sat stunned. Was this the launch of the race war everyone had been predicting? Was Carmichael about to lead a guerrilla war against white America? They rushed out to file their stories.

But over the next few weeks, there was one question no one stopped to ask. Was Carmichael for real, or was the whole performance—and with the shades and the too-cool, Franz Fanon-manqué rhetoric, it was most definitely a performance—just the latest from a charismatic fool? Or had he simply gone unhinged after the murder of a man who, deep down, he truly did respect and love?

It had been just five days since King delivered the Sunday sermon at the National Cathedral, and the chapel once again overflowed with people—this time not to hear King, but to mourn him. As people filed in, the organist played a mournful version of "We Shall Overcome," the unofficial anthem of the civil rights movement.

The president arrived a few minutes after noon, and he sat in the front row, flanked by Representative McCormack, Chief Justice Earl Warren, Justice Marshall, Secretary Weaver, and Mayor Washington.

After the processional hymn, "The Strife Is O'er, the Battle Done," the Right Reverend John Wesley Lord gave a few introductory remarks, then made way for scriptural readings by Rabbi Martin Halpern and Rev. William F. Creighton. The audience sang "Precious Lord," the hymn that King had been discussing seconds before being shot. By now, in between the strains of the verse came quiet sobs and the rustling of pockets for handkerchiefs. When the hymn ended, Walter Fauntroy, who had arrived with Johnson, took the lectern.[21]

Since his confrontation with Carmichael in the middle of U Street the previous evening, Fauntroy had spent most of the night and that morning running from radio station to TV studio to the streets and back, urging calm. It was a mission with a very personal angle. Fauntroy had first met King in the early 1950s, when King was still an unknown Alabama preacher and Fauntroy was an undergraduate at Virginia Union College with a dual interest in civil activism and the clergy. King was traveling north, and rather than demean himself by staying in "colored" hotels, he was bunking at historically black colleges along the way. While staying at Virginia Union, he fell into talking with Fauntroy, and the two ended up deep in conversation for most of the night.

Fauntroy went off to Yale Divinity School, but he and King kept in touch. When he settled into the pastorship at Washington's New Bethel Baptist Church a few years later, King asked him to be the SCLC's representative in the capital.[22] Outgoing and armed with a big smile, Fauntroy made quick work of King's charge. Soon he had established himself as one of the city's leading ministers, civil rights spokesmen, and political operatives. In 1967, Johnson appointed him vice chairman of the D.C. City Council; he would later become Washington's first delegate to the U.S. House, a post he held for twenty years.

Fauntroy led the congregation in prayer. "Forgive us our individual and corporate sins that have led us inevitably to this tragedy," he intoned. "Forgive us. Forgive us. God, forgive us." When he finished, a thousand voices muttered "Amen," filling the Gothic hall with a low rumble.[23]

The cathedral choir then sang "God Be in My Head," Rev. Francis B. Sayre, Jr. read from the Book of Common Prayer, and Rev. John Spence gave the final benediction. Then the cathedral struck up its twenty-four-thousand-pound "bourdon" bell, its heavy hammer muffled in leather.

While it struck, a clergyman read John Donne's "Meditation XVII," which King had quoted in his final sermon:

> No man is an island, entire of itself; every man is a piece of the continent, a part of the main. If a clod be washed away by the sea, Europe is the less, as well as if a promontory were, as well as if a manor of thy friend's or of thine own were. Any man's death diminishes me, because I am involved in mankind; and therefore never send to know for whom the bell tolls; it tolls for thee.

The congregation filed quietly out. As it did, a knot of boys and girls in the crowd began quietly singing "We Shall Overcome." Soon those around them joined in. Within a few verses, the entire cathedral rang with the low sound of the civil rights spiritual.[24]

Several hours earlier, just before dawn, a government JetStar airplane took off from Andrews Air Force Base en route to Memphis. Inside were Attorney General Clark; FBI deputy director DeLoach (ironically, the man who had overseen much of the FBI's campaign against King); Equal Opportunity Commission chair Clifford Alexander; Assistant Attorney General Roger Wilkins; and Cliff Sessions, the Justice Department's chief public relations officer. Clark had taken unusually direct control over the unfolding investigation, requiring that all reports be sent to him and all evidence flown immediately to FBI labs in Washington. His decision to come to Memphis, however, was largely symbolic. "I thought it was important to show that we had highest respect for Dr. King," Clark said later. "But I also felt it was important for the government to show, from highest officials, that there was concern about violence in Tennessee and Memphis."[25]

Meanwhile, most of the work on the ground was being handled by the FBI, which, at least as DeLoach told it, was making swift progress on the case. DeLoach was so sure the killer would be caught quickly that for luggage he brought only a briefcase, in which he carried some papers, a gun, and a sandwich. He ate the sandwich on the plane. To push his confidence a little farther, before they landed DeLoach bet Clark a bottle of sherry that they would have the killer in hand within twenty-four hours.[26]

The plane touched down just before 8:00 A.M. The airport had been sealed off, with Tennessee National Guardsmen at the gates and state Air National Guard cargo planes ferrying in troops and equipment. A mob of reporters and onlookers stood outside the gates, awaiting the plane carrying Mrs. King and her family.

Clark, suddenly surrounded by press, gave an impromptu statement and took a few questions. Was it the work of a lone gunman? Is there evidence of a conspiracy? Where is the investigation now? He didn't tell them that the FBI had been working furiously, that investigators had already found and interviewed the gun store owner who sold the killer the rifle. The attorney general, working on no sleep, merely told them, "All our evidence at this time indicates that it was a single person who committed this criminal act." He said he would have more answers later at a formal press conference.[27]

The King plane, an Electra chartered by the Kennedy family, arrived soon after the press conference ended. Clark and his men climbed into the cabin, where they sat with Mrs. King, her children, and King's brother A.D. Clark conveyed the president's condolences, and he asked if there was anything the White House could do for her. Mrs. King said no, but thank you. "She was very obviously in pain," recalled Wilkins. "But she was controlled, and she was grateful and sent back a gracious message to the president."[28] The King family left to retrieve the body, and Clark and his team headed into town.

The quintet launched into a day-long series of meetings. They spoke by phone with the governor, and they met with Memphis public safety director Frank Holloman, the strike leaders, and the local FBI. Holloman told them the city was on the brink of "civil war." They met with Mayor Loeb and tried to get him to concede on some of the strikers' demands, telling him it might be the only way to avoid violence. Loeb refused to budge—"I remember him being obstinate, absolutely obstinate," said Wilkins.[29] Fortunately, President Johnson was also sending Undersecretary of Labor James Reynolds to put the screws on Loeb, so the Justice team could focus elsewhere.

King's body was lying at the R. S. Lewis Funeral Home. A long line of visitors had arrived to view the body, despite the fact that no public viewing had been announced. These were not the wealthy and powerful who would clamor into Ebenezer Baptist Church at King's funeral, days later. These were the anonymous men, women, and children of Memphis, the poor and working-class blacks to whom King had dedicated his last days. Many of them cried as they passed his casket. When it was time to head out, an escort of police and National Guardsmen ferried the coffin to the airport. As the plane took off, 150 onlookers broke out in "We Shall Overcome." One man raised a fist in salute to the fast-disappearing aircraft.[30]

Before heading home, Clark held another press conference, this time at the Federal Office Building in downtown Memphis. Beside him was Wilkins, visibly shaken by the day's events. Clark explained what they had done that day in Memphis, and he laid out the progress of the investigation so far. Much of the information in his statement, prepared by Sessions, came verbatim from DeLoach, and it expressed an overly optimistic, and overly conclusive, attitude about the case. It was almost certainly a lone gunman, Clark said. The FBI was making great progress, and there was every indication that they would have the suspect soon.

What about the risk of riots in Memphis? a reporter asked. Will the White House send troops?

"Every effort will be made here to maintain order, firmly, fairly, and without repression," Clark replied. But, he said, the city and state officials "know my views, that either over-reaction or under-action can lead to rioting, that you have to exercise a very careful control, and the indications to me are that this is the policy they are pursuing here."

Someone asked about the chronology of the previous night. When had he first heard? Clark said he didn't fully recall. "It seems like it has been an awfully long time."[31]

With that, they returned to Washington. Clark would, of course, win the bottle of sherry—and another when DeLoach bet him that the case would be solved within a week. In fact, James Earl Ray would not be caught until June 8, the day of Robert Kennedy's funeral at St. Patrick's Cathedral in Manhattan.

7

April 5

"ONCE THAT LINE HAS BEEN CROSSED"

Deputy Mayor Tom Fletcher later called the morning of April 5 the "shadow war period."[1] The streets were quiet, and the running assumption among officials—from the local schools to the Pentagon to the White House—was that a riot wouldn't break out until evening; that was how riots had always worked, in Watts, in Newark, in Detroit, and in dozens of other cities over the last four years. And so that morning tens of thousands of school children headed off to class, and almost a hundred thousand suburbanites went to work in downtown Washington.

But the mood was much tenser in black Washington. "There," wrote Ben Gilbert of the *Washington Post*, "the same ominous tension that had preceded Thursday night's inner-city outbreak was noticeable, not only on the riot-torn 14th Street shopping strip but also on 7th Street and in neighborhoods in the northeast and southeast sections of the city."[2] Many people stayed home from work and idled on sidewalks. Principals were having a hard time keeping students in class; in some places, teenagers were drifting out as they saw fit. By noon, half of the seventeen hundred students at Cardozo High had vanished.

For many D.C. students, school was a distant second in their mind to the rally about to take place at Howard University. Long known as the "Black Harvard," Howard was one of the country's leading institutions for black students. It was a primary conduit for the creation of the black middle class: all the best black lawyers went to its law school, and it churned out hundreds of doctors, businessmen, and engineers each year. But the university, on the edge of a steep hill overlooking the Shaw and Cardozo neighborhoods in Northwest Washington, also was a stark emblem of the divisions within the black community: between the students and the "block boys"; between the middle and working classes; between northern (the bulk of the student body) and southern blacks; and, increasingly, between the activist community and the "go along to get along" professional classes. Even the party scene was stratified: alumni recall "brown bag parties," in which a brown paper bag near the entrance was used to judge whether someone was sufficiently light-skinned to attend.[3]

Howard, did, of course, produce some of the century's leading civil rights figures; many of the movement's brightest lights, including Thurgood Marshall, were alumni. But the belief both inside and outside the school was that activism had no place on campus and that the students would rather study, party, and prepare for middle-class careers than risk their future on the movement. "Most of the students came there to get an education," says Tony Gittens, who was a Howard junior in the spring of 1968. "Howard was known as a party school. There wasn't a lot of interest in racial issues. People were just glad to be there."[4]

By 1968, however, parts of Howard were beginning to radicalize. Socially aware students congregated at the campus newspaper, the *Hilltop*, and Ujamaa, a campus activist organization. The student government became a hotbed of political and social activity, even radicalism. Michael Harris, the president of the freshman class in 1968 and political director of Ujamaa, told an interviewer that "to me, black power is just a way of getting ready for the confrontation" between blacks and whites.[5] Moreover, as SNCC and other militant organizations moved beyond their initial southern focus, they turned to college campuses such as Howard to organize. Carmichael, himself a Howard graduate, would make appearances on campus, and student radicals would show up at SNCC headquarters. In late March 1968, Howard students even shut down the campus for a few days when they occupied an administration building, demanding more focus on Africa and black culture in the curriculum and the ejection of ROTC recruiters from school grounds.[6]

At noon, the university raised the American flag to half mast. Then, inside Crampton Auditorium, President James Nabrit spoke of King's legacy to an invited audience of faculty and student leaders. "From his blood shall rise a thousand Martin Luther Kings," he intoned. The university choir sang Brahms's "Requiem," "A Mighty Fortress Is Our God," and "Precious Lord." Several clergymen offered prayers and called for peace.

But student government president Ewart Brown (who later became the premier of Bermuda) struck a more ominous tone. "Realize, white America, that in taking this life you have removed the buffer zone between racists and those who are not moderate," he said. "The outlook for America's future is grim." His was the sole dissonant voice: at the end of the service, everyone joined hands and sang "We Shall Overcome."[7]

The real draw for the city's high school students, who began ascending the hills toward the campus as Nabrit and Brown were speaking, was the rally planned after the official ceremony was over. By 1:30, when the Crampton service came to a close, five hundred to seven hundred students had gathered on the lawn, in front of nearby Frederick Douglass Hall, many carrying black power placards. Audio speakers stood on each side of the steps leading to the building.

One female student told the crowd, "Martin Luther King compromised his life away." That wasn't for her, or the cheering crowd. "He had to avoid bloodshed. . . . If I'm nonviolent, I'll die. If I'm violent, I'll still die, but I'll take a honkie with me."[8] Another speaker announced (incorrectly, at the moment) that downtown Washington was in flames. Cheers erupted. The American flag was lowered, and in its place students ran up the *ujamaa* ("coming together" in Swahili) flag—a black background with a laurel wreath and a sword in the center, though they took it down after a few minutes. At one point six students in black turtlenecks carried a mannequin, wrapped in white gauze and stained with red, through the crowd.

Suddenly the audience began to cheer and part. Carmichael was striding across the quadrangle toward Douglass, in his uniform sunglasses and green army jacket.

He mounted the stairs and turned to the audience. All eyes swiveled to him. He looked out over the crowd. "They shouldn't have killed Dr. King," he said, reprising a theme from his press conference a few hours earlier. "They have killed the wrong man. They should have killed me."

The crowd cheered—what a martyr!

They would follow him anywhere. But where? He told them, "Do not be out on the streets for looting tonight. We mean business. If you don't come out tonight with your gun, stay at home." He pulled a pistol from his waistband and waved it in the air. Murmuring ran through the crowd. "Do you have your gun?" "I have mine." "I wish I had a gun."[9]

Carmichael repeated his warning, this time louder. Then he left the steps and dropped out of sight.

Was Carmichael trying to incite violence, warn of a planned attack on the police, or scare the students into staying away and thereby reducing the size of the disorder? If one assumes that Carmichael's revolutionary stance was real, at least in his mind, then it makes sense to assume his aim in the Howard speech—just like his appearance in the streets the night before—was indeed to tamp down a potential riot. Revolutions are planned, with leadership, while riots are spontaneous and anarchic. And while some riots are explicitly political, and many others make inchoate but clear political statements, it is still hard to imagine someone like Carmichael doing much to make an anarchic riot hew to his radical aims. Or is it possible that Carmichael had given up on revolution in all but his rhetoric?

In any case, if Carmichael was trying to lead an uprising, he failed. If he was the man of the hour Thursday night, by Friday he was a bit player, even in his own neighborhood. Emotions were building on the streets independent of any speeches of gun-waving. No one needed his radical speechmaking to foment violent thoughts that Friday, and no one outside Howard particularly wanted to hear it, either. As one looter in Washington said a few weeks later, "They've been trying to make this thing out of Stokely Carmichael and people like him, saying they had something to do with it. Nobody was listening to Stokely. I know I wasn't. I'm my own man."[10]

The expectation that more rioting was on the way was borne of painful experience; as more than one ghetto resident said that morning,

Washington had watched for years as Watts, Newark, Detroit, and countless other cities exploded. No matter what the white leadership said about progressive racial policies, the man on the street knew something big was coming.

King himself had experienced ghetto violence firsthand during the 1965 riot in Watts. Like Johnson, he was riding a high off the Voting Rights Act, and he believed he could bring the same moral suasion he deployed in Selma and Washington to Los Angeles. Instead, onlookers booed King as he walked along the riot-torn sidewalks. At a community meeting on August 18, he said, "All over America . . . the Negro must join hands." A joker in the audience shot back, "and burn!"[11]

King, and the rest of America, was learning a truth long understood in the ghetto itself. Life for blacks outside the South, though freed from Jim Crow oppression, came with its own massive frustrations, made worse by the superficially racial progressivism of the urban North. Such frustrations found expression in a library shelf's worth of literature, from *Black Boy* to *The Invisible Man* to *Manchild in the Promised Land*. In two historic waves cresting in the years after each of the world wars, millions of rural southern blacks moved north to Chicago, Detroit, Baltimore, and New York; west to Los Angeles and San Francisco; and, internally, to Atlanta, Memphis, Nashville, and Washington. A total of 1.5 million moved between 1910 and 1940. Another 5 million moved between 1940 and 1970. Though this great migration is often thought of as an interwar phenomenon, the post–World War II reshuffling was the more significant. As Nicholas Lemann notes in *The Promised Land*, in 1940 America's black population was still overwhelmingly southern and rural, at 77 percent; just thirty years later, "'urban' had become a euphemism for 'black.'"[12]

These migrants created their own communities, often much poorer and more desperate than the older, established enclaves. South Side Chicago, populated in the early twentieth century, was home to one of the wealthiest concentrations of blacks in the country. But postwar migrants couldn't get a footing on the South Side. They huddled, instead, in the newly opened ghetto of the West Side, and they did so with an alacrity that stunned observers and sent a shock through the social system. Not only did the population flip, it also exploded: Lawndale, in the heart of the West Side, experienced a 25 percent population increase between 1950 and 1960, even as its white residents decamped by the tens of thousands. Such a rapid change left many social and economic structures intact, even as poverty rates rose and services deteriorated. Stores were still white-owned, as were the machine-controlled political offices.[13] Not for nothing did locals call the West Side the "plantation wards."

Nor were white populations the only things leaving the new ghettos of Chicago, Detroit, Cleveland, and elsewhere; jobs were, too. The midcentury American city was undergoing not just an ethnic upheaval, but an economic one as well. The national economy was increasingly driven by white-collar and service sectors, which had less need for proximity to urban concentrations of workers. Likewise, manufacturing, previously the backbone of the urban economy, was moving to the suburbs as well or, increasingly, to the low-tax Sun Belt and even offshore locations. As historian Tom Sugrue and others have pointed out, the Rust Belt may have hit the national consciousness in the 1970s, but its roots—and its effects on blacks moving north—took hold decades earlier.[14] Between 1929 and 1939, central-city Baltimore lost 10.4 percent of its manufacturing jobs, even as its suburbs gained an astounding 252.3 percent. Cleveland, during the same span, lost 23.6 percent of its manufacturing jobs, while its suburbs gained 13.7 percent.[15]

Even Washington, a supposedly progressive city with a solid employer unlikely to flee to the suburbs—namely, the federal government—harbored deep racial tensions. The city had the second-worst infant mortality rates in the country (behind Mississippi). Blacks, though many with good jobs in the federal government, were still kept in menial tasks and rarely allowed to rise above clerks and postal carriers. As one looter, a college dropout, said later, "The more education I get, the less money I make. And it's continued along and all these other little subtle forms of discrimination. Every time you look for a job you have people who're finding little excuses. I mean little excuses, things that don't really matter—'Well, I think maybe you live too far away, you know.' . . . Now all these little things have been building up to the point where I've had to try and fight the system just to make a living."[16]

Poverty, jobs, discrimination, poor schools—all this in cities where blacks were supposedly free, where city leaders flatly denied the existence of squalid conditions or de facto segregation. Is it any surprise that young blacks, looking at their compromise-friendly elders in the NAACP on the one hand and the exciting, but to their needs irrelevant, southern civil rights movement on the other, would drift toward militancy, riots, and separatism? As Claude Brown asks in the foreword to *Manchild in the Promised Land*, "Where does one run to when he's already in the promised land?"[17]

The answer to Brown's question came clear that April 5 afternoon. All morning small acts of violence had been taking place around the city. Bystanders harassed white drivers entering downtown. Broken shop windows along U Street drew occasional looters, who picked over the remains of the previous night's spree. At Fourteenth and Harvard, in the Columbia Heights neighborhood, a white motorist was pulled from his Volkswagen and beaten until a passing priest intervened. Critically, many of the city's best police officers—those in the Special Operations Division and its subset, the Civil Disorder Unit—had been sent home to rest for the night.[18]

Then, at about noon, the fire department started to get calls. First one a minute, then two, and suddenly the phones were ringing non-stop. Many units were still out in the field, putting down the last of Thursday night's conflagrations. These new fires tended to be in stores that had already been picked clean by looters. But at 12:13 P.M. a call came in about a new fire at the Safeway supermarket on Fourteenth Street, just below U. Four minutes later, there was a call about a clothing store on fire at Fourteenth and Harvard, about half a mile to the north. By 1:00 P.M. seven major fires dotted Fourteenth Street. Assistant Police Chief Jerry Wilson called in the 4:00 P.M. shift early, then alerted Murphy, who was in meetings at the Pentagon.[19]

By this point, the crowds in the street stretched along Fourteenth from well below U up to Park Road; along U to Seventh Street, at the foot of the hill below Howard; and down Seventh to Mount Vernon Square, on the edge of downtown (what is today Chinatown). These thoroughfares, along with H Street in the city's Northeast quadrant, were the main commercial arteries of black Washington. Soon the adults in the crowd were joined by tens of thousands of high school students, some of whom were coming, full of anger, from Carmichael's speech at Howard.

What causes a riot? There are, first of all, the general causes. In the case of the 1960s riots, these were usually chronic problems such as police brutality, poor job opportunities, perceived municipal neglect, and abuse by ghetto shop owners, who tended to be white. There are contributing factors, such as heat: most riots occurred during the summer, when it was too hot to stay indoors, creating a natural crowd on the sidewalks. Then there are immediate causes: a particularly brutal instance of police brutality, an assassination, a passionate speech.

But such causes raise the question of why some riots occur in certain places and not others. Militants were speaking in every city, but only in a few did their words lead to action. Police brutality was omnipresent. And while more than a hundred cities rioted after King's death, many cities mired in poverty and segregation—Houston, Gary, Boston—did not. In some cases it was in part thanks to quick-thinking mayors, such as New York's Lindsay and Gary's Richard Hatcher, who had competent antiriot mechanisms in place and made the point of showing themselves in the streets as soon as possible. But would it have made a difference if Walter Washington were out in the streets that Thursday night?

The frustrating fact is that riots, like any social organism—traffic jams, stadium crowds—have an inscrutable life of their own. And like any organism, they can be generally described, but they also have unique characteristics that defy categorization. The same can be said about rioters themselves; there was no "typical" rioter. This was, essentially, the conclusion of almost a decade's worth of research by a small cottage industry of social scientists in the 1960s and 1970s, some of whom—UCLA's David O. Sears, the University of Wisconsin's Seymour Spilerman—developed entire careers around the study of riots and rioters. "Although different communities are not equally prone to racial disturbance," wrote Spilerman in 1970, "the susceptibility of an individual Negro to participating in a disorder does not depend upon the structural characteristics of the community in which he resides."[20]

Most people watching the riots on their suburban TV screens turned in disgust; they couldn't imagine themselves or any of their friends participating in such violence. But that is the mystery of rioting. It is easy to forget the extent to which the range of actions we consider acceptable is dictated by our immediate moral surroundings. That's what is so disconcerting about the famous experiments by Yale's Stanley Milgram, in which normal, self-described moral adults were willing to inflict great pain on others when given orders by authority figures. "Stark authority was pitted against the subjects' [participants'] strongest moral imperatives against hurting others, and, with the subjects' [participants'] ears ringing with the screams of the victims, authority won more often than not," Milgram wrote.[21] What the riots, and the riot research, showed was that authority and approval by an individual wasn't always necessary—if their immediate social surroundings condoned, and even rewarded, criminal behavior, then average people were more often than not likely to participate. What is necessary, as Nobel Prize–winning economist Thomas Schelling recognized, is an incident that signals to people that, rather than punishing violence, the crowd will now reward it—what has come to be known as a "Schelling incident."

Thursday night in Washington, the Schelling incident had been the moment when the crowd saw looters breaking the Peoples Drug windows. Not everyone participated, but the barrier to participation dropped immediately, while the reward—loot, the emotional catharsis of destruction—rose significantly. One anonymous looter told an interviewer, "It wasn't really safe . . . but I felt that in view of the circumstances, the risk of perhaps being apprehended or penalized for the looting was small enough to chance going in and taking those things which I felt I could use."[22]

As public safety chief Murphy later recognized, "There is a dividing line, a thin line, that keeps lots of people from breaking a window, or, once a store window has been broken, from taking what has been left exposed inside. Once that line is crossed, usually law-abiding people join in, and everything breaks out of control."[23]

By 1:00 P.M. on Friday, April 5, the city had once again experienced a Schelling incident, and the rioting was back on.

Johnson and the collected black leaders returned from the National Cathedral to the White House, where they went back into the Cabinet Room for more discussions. They pressed Johnson further on their priorities. Something concrete had to be done, they said. No more vague promises. The Great Society had resulted in significant improvements in rights, and legislation had passed that promised to make substantial material changes in the lives of poor blacks. But those promises had so far gone largely unfilled by a penurious Congress that refused to fully fund them. Johnson had been having a hard time getting even his modest funding requests on things such as housing, education, and urban renewal approved, and this year, with a budget deficit and a coffer-draining war in Asia, he faced even stauncher opposition from Arkansas representative Wilbur Mills, a conservative Democrat who ran the powerful House Ways and Means Committee.

Johnson went around the table, asking each man what he wanted to see the White House do. Young wanted more jobs programs. Higgenbotham wanted court reform. Wilkins wanted more rights bills. But Martin summed up the general sentiment when he said, "Human misery—it's still there, and it's hardly been touched."[24]

Johnson nodded in approval. He would deliver, he promised. As soon as their meeting was over, he told them, he was to give a national address from the Fish Room. There, in front of the national TV cameras, he would ask approval to address a joint session of Congress on Monday, where he would lay out a wide-ranging, concrete agenda to answer all of their concerns.

Just outside the door, Christopher, McGiffert, Temple, and Murphy were discussing the more immediate situation, escalating right there in Washington. Christopher had already recommended that the D.C. National Guard be called up on training status, which would have them ready, but not deployed; better, he felt, not to jump the gun. Busby and Clifford were working on the speech. And Washington shuttled in and out of the meeting to get updates on his city.

Johnson then went to give his address. Contrary to what he said in the Cabinet Room, there was no mention in the text of a Monday night speech. It had been a spur-of-the-moment thought on the president's part. But it was one he now intended to follow through with. "Goddamn it," he told Busby and Clifford when they handed him the speech, "this country has got to do more for these people, and the time to start is now." So Clifford hastily penciled in a few sentences about giving an address to Congress.[25]

Flanked by many of the men who had gathered in the Cabinet Room, Johnson began, "Once again, the heart of America is heavy—the spirit of America weeps—for a tragedy that denies the very meaning of the land." He dove almost immediately into the violence of the previous night. "If we are to have the America that we mean to have, all men—of all races, all regions, all religions—must stand their ground to deny violence its victory in this sorrowful time and in all times to come."

The president mentioned his meeting with the civil rights leaders, though he didn't mention what they discussed. Instead he said, "We must move with urgency, with resolve, and with new energy in the Congress, in the courts, in the White House, the state houses and the city halls of the nation, wherever there is leadership—political leadership, leadership in the churches, in the homes, in the schools, in the institutions of higher learning—until we overcome."

Then he rolled into Clifford's addition. Noting that "our work is not yet done," he said, "I have asked the Speaker of the House of Representatives, the leadership of the Congress, and the Congress to receive me at the earliest possible moment. They are in adjournment over the weekend. But I would hope that could be no later than Monday evening, in the area of nine o'clock, for the purpose of hearing the president's recommendations and the president's suggestions for action—constructive action instead of destructive action—in this hour of national need."

Finally, he read a proclamation making Sunday, April 7, a day of national mourning, shuttering government offices and directing that all flags be flown at half mast until King's burial (a strange, but perhaps politically expedient, choice of days, given that most federal offices would be closed anyway).[26] With that, he left the room.

One item Johnson did not mention, but that he was already moving on, was the stalled fair-housing bill. Long a goal of Johnson's— he had told Califano to get it moving in 1965—was a proposal to outlaw housing discrimination in almost all private real estate in the country. He had rolled out a bill to do just that in 1966, only to see it stall in the Senate after passing the House; in 1967, an identical bill never made it out of committee. In both cases, pundits chalked up the loss to the riots that annually racked the nation's cities from 1964 onward.

But the bill would have been a hard sell in any case. Unlike the Voting Rights Act, it did more than extend protection to relatively abstract political rights that most blacks already enjoyed. And unlike the Civil Rights Act, it didn't just ban discrimination in public places, a legal reality in only some parts of the country (though a tacit fact in many others). Rather, the fair-housing bill explicitly regulated the private sphere and private property, something that even libertarian-minded moderates had a hard time accepting.

Moreover, as North Carolina senator Sam Ervin noted, it would be the first civil rights legislation in which a region other than the South was targeted. Housing segregation was, perhaps surprisingly, much more prevalent in the urban North than the urban South (though the suburbs in both regions were highly segregated), in part because southern whites had other means of racial control at their disposal. And some of the most vehement opposition to the bill came not from southern legislators but from northern and midwestern members of Congress. As Califano later noted, "Urban representatives, normally civil rights supporters, were besieged by middle-class white constituents who wanted to keep blacks out of their neighborhoods."[27]

Nevertheless, Johnson saw that the King assassination represented a unique opportunity to move the legislation to the Oval Office. It had, in fact, been approved by the Senate on March 11. But it was stalled in the House, where its opponents were biding their time until the Poor People's Campaign and the expected summer riots, when they calculated that public support for civil rights would ebb and they could more easily kill the legislation.

Johnson had already sent a letter to Speaker McCormack's office that morning, copied to the rest of the House leadership, urging them to pass the bill. King's murder, the president wrote, "has caused all good men to look deeply into their hearts. When the nation so urgently needs the healing balm of unity, a brutal wound on our conscience forces upon us all this question: What more can I do to achieve brotherhood and equality among all Americans?" Perhaps implicitly recognizing that new spending programs would be a hard sell in Congress, Johnson added, "There are many actions the Congress can take on its part. The most immediate is to enact the legislation so long delayed and so close to fulfillment. We should pass the Fair Housing law when the Congress convenes next week."[28]

After more meetings with some of the remaining civil rights leaders—Rustin had already left for Memphis, and others had their own organizations to attend to—Johnson retired to the White House Residence for lunch. Things outside were not going well, he knew. At one point during his talks, Washington, coming into the Cabinet Room after getting an update about the scene uptown, had asked Johnson to step outside; there, joined by Califano and McPherson, the mayor told him that the city was sliding quickly back into disorder. It was only a matter of time before a full-scale riot broke out. Johnson called army chief of staff Harold Johnson and told him to get his troops ready.

At the dining table, flanked by Luci, Busby, McPherson, Califano, Supreme Court justice (and longtime adviser) Abe Fortas, and a few other aides, Johnson bowed his head. "Help us, Lord, to know what to do now," he prayed. Looking up, he added, "I thought I'd better get specific about it, fellas."

Halfway through the meal, one of the men got up and went to the window overlooking Pennsylvania Avenue. "Gentlemen, I think you'd better see this," he said. Through the budding trees they spied a flood of cars and people, driving, walking, running, all pushing their way frantically westward, toward the Virginia and Maryland suburbs.

Johnson and the others moved from the dining room to the sitting room. The president looked down the long hall of the White House and pointed silently. Out the window, past the Treasury building, they could see a tall column of smoke rising from downtown. "The convulsions had started," Busby recalled, as the acrid scent of burning timber seeped into the White House.[29]

8

April 5

"OFFICIAL DISORDER ON TOP OF CIVIL DISORDER"

W alter Washington arrived at the District Building to find chaos. Staffers scurried around him, trying to get through the door and out to their suburban homes. Many of those who stayed didn't know what to do. His aides couldn't even locate the police radio reserved for the mayor's office, so they had to request another from the police department itself—which, by then, didn't have any to spare. The city had been working all winter on a riot plan, but its target completion date was not for several weeks, timed for the Poor People's Campaign.

Not that it was any good to begin with. As a May 1968 study by the Brookings Institution characterized it, the plan was "official disorder on top of civil disorder."[1] Though it did a good job of preparing police officers for riot duty, the District's plan paid almost no attention to ensuring a broader command and control network over the city government operations such as the schools and public welfare. The civil defense communication network, designed to keep the government running in case of a military attack and perfectly suited for a major civil disorder, was never utilized. The plan didn't establish points of contact either, and in some cases department heads were left without any direction as to how they should respond—a critical shortcoming with regard to the schools, where principals did not know whether to send students home or keep them in class Friday afternoon. The city was simply unprepared for the convulsion that so many of its residents had long seen coming.

By now, the city was tumbling into a full-on riot. Police were using tear gas in Columbia Heights. A mob of looters, led by teens, was heading down Seventh Street, tearing up shop windows as they went. By 3:00 P.M., fire reports along Fourteenth Street alone were coming in at twenty to thirty an hour.[2] And tens of thousands of downtown workers, mostly white suburbanites, were fleeing the city. There was no subway at the time, and the buses and stoplights were not on their rush-hour schedules. An enormous traffic jam ensued—"of monumental proportions," a city report later concluded, with delays of an hour and a half just to cross the bridges—and many motorists simply abandoned their cars in the streets, joining those without cars on the long march across the Potomac bridges and into the northern Virginia suburbs.[3] From there, they could look back and see smoke clouds rising above the city.

Washington, along with Murphy, Layton, and Deputy Mayor Thomas Fletcher, immediately decided to call up the D.C. National Guard, some 1,750 soldiers.[4] But that was hardly an immediate solution. With all the mayhem in the streets, it would take hours for the Guardsmen to get to their armory, across the Anacostia River on Washington's far east side. At 3:00 P.M. they decided to set up a command center in Room 10 of the District Building, usually used as a dispatcher's station for snow equipment. The scene inside was hardly better—"pandemonium," recalled Fletcher. One staffer plotted incidents on a map; others ran in and out, delivering equipment. Washington stood at the back with a phone at each ear, carrying on a makeshift conference call. Those with nothing to do stood watching the map pile up with thumbtacks indicating looting and arson. At one point so many onlookers had gathered to watch the riot explode on the map in near-real time that Washington had to yell at them to sit down so he could see it. The mayor's next move was to institute a curfew from 5:30 P.M. to 6:30 A.M.

Then he called Cy Vance.

By 1968, Cyrus Vance was the nation's Mr. Fixit. Born in West Virginia, he was nevertheless an archetype of the East Coast establishment: boarding school in Switzerland, Yale undergraduate, Yale Law School, followed by a post at a white-shoe New York law firm. He came to Washington in 1957 to take a job as counsel to the Senate Armed Services Committee; once John F. Kennedy took office, he moved over to the Pentagon, where he became counsel to the army. A year later Kennedy made him secretary of the army, where he oversaw the service's role in integrating the University of Mississippi. Vance returned to private practice in June 1967, ostensibly because of a chronic back problem, but also because of disagreements over the course of the Vietnam War. But he remained a key informal adviser to Johnson, acting as special envoy to the Greek-Turkish conflict over Cyprus and to ongoing tensions on the Korean Peninsula.[5]

But for all Vance's foreign policy skills, he proved equally adept at dealing with domestic disorders. In July 1967, Johnson again pulled him away from his law-firm desk to be his personal liaison in Detroit during the riots. Vance's recommendations following that disorder became the founding text of counterriot planning across the government that fall and winter, with an outline that covered everything from riot training for thousands of army and National Guard troops to liaison among the local, state, and federal forces. Most important, he recommended that the police and military "use the minimum force necessary to restore law and order," i.e., no loaded weapons, and no firing unless absolutely necessary to save a life.[6] This position, which would later become very controversial, was nevertheless quickly adopted at all levels. "[T]hat is accepted now as standard practice, I think, in all riot control situations by the federal forces," Vance noted in a later interview. "I personally feel that it's better to save a life than to shoot a fourteen-year old kid who's taking a loaf of bread, and I think that by and large most police chiefs now agree with that."[7]

Johnson readily agreed to Washington's request, and by 2:00 P.M. he had Vance on the phone in New York. Ironically, Vance was already in the midst of playing riot guru; he was just finishing up a report for Mayor Lindsay on defense counsel procedures during riot-related cases. But Vance agreed to set that work aside and come to Washington. He was in the capital by 4:30. Thanks to the chaotic traffic, it had taken him longer to get into the city from his plane than it did to get from LaGuardia to National Airport.

By 1:00 P.M. rioting was in full swing across the city. All 280 men in the elite Civil Disturbance Unit were back on the streets, but even with their augmentation to the regular forces, they were easily outnumbered. Looters went about their work in earnest. "On the second day I was more aggressive," one looter, "Anonymous A," told a Howard University interviewer a few weeks later. "I knew by the second day that this was more than just a trivial event and its success would be measured by the participation of those within the area. I felt that if my people were going to go and do this thing, I may as well join them."[8]

As in the case in Watts and Detroit, the rioting population was both larger and more diverse than the media and politicians depicted it. Conventional wisdom held that rioters were generally poor and deviant, the "riffraff" theory of rioting. Only a few locals supposedly participated. It was an easy idea for people across the spectrum to support. Liberals liked it because it disarmed accusations that ghetto residents were criminals, while conservatives favored it because it contradicted the charge that ghetto frustrations were significant and dangerous enough to justify massive social spending.

But in his study of the 1965 Watts riot, sociologist David Sears found that as many as 15 percent of residents within the 46.5 square-mile riot zone participated in the looting and burning, while another 30 percent were "close spectators"—in all, some 100,000 people. Nor were the rioters drawn from the bottom rungs of society. "The disorder attracted middle-class, working-class, and lower-class people, educated and uneducated alike," Sears found.[9]

Researchers found similar results in Washington. *Washington Post* analysts estimated that 17,600 to 22,800 actively rioted, about 8 percent of residents in the affected zones—a somewhat lower number than in Watts, but the quick deployment of federal troops likely had a dampening effect on later participation. There was no "typical" rioter, but the statistically average profile was better educated and more likely to be employed than most people in the riot area (though, despite claims later made on the Senate floor, only a handful of rioters were government employees).[10]

Such results underscore an alternative theory of ghetto rioting: that it was at least as much an expression of protopolitical anger as it was of opportunism and common criminality. Nor were these factors mutually exclusive: Rioting was both cathartic *and* fun. As one looter, a twenty-three-year-old philosophy graduate student at Howard, later told reporters, "I'm not particularly fond of Washington. I'm not sorry about anything. All I worried about was whether black people would get hurt. All the white stores in town could burn down. I wouldn't care. . . . We had a ball . . . just a ball."[11] Others had a more directly political view of the looting. "I felt that for some reason or another this was the proper thing to do at that particular time—taking from the white merchants those things which I felt brothers had been denied of because of oppression and a number of other factors that have made difficult the success or liberation of the black man," one looter told a Howard researcher.[12] One factor was decidedly absent: Postriot interviews found very few people who claimed to be rioting in response to King's death.

Many interviewees later said that they were targeting specific stores because of specific grievances against the owners, particularly white-owned small businesses. (To differentiate themselves, black owners would use shoe polish to write "Soul Brother" or "Blood" across their windows; in many cases, these would be the only stores left untouched on a block otherwise devastated.) "Mom and pop," a phrase that invoked warm feelings elsewhere, was a bad word in the ghetto. It symbolized whites who raised prices unfairly and charged exorbitant interest on loans, all for low-quality goods. Nor were chains immune: Safeway, which had a reputation for discriminatory hiring practices and high prices, saw five of its stores burned to the ground, while its competitor Giant, with a much better local reputation, was completely spared.[13]

Particularly hard-hit were white-owned chain stores in the Fourteenth Street-to-Park Road area: Kay Jewelers, Carousel, Woolworth's, G. C. Murphy. A gas-filled bottle, with a lighted wick trailing from the mouth, was left in Beyda's, a clothing store. A cop saw it and, through his bullhorn, yelled to the looters to get out. The store exploded a few seconds after the last looter hit the sidewalk. Two boys trapped inside G. C. Murphy weren't so lucky: One, a fourteen-year-old, was found near the loading dock, burned beyond recognition; the other, eighteen-year-old George Neely, was found in the second-floor storage room.[14]

By then half the buildings on the two blocks of Fourteenth between Columbia and Park roads were on fire, and the rest were being ransacked. Smoke mixed with tear gas, bringing visibility to a hundred feet or less. People darted in and out, some with only a few items—a pair of shoes, a shirt; one looter confessed to stealing just a sponge—while some walked away with armfuls of goods. Two men, among the relatively few arrested that afternoon on Fourteenth, said they decided to do a little looting simply because they were on their lunch break.[15]

A recurrent image from the riots, recounted in newspaper reports and beamed into suburban homes on the nightly news, was of police officers standing by while rioters went wild. To many, this looked like they didn't care. But the reality was more complex. Many realized the futility of trying to arrest a few people out of a thousand; others feared provoking an already angry mob. Still others felt constrained by higher-ups, who they said had explicitly ordered them not to use violence. As one officer complained to a *U.S. News & World Report* journalist, "I think we could have stopped this thing if they hadn't put us under wraps so. Looters would break a window, then stand aside to watch our reaction. When we did nothing, the mob would move in and ransack the place. We just had to stand there."[16]

A French reporter on the scene likewise told an American colleague, "What you need here are a couple of squads of Parisian gendarmes. They move in, swinging their lead-weighted capes, and wielding their clubs. They go right after the ringleaders and smash the hell out of them. And I'll tell you this: that discourages a mob very fast."[17]

Standing on a Columbia Heights sidewalk, one officer on the scene, Captain Tilmon O'Bryant (one of the few blacks on the force), grew resigned. "Look at this. Just look at it," he told a reporter. "They don't know what they are doing, some of them. They are doing it just because everyone else is." He turned and, seeing a boy walking out of a store with an armful of clothes, asked what he was doing.

"I don't know," said the boy sheepishly. "I just saw it laying there."

"Put it back!" ordered O'Bryant.

The boy did as he was told.

In the early afternoon two hundred people, mostly high-school-age kids, marched down Seventh Street, a run-down commercial strip known as "Furniture Row" and the subject of Jean Toomer's famous eponymous poem:

> Money burns the pocket, pocket hurts,
> Bootleggers in silken shirts,
> ballooned, booming Cadillacs,
> Whizzing, whizzing down the street-car tracks.

Looters had largely spared the street the night before, and now it was ripe for destruction. They smashed windows as they went; some dashed in to grab loot, while others moved on. Many of the merchants who owned the stores had long closed shop and fled, but some stayed to ward off attackers.

"I saw kids, five and six years old, come out of liquor stores with bottles in their hands and throw them at police cars and other cars driven by whites," one remaining merchant said.[18] Rather than wade into the mob, police set up a barricade with their patrol cars at Mount Vernon Square, at the intersection of Massachusetts and New York avenues with Seventh Street. But the mob simply went a few blocks over and around them, all the while headed downtown.

That morning, long before looting began downtown, small groups of teenagers had run through the two biggest downtown department stores, Hecht's and Woodward and Lothrop's, harassing customers and overturning displays. Both stores quickly closed, and their maintenance crews hammered plywood boards over the large plate-glass window displays. One would have thought a hurricane was coming. And in a sense, it was.

At Seventh and P, cops tossed gas canisters at the crowd, but it just pushed people farther south. Other officers, massed at Mount Vernon Square, moved north to meet them, tossing gas. One reporter saw a grenade land in the middle of three teenage girls carrying armloads of clothes; they shrieked, dropped their loot, and ran. Another reporter watched as a Cadillac pulled up in front of a men's clothing store and its occupants loaded it with suits, shirts, and ties. But the gas only succeeded in driving rioters off Seventh, and only until the clouds cleared. Soon the crowds were back.

By 3:00 P.M., the mob had cascaded around the blockade at Mount Vernon Square and flooded into downtown. Like the night before in Columbia Heights, the police played a desperate game of cat-and-mouse with looters: pulling up to a store, watching the rioters scurry, only to have them return when the cops pushed off to another street. Self-appointed lookouts would give the looters a few seconds' warning, but arrests in any case were few. Cops had neither the time nor the manpower to respond effectively.

Fortunately for many merchants, the looting downtown wasn't very extensive. The stores were a long way from looters' homes, and many of the people who made it that far were in it for fun, not profit. Things were much worse on H Street, in the city's Northeast sector, where a long row of stores, again predominantly white-owned but black-patronized, went up in flames that afternoon. By early afternoon a few dozen cops were facing more than a thousand looters. No one paid them much attention. A thick cloud of tear gas floated overhead as teenagers ran into and out of stores.

Here, as on Fourteenth Street, the terrible ecology of looting replicated itself. A vanguard of window-smashers, often adults, would pass through, after which a wave of children and teenagers would filter in past the broken plate glass. They would overturn displays and grab a few items. But the real looters waited until the initial crowd had moved on. They would pull up in a car, pop the trunk, and systematically carry out loads of anything they could find—food, liquor, clothing, car parts. Some of them later confessed to working off "shopping lists," targeting specific stores and specific items. Others were simply going for the easiest targets.

Once the stores were empty, the arsonists arrived. Some carried gas cans and set meticulous infernos. Many just tossed Molotov cocktails. The arsonists later claimed to be solely interested in property destruction—as one anonymous fire-starter swore, "No one lived above the stores I had anything to do with"—but intentional or not, arson claimed the majority of the twelve deaths related to the D.C. riots.[19]

In one instance, arsonists set fire to the Quality Clothing Store at Seventh and Q streets. Above the store lived city bus driver Clarence James and his mother, Annie. Ms. James, fifty-two, had cared for more than forty foster children, and even adopted several herself. But her obesity—she weighed 450 pounds—severely limited her mobility. Coming home Friday afternoon, Clarence found several teenagers trying to set a fire out of a pile of cardboard and paper in the looted storefront. "Don't do that!" he yelled. "My mother lives on top of that store, and she can't get out of bed!"

They did it anyway. The building erupted in flames. Eventually firemen arrived, but by the time they got Ms. James outside, she was unconscious. Clarence and his younger brother put her in his car—there weren't enough ambulances in the city—and took her to the hospital, where she died.[20]

In all, five hundred fires erupted on Friday; at one point, two hundred were raging simultaneously. Donald Mayhew, a third-generation Washington, D.C., firefighter, had been on duty since Thursday night. That evening he was placed in charge of defending the department headquarters because, he said, "There were rumors going around that they were going to burn the communication center." Friday afternoon the department, finding itself undermanned, called in support from neighboring jurisdictions in Virginia and Maryland. Under normal circumstances, fire crews would spend several hours on a fire, first extinguishing the flames and then carefully going through the ashes, putting out embers. By Friday afternoon, Mayhew said, the order came around to simply put fires down and move on, because there wasn't enough time to do a thorough job. "We could only contain them, we weren't able to put them out," he recalled. But that only made it easier for arsonists to come by afterward and relight.[21]

The fires brought out strange extremes in the surrounding crowd. Many people, both looters and bystanders, volunteered to help move hoses, and some even brought food and drinking water for the men. Others did everything they could to hamper the efforts of Mayhew and his colleagues, from taking axes to fire hoses to opening fireplugs in order to drop the water pressure. Some even threw bricks and bottles at the open-top fire engines as they drove by. Eventually, Mayhew said, engine drivers learned to build makeshift chicken-wire roofs over their seats, while the rest of the men would lie under the hoses in back. Mayhew worked all night on Friday, and didn't go off the line for nearly two weeks.

The White House was moving to a full-on crisis mode. Califano's office, a long room with a conference table running most of its length, became the command post. At one end he and his staff stood a large map of the city on an easel; like at the District Building, they filled it with multicolored pushpins that corresponded to reports of looting and arson. Pins quickly forested the board. Outside the door they had ticker machines spitting out wire reports from the major news services.[22]

"I remember that day vividly," recalled one of his aides, Matthew Nimetz. "We got calls from the police in the afternoon saying, 'Things are going to be out of control. There is just no way we can control this city. Everything is going to go.'"[23]

President Johnson, watching the smoke rising over the city, knew he now faced one of the hardest decisions of his political life, a mere five days after deciding to withdraw from politics altogether. Should he call in troops to occupy the U.S. capital? This was different from Detroit. This was the center of the free world. What would it say about the country if the next day images of rifle patrols and lumbering tanks foregrounding the Capitol appeared in newspapers around the world? And what if a soldier killed a civilian?

Before deciding to send in troops, Johnson wanted to be absolutely sure they were needed. Yet no one at the White House, at the center of the national government, had a good sense of what was going on just blocks away. And no one wanted to rely on the District government's word alone. A little after 2:00 P.M., the president called Christopher and directed him to meet Murphy and General Ralph Haines at the White House immediately. He ordered the trio to drive an unmarked police car through the riot zone and report back to him as soon as possible. By 2:45, they were off.

The plan was for them to communicate with the White House via police radio. But "this was completely ineffective," Christopher noted later. "The police network was swamped with calls."[24] Not only could they not reach Johnson, but he couldn't reach them. They decided instead to reconnoiter as much as possible, then go back to the White House. They saw rampant looting, arson, firefighters, police, and garbage everywhere. At one point they got out to talk to people, and Haines was hit in the shoulder with a rock.

But for all the destruction going on around them, they decided that the crowds were not particularly dangerous. "There was restiveness but the people were not thoroughly out to dismiss all law and order," Haines later told congressional investigators. "I felt it was a situation where the uniform would be respected if troops entered the city."[25] In a perverse way, that made it ripe for the military to intervene. They agreed to recommend troops.

The problem was actually talking to the president. Stuck in the middle of a riot zone, it would have taken too long to get back to the White House by car and been too dangerous to go back by foot. They tried running the siren, but it didn't move the crowds at all. They decided to find a pay phone. But even in normal times, most ghetto phones were out of order; in a riot, the rest had been burned or smashed. Finally they found one, in a gas station—and someone was using it.

Since it was a bad idea to announce their presence and demand to use the phone, three of the most powerful men in Washington waited patiently in the middle of a riot zone to call the president of the United States.

After what must have felt like an hour, the phone was free. Murphy handed Christopher a dime, and Haines and Christopher hurriedly dialed the White House. "I'm sure it must have been a very odd-looking pair—General Haines and I huddled around a telephone in a service station," Christopher said. "There was a whole group of people standing outside the telephone booth not knowing what we were doing."[26]

Finally they got through to the president. "Where have you been!" Johnson yelled. "I've been trying to reach you for an hour."

Christopher explained the situation briefly. Then he recommended troops. Meanwhile, the line behind them was growing, and getting testy. Christopher mimed to them that it wouldn't be long, pointing expressively to his watch. Then he gave the phone to Haines, who said yes, troops were definitely needed.

Johnson cut him off. Fine, he said. We'll send in troops. He hung up.

The president already had a formal request from the mayor's office on his desk. "We have reviewed the situation and we conclude that Federal Troops are essential to supplement the local police force and National Guard in order to maintain safety for the citizens of the District of Columbia," it read. "Therefore, we the undersigned recommend that you take the necessary action to permit the deployment of Federal Troops as soon as possible."[27]

A few minutes later, Johnson had signed the necessary paperwork: a proclamation calling on the rioters to cease and desist, and an executive order to federalize the D.C. National Guard and send in the U.S. military.

Captain Leroy Rhode had been waiting all day. He was based at Fort Myer, an army base in the leafy Virginia suburbs, just over a hill from Arlington National Cemetery. Rhode's unit, the Third Infantry Regiment, was known as the "Old Guard," and Rhode led the 150 men of D Company. It was a good gig. The job mostly involved ceremonies of all sorts—military parades, honor guards, even social escorts for the Johnson daughters, whose husbands were both serving in Vietnam.

Rhode had joined the ROTC while an undergraduate at Stetson University in Florida, and when he graduated he was assigned to the 173rd Airborne Brigade—the "Sky Soldiers"—and sent to Southeast Asia as a second lieutenant, at the head of a platoon. "On my twenty-third day out there, I went out on an operation, to keep the NVA from cutting Vietnam in two across the Central Highlands," he said with a gruff martial swagger, a mix of pride and irony. "Intel said there were seven NVA and VC [Viet Cong] divisions in the area, and I thought, 'shit,' because a division is about twenty-two thousand men, and I asked the question, when they told me what my area of responsibility was, 'Aren't we mismatched here?' And they said, 'No no no, don't have to worry, an NVA division is only about fourteen thousand men.' And I said, 'Yeah, but I still only have about forty-two men, right?'"

Rhode's unit landed near Pleiku and helped secure an airfield, then moved on through the jungle. "Long story short we spent twenty-eight days marching across central Vietnam, kicking Charlie's ass, kicked it back into Laos and Cambodia, decimated a couple of divisions and I didn't lose a single man," he says. "As a result of that I went from there to the Third Infantry."[28] Rhode was just twenty-five years old.

Rhode joined D Company as the executive officer, then rotated out to the motor pool and then back as company commander. Few who were not West Pointers get that sort of honor, and Rhode wore it with pride. His unit was active during the March on the Pentagon in the fall of 1967, though mostly Rhode saw "action" as a member of color guards and funeral escorts.

But he was well aware that another, much more difficult assignment loomed as a possibility. In a corner of his base office sat a heavy steel safe, inside of which were dozens of operational plans for the Old Guard's other primary mission: defending the capital. If, say, the Soviets attacked, it was his job to lead D Company across the river to the White House, the Capitol, or one of a few other critical federal sites and occupy them, thereby ensuring the continuity of government. If a national emergency hit the capital—including a riot—Rhode said, "The phone would ring and they'd say okay we're on Contingency Plan Alpha Delta Snowflake Two and I'd open the safe and I'd find that folder and I'd open it up to find what the hell I was supposed to be doing."

Rhode got that fateful call a few hours after King was killed—at 10:30 P.M., the Army Operations Center put his company on thirty-minute alert. "I got the plan out of the safe, and we were to protect the White House," he recalled. "There were certain weapons we did take, certain weapons we didn't take, that sort of thing. And so they'd call up and say get ready to go and I'd load all my people and equipment on the trucks, and sit there for an hour or two. Then they'd call back and say it's all changed now, we're going to do something else. So I'd unload my people and we did that about six or seven times." This went on most of the night and on into Friday. "Finally," a little after 4:00 P.M., "they called us and said we're going in."

Rhode's unit saddled up in their trucks and, behind a Military Police escort, headed for the White House, with Rhode in the lead jeep. To get there, they had to cross Memorial Bridge, a main conduit spanning the Potomac between Arlington National Cemetery and the Lincoln Memorial. It is one of the capital area's most picturesque locales, but that day it was a nightmare. Tens of thousands of people—in cars, in buses, on foot—were headed out of town in a mad rush, taking up both sides of the road. In the background rose dense smoke plumes, circled by police and television helicopters.

The convoy blared its horns and slowly edged the river of cars aside. But no one seemed to mind. "Even though we were interrupting the people getting the hell out of there, a lot of them pulled over and got out of their cars and applauded as we went by," said Rhode.

The Third Infantry may have been the first unit into the city, but it wasn't the only one. The Sixth Armored Calvary Regiment, based at Fort Meade, was also on the way, trundling down the leafy Baltimore-to-Washington Parkway; they bivouacked at the Old Soldiers' Home

in upper Northeast Washington and were on the street patrolling by
6:00 P.M. In the head jeep rode Sergeant Paul Devrouax, a lanky young
black soldier from New Orleans, whose training as an architect had
kept him out of Vietnam and on the Sixth ACR's planning staff. As
one of the few black soldiers in the unit, Devrouax had been stuck at
the head of the column by his commander, who wanted him there as a
signal to locals that the army was not just a bunch of whites coming to
put down the city's black population.

It wasn't a role Devrouax felt comfortable playing; he spent his days
on patrol looking out on the city with mixed emotions. "It was something I was obligated to do," he said. "If I hadn't been in the army,
if I'd been on the other side, I don't know what I'd have been doing,
whether or not I'd have been part of the anger that came out from a
lot of blacks at the time."[29]

Elsewhere, elements of a Marine Corps battalion headed for
a staging area in Southeast Washington. The 91st Engineering
Battalion, 850 men, headed out from Fort Belvoir. From Fort Eustis
and Fort Lee, to the south of the city, came, respectively, the 716th
Transportation Command Group and the 544th Supply and Service
Battalion. And, at 9:00 P.M., the first planes carrying the mighty 82nd
Airborne, the only fully ready army division left in the country, took
off from North Carolina.[30]

Rhode and D Company headed to the White House, but at the
last minute the Pentagon changed its orders again and sent them to
the Capitol, directing another 3rd Infantry company, right behind
Rhode's, to the White House instead. The White House gates were
sealed, and troops were soon patrolling behind small hills of sandbags
all around the perimeter fence. Bright floodlights bathed the com-
pound in a sickly yellow glow.

Rhode and his troops headed down the center of Pennsylvania
Avenue. At the Capitol, "I drove up the steps that look toward the
Lincoln Memorial in my jeep and parked it up on top of that area
and set up my radios and everything like that and deployed my men
around there and sent some people across the street to break into the
office buildings so we could get on roofs so we could have fields of
fire," he said. "And there was one or two poor policemen inside the
Capitol building and God were they happy to see me." Rhode's company soon had machine-gun posts around the building and out on

the Capitol grounds. They set up their command post on the Portico, overlooking the Mall.

Columnist Mary McGrory, writing that week in the *Washington Star*, said the gun emplacements on the steps of the Capitol gave it "the air of a parliament of a new African republic."[31] It was 5:20. By 9:30 P.M., 3,850 troops would be on patrol in the city.[32] The occupation of Washington had begun.

9

April 5

THE OCCUPATION OF
WASHINGTON

That Friday afternoon tens of thousands of D.C. workers fled the city to the Maryland and Virginia suburbs. Suburbanization had been a reality of American life since the early part of the century, picking up significantly after World War II with the flight of thousands of newly enriched whites into racially restricted, middle-class communities. But until the 1960s those communities were still intricately tied to the urban core, even as it showed significant fraying at the edges. Not only did most of their adult residents still work in the city, but at night and on the weekends those same workers came back with their families to shop, eat, and go to the movies. Downtown Washington, in particular, was in 1968 still the retail center of the region, with its massive department stores and long streets of stores selling jewelry, shoes, and fancy dresses.

While the overwhelming majority of new suburbanites were middle-class whites, racial fears, before the 1960s at least, were not the main reason for their decamping. Rather, race drove such geographic realignment in less direct ways: racial exclusion from good jobs and from federal benefits programs made it financially impossible for blacks to move outward, while racially restrictive residential covenants, tacitly blessed by the Supreme Court in 1917 in *Buchanan v. Warley*, excluded even middle-class blacks from the same movement (the Court explicitly reversed that position in 1948 in *Shelley v. Kramer*, but by that time residential patterns were well defined).

And, as historian Kenneth T. Jackson documents assiduously in his classic *Crabgrass Frontier*, federal programs further reinforced the growth of the suburbs: the overwhelming majority of Federal Housing Administration (FHA) funding in Washington, among other cities, went to the outlying parts of the city, while two-thirds of all spending in the region went to the northern Virginia and Maryland suburbs.

Meanwhile, the FHA helped usher in urban decline by declining to insure vast sections of black-majority Washington while also refusing, as a matter of policy, to insure mixed-occupancy housing projects—a policy replicated across the country.[1] Add to that the billions in federal dollars spent on limited-access highways into and out of the city centers, and the nation had nothing less than a strategy for resegregating the American populace geographically at precisely the moment when so many of the buttresses supporting legal segregation were collapsing.

Nevertheless, suburban whites did not immediately sever their relationships to the city. Not only did they return to work and shop, but they also maintained strong political allegiances. Throughout the 1950s and early 1960s, scores of American suburbs allowed themselves to be annexed by their urban neighbors. In short, though racial fear was not an insignificant motivation for the movement of many whites to the suburbs, up to the late 1960s it was not the predominant motivation, either.

But racial fear was very much in the minds of the tens of thousands of whites who fled Washington that Friday afternoon. They had reasons to be frightened—not only was a major riot taking place blocks from downtown, where most white commuters worked, but also many had to pass through the edges of the riot zone to get home. It was a frenzied exodus, with every street out of the city turned into a parking lot. A man at Fifteenth Street and L was doing his best to direct traffic with an umbrella, but it didn't make much difference.[2]

Mobs pitched rocks and bottles at whites as they drove north along Sixteenth Street, and they dropped bricks from the overpasses on Kenilworth Avenue, to the east of the disorder's center. "It's every man for himself," one frightened commuter told the *Washington Post*.[3] Another man, desperately looking for a bus, told *U.S. News & World Report*, "We've got to organize 100 percent to defend ourselves against the blacks."[4]

The media had prepared them for this. All winter Americans had been reading newspaper articles about a coming "race war," in which black urban guerrillas would go on terrorist campaigns to destroy the inner cities. That spring *Reader's Digest* took out ads in major newspapers featuring a photograph of cops taking cover behind a police cruiser, aiming their rifles up at an unseen target. "Does the United States Face Insurrection? An Expert Says, 'Yes, It's Quite Possible,'" read the headline, above smaller headlines for "The Pill and the Teen-Age Girl" and "7 Ways to Get More Out of Life."[5]

As the suburbanites fled across the District lines, the adjacent county governments, and the Virginia and Maryland state governments, closed the borders against the expected coming hordes. Things were particularly hairy along the Maryland side, where major streets cross over from Washington with little more than a change in signage. At several crossings Friday afternoon, dozens of heavily armed state troopers took up position. "The atmosphere was electric and riot police with shotguns and helmets stood ready to repel any invasion," reported the *Washington Post*.[6]

Long before rioting broke out in Baltimore, Governor Spiro Agnew and his staff worried that their biggest threat came from Washington; at 11:00 P.M. on Friday, he alerted the Maryland National Guard and called General George Gelston to duty, deploying him not to Baltimore but to the state armory in Silver Spring, a D.C. suburb.[7] The Guard even had an emergency plan, Operation Tango, for riots that spread north from the District.[8]

A scene on Saturday along Southern Avenue, the border between Southeast Washington and Prince George's County, Maryland, drove home the stark divide between city and suburb. A five-store strip mall on the District side burned for hours, even as teams of firemen fought to contain it. Down the block three hundred people were looting a grocery, a deli, and a liquor store. Across the street, in Maryland, a line of policemen armed with dogs, gas, shotguns, and rifles stoically watched the conflagration, on guard for any spillover rioting. Two Maryland state police sharpshooters perched atop a liquor store with high-powered rifles. Others sat inside stores and cars, their weapons pointed toward the capital. The troopers had explicit permission to fire on any looter crossing the state line, passed down from County Commissioner Gladys Spellman.

One D.C. National Guardsman on patrol in the area, Major Robert Donlan, said he was "scared stiff" of the small army amassed across the street, "armed to the teeth, just waiting." With a bullhorn in hand, Donlan tried to get the looters away from the border, lest they cross it and spark an even bigger crisis. "I told the people in Washington to stay within the city limits and go home," he told the *Washington Post*'s Ben Gilbert. "I told them if they crossed into Maryland they would probably be shot. Nobody crossed the line."[9]

While most of the Washington deaths resulted from the fires, two died Friday night of police gunshots. By late afternoon looting had begun to spread eastward from the H Street corridor to Anacostia, the agglomeration of poor black neighborhoods on the other side of the Anacostia River. At 6:00 P.M., three cops responded to a burglar alarm at the Young Men's Shop at the intersection of Minnesota Avenue and Benning Road. They found looters on the scene, and one of the officers, David Tompkins, grabbed fifteen-year-old Thomas Williams as he ran out the front of the store. Tompkins pushed him up against the wall. According to a later investigation, another looter then ran past Tompkins, bumping him and setting off his gun, killing Williams. Tompkins was cleared by a coroner's jury, which ruled the death accidental, though witnesses said the officer had earlier been seen firing warning shots over the heads of looters.[10]

Three hours later, a similar incident occurred along South Capitol Street. Three officers, including Private Albert Lorraine, responded to reports of a looting. Lorraine, thinking one of the looters had a gun, shot him in the back. Ernest McIntyre, a twenty-year-old janitor who lived with his wife and daughter about a block away, stumbled into a nearby alley, where Lorraine and his colleagues found him dead a few minutes later. In his hand was a piece of glass. Like Tompkins, Lorraine was cleared, in his case by a U.S. grand jury.[11] In both cases, the officers became causes célèbres in the white suburbs and avatars of police brutality in the black community, further driving a wedge between the two.

Meanwhile, federal troops poured into the city. Some came by land from nearby bases; others landed at Andrews Air Force Base in suburban Maryland and the much smaller Bolling Air Force Base in Anacostia, which had recently closed its fixed-wing-aircraft field but still had the capacity to receive flights in emergency situations. As they arrived, the troops fanned out in two directions: one set, including Rhode's unit, went to protect local and national assets, from electrical facilities to federal office buildings. The others went directly into the streets. Soldiers weren't allowed to make arrests themselves, but they could detain suspects, and in many cases cops and soldiers worked in tandem to isolate and then arrest hordes of looters. In other cases simply having the troops around to break up masses of looters made the task of actually arresting them easier—which explains the skyrocketing arrest rate after midnight.

By six, troops from the Sixth Armored Calvary Regiment were massed at Fourteenth and S; they marched north slowly, stretching across the entire street and sidewalks, unsheathed bayonets fixed to their rifles. Many were already Vietnam veterans, and they trembled at the thought of shooting American citizens. Others were fresh recruits and feared that their first combat experience would be in their nation's capital.

"I noticed a large group of kids following us down the street," recalled Specialist Fourth Class Jack Hyler of the 503rd Military Police Battalion. "They were yelling things and threatening us. Physically we were trapped by row houses, and the fire burning out of control at the other end. I started worrying about what we should do if those kids tried to attack us—use gas, load our guns, or what."[12]

Others weren't so cautious. Over the course of the riots the military used eight thousand gas canisters. Fortunately, they only fired three bullets, hitting no one (that didn't mean there were no deaths in the area: later that night twenty-nine-year-old Ronald James Ford was found near Cardozo High School, down the street from Howard; his throat was cut and a bloody trail led back from his body to a broken window).

Such restraint had been drilled into them during the extensive riot training the units had undergone over the winter. Each soldier also carried a laminated card outlining their rules of engagement: from "I will not load or fire my weapon except when authorized by an officer in person" to "I will not discuss or pass on rumors about this operation."

At the Capitol, Rhode quickly realized that there was not, in fact, going to be a massive assault on the federal government. After several hours, he and most of his men were redeployed, this time to H Street, which was still raging out of control into the evening (his unit was later replaced at the Capitol by marines). Rhode loaded his men into their trucks and headed the short distance from Capitol Hill to the eastern end of the riot zone, at H Street and Bladensburg Road.

"I looked up and there were a thousand people in the street just going hog wild," he recalled. The police had a few blocks of H Street, up to Ninth, under control. But beyond was anarchy—flames, mobs, fights, a Boschian hell-scene. At the intersection sat two lone squad cars, each with a single police officer—one in an arm cast—leaning over the hood, pistol pointed toward the approaching mob.

"I blew my horn and nothing happened, except the guy with the cast on his arm kind of dodged out of the way and I just pushed the lead deuce-and-a-half [two-and-a-half-ton truck] ahead and pushed his car out of way so we could get past." Rhode pulled his troops into the middle of the street and set them up into wedge formations from side-walk to sidewalk. Then they pressed forward. "I turned around and the street was empty," he said. "That was all we had to do. Everyone had just disappeared."

Once they had cleared the eastern end of H Street, Rhode walked back to the two officers to make sure they were all right. "When I walked up there I said, 'Jeez, I'm sorry I busted your car, you know,' and he ran up to me and put his arms around me and he said, 'God, you're so goddamn ugly, but God, I love to see you. If you ever need anything let me know." Soon more cops arrived, and together with the troops they started making curfew arrests, sending some downtown but putting most of them in a local playground.

At one point shop owners started to arrive, some of whom were lucky enough to find their stores still intact. They begged Rhode to place guards in front of their stores. "I just couldn't do that," he said later—not enough men. Instead, "A lot of 'em asked me to use a real strong form of tear gas, throw it in their stores to try to keep people out until they could get back in and clean it up, hose it down, and recover their merchandise." Rhode gladly obliged.[13]

While Rhode and his Third Infantry Regiment company worked H Street, another Third Infantry contingent tackled Seventh Street. Seven hundred soldiers from the 91st Engineering Battalion responded to scattered violence in the city's Southeast quadrant, while the D.C. National Guard—at full complement, it totaled just two seven-hundred-man MP battalions—spread out to protect firemen and the city's power and water supplies. The D.C. Guard included two professional athletes, Baltimore Orioles pitcher Pete Richert and Washington Redskins All-Pro tight end Jerry Smith, who duly reported for duty.

By Wednesday, April 10, the peak of the Washington deployment, there were 15,530 army and National Guard soldiers in and around Washington, hailing from as far away as Fort Carson, Colorado (the Second Brigade, Fifth Infantry Division), and Fort Sill, Oklahoma (the III Corps Artillery Brigade).

By nightfall Friday the hectic command and control situation had congealed into three headquarters: the city government, working out of the District Building, at 300 Indiana Avenue; the military (Haines and twenty-eight staffers), working out of another office in the same building; and the White House. The District Building was just east of the downtown core, so that less than a mile separated them from the White House, making it easy for Vance, Murphy, and others to shuttle among them—which they did, all night. Subsidiary power centers emerged at the Department of Justice, the Pentagon, the police precincts, and the various field posts established by the arriving units. At times, Deputy Mayor Fletcher recalled, he would look out the District Building window at the burning city and ask himself, "My God, what am I doing here?"[14]

Flying home from Memphis that evening, Attorney General Clark and his staff had the pilot circle the city before landing at Andrews. Wilkins recalled seeing fires everywhere, obscured by massive, billowing smoke. "Coming up the river, looking out the window, I saw a great big orange ball with a needle in it. All of a sudden I said, 'Holy shit, that's flames, and the needle I'm seeing is the Washington Monument. The city looked like it had been bombed from the air.'"[15]

One of Califano's staffers, Larry Levinson, had been on vacation in the U.S. Virgin Islands when King was killed. His boss called him that night and told him to get the first commercial flight back. Levinson finally arrived at the White House Friday evening. He rode in through the South Gate. "I was just sitting there stunned to find sandbags on both sides of the entrance to the White House, floodlights on it," he recalled, "manned by the military with full battle gear and a fifty-caliber machine gun at the center of the entrance."

Inside, Levinson found weary staffers running at a hundred miles an hour. "It was like coming back to another planet."[16] He went to find Califano. White House aides flew in and out of his boss's office, and meetings both spontaneous and planned took place in the Oval Office, the Cabinet Room, and at points all along Califano's giant conference table. Outside the door they had ticker machines spitting out wire reports from the major news services. "I remember that day vividly," said one of his aides, Matthew Nimetz. "We got calls from the police in the afternoon saying, 'Things are going to be out of control. There is just no way we can control this city. Everything is going to go.'"[17]

Everyone's desk had a phone, and many of them had direct lines to the president. "He had a hotline from his office and his bedroom and he ran lines to three or four top aides," said Califano. It even had a special ring. "It was a phone that just rang without interruption. It just rang. So you knew it was him."[18]

Despite the world-historical events going on outside, all pretense of hierarchy among the White House core staff was gone. "By '67 we had a very good sense of mutual trust and collaboration," said Levinson. "Nobody had an individual agenda, no one was trying to say, 'I'm the guy trying to solve this crisis.' We had a pretty integrated team." At one point Supreme Court justice Abe Fortas stopped by to talk. Levinson, a recent Harvard Law graduate, was speechless. "As a young lawyer, it was very hard for me even to say 'Justice Fortas,'" he said. "But he just said, 'Call me Abe.'"[19]

Though Johnson was officially in charge, Califano assumed much of the executive duties. If Johnson could sometimes seem a Quixote-like figure,

tilting at imaginary enemies, then Califano was his Sancho Panza: pragmatic, at times skeptical, but extremely loyal and able to at least keep the
president on his horse. Officially the president's domestic policy adviser,
he had used his sharp elbows and organizational acumen to establish himself as first among equals in the White House staff; only McPherson had
as much sway with the president.

And Califano fit the part: born in Brooklyn and educated at Holy
Cross, he had gone on to Harvard Law School and a fast-track job
at the Department of Defense. Short and compact, Califano quickly
climbed to general counsel of the army and, soon after, special assistant to Secretary McNamara. There he imbibed McNamara's mana-
gerial wizardry as he helped the former Ford president implement a
thorough restructuring of the military. He also acted as liaison to the
White House, and soon after his 1965 inauguration, Johnson decided
he wanted Califano for himself. He stayed for the entire second term.
Like McPherson, he was one of the few men who could live—indeed,
thrive—in close proximity to the stinging wrath of Johnson's ego, like
clown fish around a sea anemone. He proved so competent in that
post—again, like McPherson, switching from speechwriting to policymaking to liaison with departments and Congress—that the *New York
Times* called him "the deputy president for domestic affairs."[20]

At eleven Johnson met with Califano, Vance, and Washington
to take stock and plot the next day (McPherson would have been
included, but his daughter Coco had fallen out of a tree that evening
and cracked her head open, and he had rushed to the hospital to be
with her). Vance said there weren't nearly enough troops on hand,
so Johnson ordered up more units from the Eighty-second Airborne.
Washington complained that too many arrestees were being arraigned
and released. "I don't give a damn what they have to do," the mayor
said. "I don't want them released tonight. Apparently the troops are
starting to release some people they picked up for looting. That's just
insanity. I don't give a goddamn what the Constitution says. We
just can't release them and let them go out again."

After Vance and Washington left, Califano handed the president a
report saying that Carmichael was planning a march on Georgetown,
the leafy enclave home to many of the northeastern elite Johnson so
disdained. "Goddamn!" the president cried. "I've waited thirty-five
years for this day."[21]

By 1968 Johnson had managed to achieve what drew such praise for his predecessor: a highly efficient, intelligent, loyal White House staff. Califano, Clifford, McPherson, not to mention a dozen aides underneath them—these men were, like Sorensen and McNamara before them, among the nation's best and brightest. But they faced a wholly different, more intractable set of problems: a quagmire in Asia, constant riots at home, a surging deficit, and an increasingly antagonistic public. They, too, were technocrats of the Greatest Generation, but for the past few years they had seen the world refuse to work with them. Then, just at the moment when they thought they had managed a breakthrough with Johnson's withdrawal, King died and the city descended into rioting. It was a tragic reminder that no matter how well organized the White House, no matter how hard they worked, no matter how many Ivy League degrees filled the Cabinet Room, no matter how great their policy proposals looked on paper, reality had a way of working along its own course. "We were scared to death," recalled White House aide and former Supreme Court clerk James Gaither. "The country was exploding, and it was pretty hard to figure out how the hell we were going to contain it."[22]

At one point later that night, Califano and the president stepped onto the North Portico to talk privately. "You could see the smoke from Fourteenth Street," Califano said later. "It was one of the most stunning experiences of my life, I think, certainly for me. And I guess for him, too."[23]

Before coming to the meeting, Vance had gone out to see the rioting firsthand. John Hechinger, the head of the City Council and one of the city's liberal business elite—he ran his family's chain of hardware stores—offered to take him for a ride in his black limousine. The pair headed toward H Street. After touring the edges of the disorder, Hechinger said he wanted to check on his company's lumber supply outlet just east of the rioting. His office was on the top floor.

As they approached, their headlights illuminated dozens of looters carting off goods, quickly but methodically. "My God!" he said. "They're using forklifts!" They called the police, but none was available. Vance told the driver to head into the lot at full speed. When the looters heard the big vehicle approaching, they ran off.[24]

At 1:20 A.M. Vance and Washington held their first press conference. Washington reported that the city was "quite calm," and they both expressed hope that the drop in violence since the curfew and troop deployments would continue. "We talked with the police and with federal troops and National Guard," Vance said, "and were informed that the cooperation among them was excellent. The situation appeared to be quieting down and, as of the moment, to be in hand."[25] Though incidents of looting continued to be reported through the night, by 4:00 A.M. the Secret Service reported to the Oval Office that "looting has slowed to an almost negligible point."[26]

Finally, Vance went back to the White House and, at 3:00 A.M., met Califano for a scotch and soda. Vance had endeared himself to federal officials during the Detroit riots by holding an evening cocktail hour each day (with booze, otherwise unobtainable in the city, provided by Mayor Jerry Cavanaugh); by now, a scotch and soda after a long day's work fighting a riot was probably a deeply ingrained routine for him.[27] As they chatted, the president came wandering in from his bedroom, still in his pajamas. As usual during crisis situations, he couldn't sleep, and he'd been wandering the halls, reading wire reports and checking up on the situation in Vietnam.

"No wonder the nation is going up in smoke and riots and looting," Johnson said, standing in the doorway to Califano's office. "My two top advisers are sitting around drinking!"[28]

10

April 5

"There Are No Ghettos in Chicago"

Washington wasn't the only city hit by rioting Friday. Police in Flint, Michigan, used tear gas to push back rioters. About two hundred people marched through downtown Jefferson City, Missouri, breaking store windows and looting merchandise. The Hill District in Pittsburgh, a predominantly black neighborhood, experienced widespread vandalism. Twenty people were arrested and one man, a white bystander, was shot and seriously wounded. Three people, including a fireman, were wounded in sporadic violence in Savannah, Georgia. A band of rioters in Tallahassee unleashed a volley of arrows at police officers.[1] And in still-scarred Detroit, three thousand Michigan National Guardsmen deployed after scattered looting; police shot several rioters, killing one. Mayor Cavanaugh, voicing an attitude widespread among many municipal leaders that day, told the press, "It is better to overreact than underreact."[2]

The violence contrasted sharply with the deep outpouring of grief across the country and around the world. King's death made the headlines of every major international newspaper. A thousand people in New York, led by Dr. Benjamin Spock, marched in silence from

Central Park, down Broadway to City Hall. Seven thousand participated in an open-air memorial service for King in San Francisco.

In Boston, the city underwrote a concert by soul singer James Brown that was aired on the local public broadcasting channel. During the song "Has Everybody Got the Feeling?" his fans rushed the stage, trying to touch him. Police pushed them back as the Godfather of Soul pleaded, "Let me finish the show! We're all black. Let's respect ourselves. Are we together or are we ain't?"

"We are!" shouted the crowd. And though there was scattered violence that night, primarily in Roxbury, the predominantly black part of the city, the expected riot never materialized. How could it, when so many would-be rioters were at home watching Mr. Dynamite on TV?[3]

In Cleveland, Bobby Kennedy repeated his soul-searching efforts to connect with the country's grieving black population with a short speech Friday night at the City Club. He had canceled the rest of his Indiana tour, but before returning to Washington he felt he needed to make another public statement. He and three of his closest advisers— Ted Sorenson, Jeff Greenfield, and Adam Walinsky—had stayed up all night writing it.[4]

Cleveland was safer from rioting than most cities at the moment, thanks to its popular black mayor, but it was hardly violence proof. Kennedy had spoken off the cuff the night before in Indianapolis; now, with time to reflect, he wanted to address more fully the issue of violence in America.

"This is a time of shame and sorrow. It is not a day for politics," he began. "I have saved this one opportunity to speak briefly to you about this mindless menace of violence in America which again stains our land and every one of our lives."

Kennedy refused to talk about violence against only one race—"the victims of the violence are black and white, rich and poor, young and old, famous and unknown." And yet, unlike Johnson and other liberals who sought a middle ground by denouncing both the Ku Klux Klan and SNCC, both King's killer and Stokely Carmichael, he transcended that divide. "Whenever any American's life is taken by another American unnecessarily—whether it is done in the name of the law or in the defiance of law, by one man or a gang, in cold blood or in passion, in an attack of violence or in response to violence—whenever we tear at the fabric of life which another man has painfully and clumsily woven for himself and his children, the whole nation is degraded."

This, to him, was a basic principle in American society. And yet in recent years, that principle had eroded. Why? "Too often we honor swagger and bluster and the wielders of force; too often we excuse those who are willing to build their own lives on the shattered dreams of others," he said. "Some Americans who preach nonviolence abroad fail to practice it here at home. Some who accuse others of inciting riots have by their own conduct invited them. Some look for scapegoats, others look for conspiracies, but this much is clear: violence breeds violence, repression brings retaliation, and only a cleaning of our whole society can remove this sickness from our soul."

The real culprit was the dehumanizing effects of modern American social and political institutions. "For there is another kind of violence," he went on, "the violence of institutions; indifference and inaction and slow decay. This is the violence that afflicts the poor, that poisons relations between men because their skin has different colors. This is a slow destruction of a child by hunger, and schools without books and homes without heat in the winter. This is the breaking of a man's spirit by denying him the chance to stand as a father and as a man among other men. And this too afflicts us all."

What was needed, he said, was not more social spending—that was beside the point—but a massive public effort to "achieve true justice among our fellow citizens. The question is now what programs we should seek to enact. The question is whether we can find in our own midst and in our own hearts that leadership of human purpose that will recognize the terrible truths of our existence." What America needed, in short, was a renewed sense of a common goal. "Surely," he concluded, "we can learn, at least, to look at those around us as fellow men and surely we can begin to work a little harder to bind up the wounds among us and to become in our hearts brothers and countrymen once again."

And with that he finished his short speech and flew back to Washington.[5]

In New York, Mayor Lindsay went back to work after just a few hours of sleep. Another visit to Harlem at 7:30 A.M., and then he headed to City Hall for a long series of meetings: a talk with his cabinet in the Blue Room, a meeting with the police and fire chiefs, an

11:30 press conference, and finally a huddle with his eighteen neighborhood task force leaders. By 2:30, he was back on the streets. This
time he ventured into Brooklyn, to Bedford-Stuyvesant, a poor black
area that in 1964 had also erupted in rioting. Finally he returned to
Harlem, his fourth visit in less than twenty-four hours.[6]

New York may have looked fine on the surface, but Lindsay knew
better. Rumors flew about everything from blacks shooting white store
owners in Williamsburg to guerrilla bands planning to dynamite the
Hudson River tunnels and attack the stock markets. None of it was
true, of course, but it didn't help that evening when several radicals,
including housing-activist-turned-black-nationalist Jesse Gray and militant Charles Kenyatta, held a rally at 125th Street and Lenox Avenue.
Despite Lindsay's best efforts, they excoriated him for not reaching
out to "the people." But, Kenyatta said, rioting in Harlem wasn't the
answer. "Don't be snatching no drawers or shoes or nothing—we must
have a higher revolution than this. If this city must be flattened, let's
do it downtown!" he shouted. "This country is up for grabs. We gonna
move this thing until King's dream turns into violence."[7]

What was becoming apparent in New York, Detroit, Washington,
and elsewhere was that behind the pain of King's death was rising a
deeper anger in the ghetto. This wasn't about the murder in Memphis.
King's assassination merely dramatized what black people everywhere,
young and old, moderate and radical, middle-class and poor, had been
feeling all their lives: a studied indifference, a not-so-benign neglect
of their real problems. Crime, unemployment, bad housing, the list of
long-standing grievances went on. As one Washington looter told a
Howard interviewer, "Burning and mass-scale looting, which is a part
of rioting, as it goes today, was something that was inevitable here in
the District as well as in a number of other ghettos across the nation.
This is something which has been building up over the years."[8]

Only Bobby Kennedy seemed to understand that, and he was just
one man running an upstart presidential campaign. Meanwhile, no
matter how blacks voiced their frustration, the white establishment
found a way to ignore them or repress them. Now, finally, black
America was making itself heard, and heard loudly, in almost every
major city across the country—including the place where the hypocrisy of big-city white liberalism was the most obvious, the place
where claims to racial progressivism were belied daily by rat-infested

public housing, viciously racist suburbanites, and uncaring bureaucrats: Chicago.

The Second City was supposed to be a relatively modern place, racially. It had a powerful mayor who funneled millions in federal urban renewal funds into inner-city housing projects, and it had a politically empowered black bourgeoisie that dominated the city's South Side.

But such superficial qualities hid a pernicious and long-running tradition of racial antagonism and exclusion. In 1919 a bitter race riot broke out after a fight at a segregated beach; in the resulting three-day war that raged across the city, white and black gangs attacked each other's neighborhoods, destroying property and killing twenty-three blacks and fifteen whites. "Dozens of white mobs prowled the streets," wrote *Chicago Sun-Times* columnist Mike Royko. "Blacks going home were dragged from streetcars, beaten, and killed. Raiding parties drove into black areas and lobbed bombs into homes. The blacks retaliated by killing white deliverymen and greeting white raiders with gunfire."[9]

After a few decades of relative peace the city erupted again in the early postwar years, with two riots in 1949; another in 1951 was so large it required the Illinois National Guard to put it down. And those were just the proverbial tips of the racial iceberg. In the words of historian Arnold Hirsch, a "persistent undercurrent of violence lurked beneath the headlines, just beyond the recall of popular memory."[10] Individual instances of racial violence—beatings, harassment, bricks thrown through windows—became regular occurrences during the following decade as a burgeoning black population pushed out from the ghetto into surrounding white neighborhoods.

Simultaneous with simmering white-black tensions was the postwar inflow of millions of poor southern blacks to the city's West Side. This second great migration was much larger than the first, which had funneled blacks to the South Side. In 1920, blacks represented 4 percent of the city's population. In 1940, at the end of the first great migration, they were only 8.2 percent. Twenty years later, they represented 22.9 percent. And almost all that growth took place west of the Loop.[11]

Chicago's West Side had been largely Jewish. But as in many urban neighborhoods across the country, the second- and third-generation immigrants in places such as the West Side looked a little farther out and saw cheap housing, with immaculate yards, which their rising incomes could suddenly afford. And so they moved, oftentimes with shocking speed. The West Side was 87 percent white in 1950; a decade later, it was 91 percent black.[12]

To make things worse, Chicago's machine-driven political system didn't easily accommodate rapid population change, and no part of Chicago was more machine-driven than the West Side. The machine ensured political stability, but it was predicated on demographic stability: because elected ward officials were more or less appointed, the system depended on their ability to build personal ties in the community. With the community turning over so rapidly, the ward bosses suddenly found themselves with unfamiliar constituencies with vastly different needs. These new residents, largely rural and agricultural in background, required job training and social services, things the old guard couldn't and didn't want to deliver.

Moreover, the jobs these migrants came for—the West Side was once home to one of the country's largest agglomerations of urban industrial plants—were themselves fleeing to the suburbs and beyond, leaving the newcomers trapped in a cycle of unemployment, dependency, and frustration. And because the machine didn't allow voters to turn over their elected officials, the political system remained led by the same white politicos who had run the West Side for decades, even though many lived in luxury high-rises along Lake Michigan: Bernie Neistein in the Twenty-ninth Ward, Carmen Fratto in the Twenty-fourth, Ed Quigley in the Twenty-seventh.[13]

Chicago's solution for the overcrowding and poverty hitting the city was to tap the federal funds available through urban renewal. It tore out blocks and blocks of slums and replaced them with high-rise apartment buildings. But instead of scattering the projects around the city or pushing for racial integration within their tenancies, the Chicago Housing Authority purposely massed them in black neighborhoods and filled them almost completely with black residents. Because the machine system regarded the projects as political boondoggles rather than civic missions, they allowed allied construction firms to make millions through scrimping on materials and building shoddy structures.

As a result, by the mid-1960s the city's housing projects were little better than the slums they had purportedly replaced. In fact, they represented a much more segregated population than before: Of the thirty-three Chicago Housing Authority projects put up between 1950 and 1965, only one was in an area that was less than 84 percent black already; many went into a long thin stretch of land running south along the Dan Ryan Expressway, creating a literal wall of poverty between the black South Side and the white ethnics of the city's vast southwest.

Even worse, the buildings were stark, nearly Soviet in their disregard for aesthetics and human needs. Hallways opened to the elements, treeless courtyards channeled heavy winds through the high-rise canyons, dark corners and lonely stairwells encouraged crime. As one project resident told Royko, "See that balcony, these outside hallways? That's my kid's playground. And when that wire fence tears through those little babies fall through and die. Man, this is real isolation. Even the police are afraid to come here."[14] When city social workers began to be attacked in stairwells, the city commanded them to only use the elevators; since those often malfunctioned, visits from the city—a vital lifeline in the health of the ghetto family—were significantly curtailed.

Sitting atop this urban morass was perhaps the greatest urban chieftain in twentieth-century America, Richard Daley. A true son of the city, he had grown up in Bridgeport, an Irish neighborhood southwest of the Loop. As mayor he lived less than a block from his boyhood home. He had attended local colleges and entered the city's political system at the ground level, working his way up to the mayor's office in 1955. Daley was one of the few American mayors to be a true force on the national scene—because he could reliably deliver Chicago's millions of votes to a Democratic candidate, he was an object of fealty from even sitting presidents. He had a small room off his office that he liked to tell guests was where he took calls from the White House. When Daley opposed the War on Poverty's community action programs (CAP), fearing that they would empower local leaders outside the machine and thus upset his power base, Johnson immediately conceded by giving City Hall control over most CAP hiring.

But even a politician as astute and powerful as Daley was unready for the social upheavals wrought by the 1960s. For him, Chicago's segregation was simply an extension of the city's long-standing ethnic divisions—Germans lived north of the Loop, Poles to the northwest, Italians and Jews to the west, and so on. The communities, each of which had its own submachines, provided the filters for city services, and social spending was kept down through the actions of the church and a constellation of ethnic benevolent societies. Even the black South Side had its machine, run by U.S. representative William Dawson.

Why should blacks want to live anywhere else, when the system provides for them perfectly as is? Such was Daley's thinking. At a 1963 NAACP rally at the Grant Park bandshell, he told the crowd, "There are no ghettos in Chicago." He was booed offstage.[15]

Something was clearly amiss. Daley knew racial unrest had long been a reality in Chicago; Bridgeport was the scene for heavy fighting during the 1919 riots, and a group he belonged to, the Hamburg Social and Athletic Club, participated in attacking lone blacks. In 1964 there had been rioting a block and a half from Daley's house. In 1965 the black comedian Dick Gregory led a march into Bridgeport to protest housing and police discrimination; on the second night more than a thousand whites greeted them, chanting, "Oh, I wish I was an Alabama trooper, that is what I'd really like to be. Cuz if I was an Alabama trooper, I could kill the niggers legally."

Daley didn't come out his front door to witness the ensuing fights, or to watch the police arrest the black protesters for their own "protection." But he did respond by boosting police spending; by 1967, Chicago's police force was seen as a model for antiriot preparedness.[16]

In 1965 he and several other big-city mayors were called, at the federal government's behest, to strategize about ways to prevent riots. Daley refused to go, saying he didn't need it. The next year the city saw two more riots, one among Puerto Ricans in which a teen was killed, and one on the West Side, which resulted in two deaths despite an intercession by Martin Luther King, who was living in the city's slums for a summer. The riot was finally put down by forty-two hundred National Guardsmen, but not before it caused $2 million in damage to the West Side. Nevertheless, Daley continued to believe that Chicago was fundamentally stable.

On the evening of April 4, 1968, Daley was at home eating dinner with his four sons when an aide, Jack Reilly, called with the news of King's assassination. Daley and King had sparred fiercely over the

D.C. mayor Walter Washington meeting with reporters at the 3rd Police District headquarters on April 4. He had just returned from a tour of the riot zone.

Washington Police line up at 14th and U Streets on the night of April 4. Peoples Drug is in the background. The Washington SNCC office is to the extreme left.

Lyndon Johnson meeting with black leaders on the morning of April 5. Supreme Court Justice Thurgood Marshall is seated to his right.

Howard University students protesting outside Frederick Douglass Hall on the afternoon of April 5, while university president James Nabrit held an official ceremony in nearby Crampton Auditorium.

Fires raging on Chicago's West Side Friday night, April 5. In all, rioting partially or completely destroyed three hundred square blocks.

U.S. troops camping out in a Washington Laundromat. Soldiers caught sleep wherever they could; other units bivouacked in parks and school gymnasiums.

Lyndon Johnson and Joseph Califano Jr. examining a map of the Washington, D.C. riots. The push pins represent reported looting and arson incidents.

Washington Public Safety chief Patrick Murphy surveying the riot damage.

Baltimore police officers taking cover from sniper fire. Unlike the situation in Washington and Chicago, rioting in Baltimore didn't pick up until Saturday afternoon.

Robert Kennedy walking through the riot-torn Shaw neighborhood in Washington on Palm Sunday, April 7. At one point an elderly woman grabbed his hand and said, "I knew you'd be the first to come."

Lyndon Johnson surveying the riot damage in Washington from a helicopter on Sunday, April 7.

A local man at P and 7th Streets in Washington, after the riot. A year later, the debris had been cleared but nothing had been rebuilt. The destruction led to a mass exodus of the city's black middle class, an average of one percent per year for the next twenty-five years.

Stokely Carmichael jostling his way into Atlanta's Ebenezer Baptist Church on the morning of Martin Luther King Jr.'s funeral.

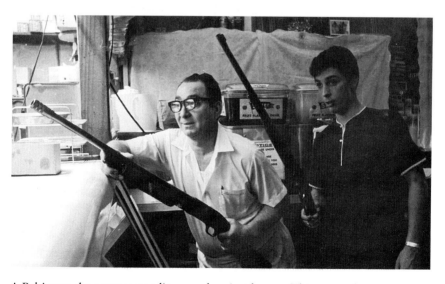

A Baltimore shop owner standing guard against looters. Thirty years later, one former merchant said, "If you ride through [East Baltimore] today, you're gonna find all the places have been bricked up . . . none of this existed before the riots."

Maryland governor Spiro Agnew confronting Baltimore civil rights leaders on April 11. He said the speech was "political suicide," but a few months later Richard Nixon made him his running mate.

Richard Nixon, HUD secretary George Romney, and Washington mayor Walter Washington examining riot damage on January 31, 1969. "Those who have been left out, we will try to bring in," Nixon said at his inauguration. But in many cities the riot scars would remain for another thirty years.

preacher's 1966 efforts to desegregate Chicago suburbs and boost funding for black-majority schools. If Daley had misgivings about honoring his former adversary, though, he didn't show them. He immediately ordered the city's flags flown at half mast, and he issued a public statement of condolence. "Chicago joins in mourning the tragic death of the Rev. Martin Luther King Jr.," the statement read. "Dr. King was a dedicated and courageous American who commanded the respect of the people of the world."[17]

Daley's immediate concern was disorder. He quickly headed to City Hall, where he got updates about unrest around the country, including Washington. The Chicago Police Department canceled all leave for its officers, and it activated its "Departmental Mobilization Guidelines," which put ten heavily armed "incidence response teams" on the streets by 8:20 and had more than three hundred specially trained antiriot officers out by 9:30. By eight the next morning, the department had four thousand officers on patrol; by 4:00 P.M. it had six thousand. Though isolated instances of violence and harassment broke out that evening, a later report by the city found it "abnormally quiet."[18]

General Richard Dunn, commander of the Illinois National Guard Emergency Operations Center, met that night with Deputy Superintendent of Police James Rochford. Did the city need troops? Rochford said no, and so the next morning the general headed south to Bloomington, where he felt he could better respond to expected outbreaks in East St. Louis. It was a costly mistake.

April fifth began normally enough. The morning was cool and clear, with little wind. Students went off to school, workers to their jobs. At the city's black-majority high schools, some principals and teachers tried to release tension by holding memorial services and allowing student leaders to address their peers. And, in some cases, their efforts paid off, particularly in those schools where social cohesion and teacher involvement were already well-established patterns.

At others, however, the student populations began dwindling fast by late morning. As in Washington, some students headed home, while many others wandered around, checking out the action. Lots of people were already in the streets. Some had skipped work, while others didn't have a job in the first place. A large group of students from Marshall High School watched a klatch of militant speakers in Garfield Park, along Madison Street in the center of the West Side. "Go out and get whitey!" one speaker yelled. "Go out and burn!"[19]

Leaving the park and heading west on Madison, the students encountered police, who ordered them to scatter. When they didn't, an officer fired his gun in the air. It was, by 1968, a classic error: an overly aggressive show of force by police that simply angered the crowd and pushed them in another direction. Soon the students were running east along Madison, breaking windows and pulling fire alarms as they went.

Elsewhere white shop owners were giving in to their nerves and closing up their stores, often on the whispered tip of a customer. Many were so convinced they were about to be looted that they were running impromptu fire sales, selling off their merchandise at cost rather than losing it to looters or arsonists. Parents rushed to schools to pick up their kids; most of the schools gave up and began shuttering at noon.

As the day slid into the afternoon, the city slid into disorder. Serious looting began on West Madison shortly after midday; at 3:45 the first fire broke out, at 2235 West Madison. The store had already been looted, and investigators later suspected it was started by a Molotov cocktail. Things got worse from there.

One thing that distinguished the Chicago riot from those in Washington and elsewhere was the aggressiveness of the crowds. In Washington observers often spoke of a "carnival" atmosphere. But not in Chicago. Rioters set up several roadblocks, and as white drivers slowed down to make their way through they were harassed, some even pulled from their cars and beaten. Counterrioters made their way along the streets, but according to the city's report, "tensions and emotions were at too high a pitch to be significantly affected by these efforts."[20] In other places rioters attacked fire hoses with axes, and in some instances even went after the firemen themselves.

Matters were compounded by the minimal police presence. Until well into Friday afternoon, the city concentrated much of its manpower in the Loop—on the assumption that blacks would take out their anger by attacking symbols of the white power structure. So sure was the CPD of impending downtown violence that it kept a large force there even after it became evident that the real action was going down more than a mile to the west.

Not that nothing happened downtown: four hundred black teenagers marched into Civic Center Plaza and sat for an hour, while four hundred cops stood around them. When they left, they marched past the massive Carson Pirie Scott department store, which had suffered a fire a week before and was covered with plywood; some kids tore off the siding and threw it in the streets.[21] But the idea that the city center was under threat of a massive attack was absurd, and the decision to keep the force there for so long contributed greatly to the extensive damage on the West Side.

At 2:00 P.M., Daley, ensconced in his office on the fifth floor of City Hall, called Acting Governor Samuel Shapiro and requested National Guard troops (Governor Otto Kerner was away on business). Dunn was called back from Bloomington, but in the face of traffic streaming from the city he didn't get to the Emergency Operations Center, on Madison, until 6:45 P.M., delaying the effective deployment of troops.

Nevertheless, by that evening the state had three thousand National Guardsmen on the streets. At a press conference, Dunn said, ominously, that "orders to shoot to kill will depend on the commander on the spot"—a much more aggressive posture than that taken by Patrick Murphy and Cyrus Vance in Washington. Two more battalions, totaling sixteen hundred men, were put on standby in Rockford and Bloomington.[22]

By the time the Guard arrived on the Chicago streets in force, however, it was too late to stop the worst of the looting. Between 4:00 P.M. and 10:00 P.M. there were thirty-six major fires, including the entire 3300 block of Madison. Some two thousand firefighters, many from the suburbs, worked a hundred different apparatus that night. Even the firefighting training centers sent equipment, and the Bureau of Sanitation contributed another thousand men to back them up. Snipers proved a big problem for the firefighters; after a few firemen were hit (none lethally), police detachments were deployed to provide them cover, siphoning off more officers from the antilooting efforts.[23]

Not that it made a difference. "The only concession the looters made to police was to detour around them," *Tribune* reporter William Jones noted. As he drove north on Homan Street, beneath its intersection with Madison, he saw two oddly uniform lines of people: Those headed north, toward the center of the looting, were empty-handed; those headed south bore televisions, radios, and alcohol by the gallon. He saw a boy of about seven struggling under the weight of a carton of beer.[24]

Eventually the Chicago Transit Authority shut off bus service to a twelve-square-mile area around the riots. Before they did, though, John Taylor, a reporter for the city's leading black paper, the *Chicago Daily Defender*, caught one headed out of the riot zone. As he boarded, the white driver told him, "I'd advise you to take cover. They threw at me when I came down." His fellow passengers included several women with children, presumably shepherding them to safer environs. The bus headed north. Suddenly it passed through a swelling crowd, who pelted it with bottles and rocks. "The bus resounded with the whang of brick against metal," Taylor recalled. "The windows shattered; glass flew everywhere," cutting up the driver's face. Everyone else had taken cover on the floor and beneath seats.[25]

Amid the looting, arson, and random violence, nine people were dead by midnight. Like most of the looters in Washington, William McMullen died in a fire, trapped behind burning timbers in a looted store set ablaze by arsonists. But the rest died in more violent ways. One, Curtis Jefro, was found dead on the twelfth floor of a housing tower from which a sniper was firing at police; it was never clarified whether Jefro was the sniper himself, or had somehow gotten caught in the middle. Marvin Carter was shot and killed by police on the South Side. Two deaths—of Clayton Webb, who was shot in the throat, and of John Sandifer, who was stabbed in the leg and bled to death—were ruled accidental.[26]

The other four deaths all took place within three and a half hours of each other, and all within two square blocks of Madison, between Karlov and Kildare streets. All appeared to have been shot from the street—Ponowel Holloway and Cyrus Hartfield in stores and Paul Evans and Robert Dorsey in alleys. The murders were never solved, but according to the report, "Allegedly two police cars containing two to four white policemen in each car who were armed with rifles were in the two block area at this time and were seen shooting on level into stores in these two blocks and shooting on the level in the alley in question."[27] The report notes that the incidents were referred to the state's attorney. But nothing came of it.

Notably, almost all the violence took place on the West Side, and almost none on the South Side. Only two of the thirty-six large fires set that night were there, and only one of the nine deaths. At the time this was thought surprising, but in hindsight it made perfect sense. While the South Side certainly had its problems, it was also a world apart from the West Side. A powerful and effective political machine, with lines of influence into both the mayor's office and the U.S. Congress, brought back significant rewards in the form of social programs and education funding. The area had its share of poverty, but it also had a sizable black middle class that had proven fairly porous to those rising from the bottom. And because the West Side blew first, it's a good bet that many would-be looters and arsonists from the South Side flocked there, rather than risk being caught out among the few lawbreakers in their own neighborhoods.

Yet another reason why the South Side didn't blow was that its youth were dominated by a handful of powerful street gangs, including the Vice Lords, the Blackstone Rangers, the Egyptian Cobras, and the Eastside Disciples. Though the gangs participated in their share of illegal activity through the years, they were much more in the tradition of Daley's own Hamburg Social and Athletic Club—independent, youth-run organizations that provided street kids with discipline and community. That discipline, in turn, kept them away from looting that weekend. Many of them had been partly co-opted into the political system through the CAPs on the South Side; some of them even received federal grants for participating in antipoverty efforts. Whether such funding was a good idea in general—these were, after all, gangs— it likely had a tempering effect when it came to the riots.

It also likely helped that less than two years earlier King had spent untold hours huddled with Chicago's various gang leaders preaching nonviolence, and he used them as marshals in his 1966 open-housing marches. Those lessons, combined with the urge to honor King's legacy, brought out scores of gang leaders to the city's schools on Friday morning; they participated in the memorial services and gave speeches about the need for Chicago's youth to protect their communities. Afterward one gang, the Vice Lords, printed thousands of antiriot flyers and handed them out among the looters.

"Little Brothers and Sisters, our Moses is DEAD," the flyer read. "But let's not destroy our hopes or his dreams for equality. We realize, we as brothers and sisters who share your grief of this violent murder, that there isn't too much we can ask of your personal feelings, but let last night be the last night of destruction."[28]

Though they didn't stem the tide of the riots writ large, the Chicago Study Committee report concludes that "in areas where the youth is dominated by powerful neighborhood gangs or where a great portion of the youngsters are themselves affiliated in well-disciplined organizations, and the leadership of these gangs committed their groups to maintaining social peace, there were few incidents of serious civil disorder."[29] The South Side, in other words, had vents for its frustration—something the West Side sorely lacked.

Daley stayed in his office all day. From the fifth floor he could watch as the four hundred black students massed below his building. He was safe, however, behind the hundreds of cops surrounding them and a backup contingent waiting secretly in the City Hall basement (another contingent was waiting at Soldier Field). He set a 7:00 P.M. to 6:00 A.M. curfew, and he banned liquor and gun sales. At 4:20, after a brief press conference, he went on radio and TV to announce that he had called in the National Guard.

"Stand up tonight and protect the city," he pleaded. "I ask this very sincerely, very personally. Let's show the United States and the world what Chicago's citizens are made of."[30] It wasn't to happen—all night Daley listened over the police bands as looters tore up vast sections of his beloved city.

At about five thirty, Daley received a call from Johnson, who had just ordered troops into Washington and was calling with Harry McPherson, listening in on speakerphone, to see how things were going. The mayor told him about the Guard call-out and said there were fires on the West Side. Daley "started telling him Chicago was getting out of control," McPherson recalled. "We were in the family sitting room in the mansion of the White House and behind him, way down the whole length of the White House, you could see, out one of the windows that faces out to the Treasury, a tower of black smoke rising from some burning department store."[31]

It was a moment when two oddly parallel political lives intersected. Two elder statesmen who had achieved their posts through ruthlessly skillful politics, two men who had cut their teeth on Rooseveltian New Deal politics and had cemented their reputations on bold, progressive gestures and massive public programs, now watched out their respective windows as forces they could not understand tore apart what they had built. (Daley, of course, was also less reflective than Johnson.

Unlike the president, he didn't take it personally, and he didn't try to see the looters as anything other than lawbreaking miscreants.)

After dinner across the street and a short nap, Daley met with John Stamos, the Illinois state's attorney, who had just toured the riot zone. Things were looking bad, Stamos said. Maybe even too much for the National Guard to handle. At 2:00 A.M., Daley decided to look for himself; as he left City Hall, he told a clutch of reporters that "things are under control."

In an unmarked police car, he and four detectives toured the West Side, followed by another unmarked car, also full of police detectives. By then most of the looters had gone home for the night, but the fires still burned brightly, reflecting orange and yellow off the dark tint of the sedan windows.[32]

11

April 6

ROADBLOCKS

A pril 6 dawned on an apocalyptic sight. Smoke from still-burning buildings obscured the Capitol dome. Thousands of soldiers and Marines patrolled the Washington streets on foot and in jeeps. Four people were known dead (more bodies would be found in the charred rubble later), 250 major fires had been reported, and 2,021 people had been arrested—more than 1,200 of those since midnight.[1]

On Seventh Street, Private First Class Richard Zimmerman, twenty-one years old, told a reporter, "It was like how I always imagined Berlin must have looked after World War II. . . . Everything was burned, gutted, and crumbling."[2] Merchandise dropped by looters—shoes, clothing, appliances—littered the streets beside broken glass, cans, and bits of metal. A few drunks, too inebriated to make it home, lay passed out in alleyways. The cops rousted and arrested them, as well as a few scattered looters and rioters they found still making trouble.

When two young boys chucked pebbles at a four-man army patrol near Georgia Avenue at 3:00 A.M., two dozen soldiers and thirty police officers surrounded them within minutes.[3] H Street and Seventh were literally sealed off, with troops refusing both cars and pedestrians. At 4:00 A.M., the Secret Service command post at the White

House, which was keeping track of incidents around the city, reported optimistically, "Looting has slowed to an almost negligible point."[4] Scenes of near normalcy cropped up: Two boys played basketball at a court along Eighteenth Street, the lower half of their faces obscured by bandanas to avoid breathing the smoke and gas that still lingered in the morning air.

But the rioters weren't done with Washington yet. Looting and arson picked up almost as soon as the sun rose and the curfew lifted. Much of the early violence took place outside the three centers of Friday's activity—Fourteenth Street, Seventh Street, and H Street— away from the heavy law enforcement and military presence. The first report of looting came at 6:30 A.M.; soon calls were coming in at the rate of two per minute, sending cops and army patrols into the far corners of the city, from Minnesota Avenue in Anacostia to Georgia Avenue in the far northern reaches of the District (though not a single incident was ever reported west of Rock Creek Park, the leafy trough running between Georgetown and Dupont Circle).

By midmorning the rioting was back in full effect. The looting was more systematic this time; people were seen loading goods into trucks and carrying boxes into cars. They were more aggressive, too: At Sixth and M streets, NW, a crowd overturned a car filled with three whites. The occupants were dragged from the cars, but National Guard troops arrived to save them.[5]

In all, 120 new fires were set that day, along with scores more that rekindled, either on their own or with help. At a little after eleven thirty a fire erupted at D.C. General Hospital, forcing the evacuation of twenty-five young patients. At almost the same time a fire broke out at the American Ice Co., near the H Street riot zone. It was an enormous building, and the blaze attracted hundreds of spectators—until someone realized that it was insulated with cork walls and that if they caught, the building could virtually explode, setting off a fire in an ammonia storage tank next door. Police set off gas canisters, and the crowd soon dispersed.

Inside the city's emergency operations center, Washington, Vance, and the rest of the staff agreed that the riot was settling into a pattern. This was not going to be the racial cataclysm that the media and black radicals had predicted. Instead, at least in Washington, it was a relatively conventional commodities riot—looting and burning in the ghetto, but little other damage and little risk of it spreading to other parts of the city, let alone to the suburbs.

Not that they took no precautions. Roadblocks went up on the Baltimore-to-Washington parkway, the Virginia bridges, and other main routes into and out of the city. A barrier was erected at Thomas Circle, which separated "black" Fourteenth Street from downtown. Mayor Washington tightened the curfew from 5:30 P.M. to 4:00 P.M. Local utility workers cut gas lines, just in case a raging fire reached a main. The Federal Aviation Administration ordered planes diverted from National Airport to Dulles; those that had to land at National were told to keep to six thousand feet as long as necessary, just in case snipers decided to aim their rifles skyward.[6]

People outside the government likewise tried to combat the rioting. NAACP workers handed out flyers saying that "hotheads" would end up "dead." Counterrioters, wearing yellow armbands, walked the streets begging looters, in midloot, to go home. Even James Brown, fresh from his Boston show, flew to Washington and addressed residents in a televised address from the District Building. "I know how everybody feels. I feel the same way," he said. "You can't do it by blowing up, burning up, stealing, and looting."[7]

Across downtown, at the White House, Johnson had his staff set on a different set of tasks. While Califano kept a close watch on the progress of civil disorders around the country, McPherson (back from the hospital), Busby, and Levinson—along with a small army of staffers and advisers drawn from the various departments—were brainstorming ideas for the president's big address to Congress Monday night. At dinner Friday, Johnson had leaned across the table and told Busby that the speech "can make or break us. The speech Sunday was good and accomplished what we wanted, but King's death has erased all that, and we have to start again."[8]

Saturday, then, saw the White House again buzzing with activity. Johnson's administration had always had a strong collaborative element, and that came through now. Proposals poured in from everywhere and from every angle. His congressional liaison, Harold "Barefoot" Sanders, suggested raising taxes above the 10 percent surcharge.[9] George Reedy, his former press secretary who had returned a few months earlier as a special assistant, wrote in a memo, "It is vitally important that your speech to the Congress be addressed to the problems of the here and now. . . . This is not a moment in history when either whites or Negroes will have much interest in new programs for social reform."[10]

Another, from a staffer in the Department of Health, Education, and Welfare, suggested that the speech tap "the rich vein of the American volunteer spirit. . . . I would like to see the citizens of every neighborhood and every city get together and learn what their problems are, and make suggestions about how to solve them."[11] And adviser Arthur Krim noted to Busby, "Above all, the speech must be one of passion and identification with the mood of the Negroes."[12]

Most proposals, though, focused squarely on money and concrete policies. The Labor Department suggested a renewed effort to rehabilitate the ghetto.[13] Gardner Ackley, the chair of the Council of Economic Advisers, suggested a "Bill of Economic Rights" that would lock in programs for housing and income assistance.[14] Doris Kearns Goodwin, then a White House fellow assigned to Labor, recalled working late into the night on the speech, then "driving home exhausted through uncanny, deserted streets, halted periodically at barricades where armed soldiers looked inside the car."[15] At one point, Califano's staff tallied $5 billion in new plans to include in the speech.[16] "One thing people were of a single mind about," McPherson recalled, "was that it shouldn't be any small measures."[17]

The press expected big measures, too. Some guessed Johnson would call for implementing the recommendations of the Kerner Commission.[18] "He is expected to speed action on several other programs he already has recommended," reported the *Washington Star*, "including a $1 billion model cities program to rebuild the centers of American cities, a ten-year campaign to build six million housing units for low- and middle-income families, and a $2.1 billion manpower training program."[19]

Such speculation was fueled by dueling anonymous leaks from inside the White House. In a Monday piece in the *Wall Street Journal*, one unnamed adviser said, "The death of Doctor King brings us to the crossroads . . . one road is violence and repression. The other is prompt action." But a contrasting quotation from a different leaker appeared further in the same piece. "What's the use of escalating the demands for the Negro when Congress won't move on what we've already sent up there?"[20]

As the weekend crept on, more and more staffers began to wonder just why they were working so hard on a proposal that, they increasingly expected, was going to go nowhere. And some, even dedicated liberals, wondered if the conservatives weren't right after all—weren't they throwing good money after bad, rewarding rioters with big-ticket programs that, as the violence attested, didn't seem to be doing much good? They might not have known it at the time, but many looked back later and decided that this was the moment when liberalism, at least as they had always known it, finally cracked.

Califano was handling more than just riots and speechwriting. At 2:00 P.M. West Virginia Democratic senator Robert Byrd called to say he wanted looters shot to "wound" and demanded to know why martial law had not been imposed. At about the same time, Johnson's mentor, Georgia Democratic senator Richard Russell, called to say he had heard rumors that the troops guarding the Capitol were not carrying ammunition, sending Califano on a string of calls to the Pentagon to verify that the soldiers did, in fact, have bullets in their belts. Back at the office, he found a memo from Sanders noting a worrisome ad from a gun store in that day's *Washington Post* urging D.C. area residents to "come buy guns." Sanders asked if Califano could get the Department of Justice to have the ad yanked from future editions.[21]

Califano was also juggling the White House's plans for King's funeral on Tuesday. The president was leaning against going, so Humphrey needed to go in his place. A Nixon fund-raiser called to suggest that the president and the presumptive GOP candidate go together, to dispel talk of partisan politicking (though seeing the president in Nixon's vicinity would obviously do wonders for Nixon's own mediocre civil rights image). Dozens of congressional offices needed help coordinating trips, as did scores of ambassadors and diplomats.[22]

Eventually Califano took a break and, with Louis Martin at the wheel, went to check out some of the riot damage along Fourteenth Street. "When we came back, we got stopped at the gate, and I didn't have my White House pass with me," he recalled. "I had nothing, no ID at all. And remember, this is the world of no cell phones. So I said to this big black cop, I said, 'You gotta let me in. I'm Joe Califano. And the cop says, 'Yeah, and I'm Walter Washington.' And Louie just started laughing. We had to go back out to a pay phone, call the White House, to get them to let us back in."[23]

If the riots were the first thing on Johnson's mind, they weren't the only thing. After all, had events gone according to plan, he would have been spending that Saturday in Hawaii meeting with Westmoreland. Instead, Westmoreland came to Washington, arriving before eight o'clock on Saturday morning. On the way to the White House, the general looked out at the destruction in the nation's capital; as he later recalled, it "looked worse than Saigon did at the height of the Tet Offensive," and he joked that while the British had burned Washington in 1812, this time Washington was burning itself.[24]

Fortunately, along with Westmoreland's acidity came good news from Vietnam. The siege of Khe Sanh had lifted the day before, the North Vietnamese were responding well to the bombing halt, and it looked like peace talks could be in the offing. Westmoreland had breakfast with the president as soon as he arrived, and the two met for nearly four hours after lunch with Clifford, Walt Rostow, General Wheeler, Harriman, Katzenbach, CIA director Richard Helms, and General Maxwell Taylor; they even pulled McPherson and Busby away from writing duty to sit in on the talks.

Westmoreland stayed for dinner, planning to fly home the next morning. It was his valedictory visit with the president as commander in Vietnam; Johnson had already decided to kick him upstairs to be army chief of staff. But the president nevertheless continued grilling him. What did he think of the Vietnamese leadership? What did he make of the embassy attack during Tet? How was the medical care for the troops?

At one point Lynda, who had joined them, asked Westmoreland what was the best way to package cookies to send to her husband, Chuck. The general smiled. In all his decades of service, he told her, no one had ever mailed him a cookie that arrived intact.[25]

Just before dinner, Johnson had finally received the telegram everyone knew was coming. Sent by Illinois acting governor Samuel Shapiro, it read, "Under existing circumstances, the law enforcement resources of the state are unable to supress [sic] the serious violence in or near the city of Chicago . . . I therefore request you as the president of the United States to send to this area up to five thousand troops."[26]

Johnson immediately authorized the army to prepare to move five thousand troops to staging areas around Chicago, including elements of the First Armored Division from Fort Hood in Texas and elements of the Fifth Infantry Division from Fort Carson in Colorado. He held out, however, on signing the necessary paperwork to federalize the Illinois National Guard and send the army into the streets.

The troops coming from Fort Hood were flown out of Bergstrom Air Force Base, seventy-eight miles away, which in turn was just fifty-five miles from the Johnson ranch. Whenever Johnson came home (something he did often), this was where he would land; he would then fly by helicopter to the ranch. This was Johnson's air base. But that day it wasn't *Air Force One* alighting on the tarmac but a flock of enormous C-141 cargo jets. Then, recalled Bob Walton, at the time a firefighter on base, "A huge army convoy from Fort Hood arrived at the same time. The jeeps and trucks were covered with barbed wire. All the soldiers looked grim, knowing that they to be flown to duty not in a foreign land with rifles, but to our own American cities."[27]

As in Washington, the violence in Chicago had begun to settle into the usual pattern—wanton destruction, limited to the worst parts of the ghetto. As of Friday night, almost 1,000 people had been injured and 9 were dead; there had been 575 fires and 3,273 people had been arrested. Sometime on Saturday *Chicago Tribune* reporters made an aerial survey of the West Side, after which they reported 20 different major pockets of smoke, bounded by Madison and Cermak streets on the north and south and Western and Central streets on the east and west. It was a devastating sight. Along Madison, "The destruction was total." They watched police stand by as looters rummaged through a burned-out market; they reported seeing small gaggles of families standing on street corners surrounded by small piles of possessions, presumably burned out of their homes. "Acrid smoke filled the helicopter," they wrote in an unbylined piece. In purple prose they added, "The looters, like vultures, fed on the ashen carcasses of scores of stores. Loaded with booty, they looked like an army of worker ants as they scurried off to the side streets and alleys."

All the while, traffic along the Eisenhower Expressway, which cuts a clear gray line diagonally through the West Side, flowed unabated out to the Chicago suburbs.[28]

Saturday saw more surreal and tragic scenes. That morning, as firemen battled flames on Madison, a man ran at them from a nearby doorway with a knife. "We're going to burn down the whole town and you with it!" he screamed. A few cops chased him down the street and tackled him, but he broke away and escaped. A few streets away Everett Austin, just ten months old, burned to death in an apartment fire. And in a bizarre coincidence, twenty-seven-year-old Oscar King was taking potshots at passing cars at the corner of Larabee and Division when he accidentally shot and killed his sister, Barbara Walker, as she and her father drove by. King later turned himself in.[29]

Attorney General Clark, back at the Department of Justice, had been in touch with Chicago all day. Technically, he had to formally agree with the decision to send troops, and he was decidedly against the idea. But he also understood the political pressures involved, the protroop opinion weighing against him. Still, he wanted to be sure. So he called Christopher and told him to assemble a team and head to Chicago. Christopher soon left for the Windy City on a department JetStar.

Two hours later he was in a briefing room at O'Hare with Lieutenant General George Mather, who was leading the federal forces, and Brigadier General Dunn.[30] The National Guard already had four thousand men deployed in the city, Dunn told him, the bulk of them on the West Side and almost none in reserve. About twenty-five hundred more were already being committed, and another two thousand were available downstate. But Dunn was still worried about potential violence in East St. Louis—minor rioting on Friday had left eleven businesses damaged and a car ablaze. Moreover, there was sporadic disorder in Evanston, a well-to-do suburb to Chicago's north, and Joliet, where rioters had set a block-long warehouse ablaze, raising concerns about the security of a massive nearby army munitions factory.[31]

Where do things stand on the West Side? Christopher asked.

The West Side was coming under control, Dunn said, but the South Side was causing some concern. Scattered "riot-type incidents" continued to pop up, and if they boiled over, the National Guard would be unable to contain them.

Then Mather and Christopher made an hour-long helicopter reconnaissance of the city. "Even at a thousand feet, it was evident that the situation was grave," Christopher later said.[32] The two decided that the city needed at least a battalion of federal troops on the streets to buttress the already committed forces, with more troops held in reserve. Christopher met with Daley and then, at midnight Central Time, called the White House to recommend troops.

Johnson had just gone to bed when the call came through. Christopher recalled the president sounding "weary and disheartened" as he listened to his report. The case was, Christopher admitted in a later interview, "marginal"—despite the horror stories coming out of the West Side, the riots there were likely to burn themselves out, and the combined police and National Guard presence would keep them from spreading. But the possibility of a spillover to the unprotected South Side made a strong case for troops as a prophylactic measure.

For all his legislative activism at the federal level, Johnson was a strong believer in local government and a long-standing opponent of centralized intervention in law enforcement matters. Despite occasionally looking the other way when it suited his political needs, he had taken firm stances against FBI wiretapping, and he had long opposed federal aid programs to police departments, seeing law and order as a states' issue. And while he had signed the Law Enforcement Assistance Act in 1965, it was a relatively small effort designed to thwart conservative law-and-order posturing. Perhaps his views had grown from stories, heard as a child, of venal federal troops enforcing Reconstruction in Texas following the Civil War. Perhaps they came from the civil libertarianism common among children and grandchildren of the western pioneers.

Whatever the source, his localist views on law and order had guided much of his approach to the riots. He had outright refused to send anything but indirect assistance to the California National Guard during Watts, and he had resisted, for too long, the need to send troops to Detroit. Even after Detroit, Johnson continued to see the army as the last of last resorts. It should be used sparingly, and only as a suppressive tool. But here was Christopher telling him troops should be sent to Chicago as a preventive measure. Once troops were deployed in Chicago, where could he draw the line? With the army already spending millions on riot control, what would keep it from pushing for preventive occupations of every at-risk city, every year? Was this the legacy he wanted to leave behind?

Califano, who had brought the necessary papers to his boss that night, remembered him sitting in bed, talking to Christopher. "Johnson's eyes were heavy with fatigue, his jaw sagging," he said. After Johnson hung up, he took the sheets from Califano. "Lying on his back in bed, he signaled me to hand him a pen, and signed the papers as he held them up over his head, which he was too exhausted to raise from the pillow."[33] Within an hour the troops were headed into the city, and by 11:00 A.M. the next morning dismounted army foot patrols coursed through another American city. By midnight Sunday a total of 11,709 soldiers, National Guard and army, were in Chicago.

Violence continued to rack urban centers across the country, with heavy responses from local and state officials. The entire Michigan National Guard had been called out to control disturbances in Detroit, Flint, Kalamazoo, and Grand Rapids, among other cities. In Nashville four thousand National Guardsmen supported local and state police as they cordoned off the Capitol and the campus of Tennessee A&I, a predominantly black school on the city's North Side.[34] With New York still on edge, Lindsay toured Brownsville and Bedford-Stuyvesant in Brooklyn, then Harlem again before going on that neighborhood's WLIB radio, taking calls for a couple of hours. In Oakland, already high tensions rose after police engaged in an hour-and-a-half shoot-out with members of the Black Panther Party, resulting in the death of seventeen-year-old Bobby Hutton. Contrary to initial police reports, Hutton was unarmed—in fact, he'd already surrendered and had been stripped to his underwear—when he was shot twelve times.

Pittsburgh was also quickly falling into disorder. Scattered violence on Thursday and Friday had swelled into major rioting and arson Friday night and Saturday, primarily in the city's Hill District, a collection of black neighborhoods just east of downtown. The weekend saw 505 fires in that neighborhood alone. Pennsylvania governor Raymond Shafer quickly deployed 3,400 National Guardsmen and 300 state police, but by Saturday night it was looking likely that the governor would have to call in federal troops as well. A memo from U.S.

attorney Gus Diamond, who was keeping tabs on the situation for the Department of Justice, noted that by Saturday night "practically all of the white business establishments have been burned or looted."

The real concern, said Diamond, was the city's Homewood District, a destitute ghetto: "The police have been holding their breath regarding the North Side area where not much trouble is reported, but where they thought the worst hooligans lived." If that went, troops would almost certainly be required.[35]

12

April 6

AN ERUPTION IN BALTIMORE

While Pittsburgh simmered, Baltimore began to boil over. Like Washington to its immediate southwest, Baltimore was not an obvious city to fall into civil disorder. Before the Civil War it was home to one of the country's largest number of free blacks—90 percent of its black population—and up to the early twentieth century few of its neighborhoods were segregated. It had relatively progressive leaders at the local and state levels, a strong black middle class well integrated into the political structure, and a good history of race relations. It had the second-largest NAACP branch in the country (behind New York City), and local civil rights leaders had succeeded in opening up the city's vast port and manufacturing industries to black workers. Blacks proved decisive in the election of Theodore McKeldin, a progressive Republican, as mayor and later governor, and during the 1950s the city and state moved forward on a number of racial fronts. School integration occurred peacefully and quickly. The City Council passed an equal employment law with real teeth. In 1959 alone, the Maryland General Assembly considered more than thirty antisegregation bills.[1]

But once again, superficial progress masked a deeper tension. Stuck between the North and the South, Baltimore combined elements of both—like a northern industrial metropolis, it had a heavily ethnic population, largely employed in blue-collar manufacturing jobs and protected by powerful unions. Like southern cities, it had a history of legal segregation—after the relatively halcyon days of the early twentieth century, a hard-nosed Jim Crow regime set in, drawing stark lines between the races in all facets of life.

Indeed, like Chicago, Baltimore was a city that had a series of supposedly progressive mayors and a solidly liberal voting public, but also a long rap sheet of racial transgressions. It was, noted historian George Callcott, the only city in the country to have legally separate housing blocks for blacks and whites. Police brutality was common: in February 1942 an officer shot a black man after resisting arrest for riding in an unlicensed cab; nine more blacks were killed by police in the next four years. And despite legislative progress during the 1950s, by the early 1960s Maryland was falling behind the rest of the nation: in 1962 Governor J. Millard Tawes failed in his push for a law banning segregation completely, even after it was changed to include only Baltimore and nine counties (Baltimore and Montgomery counties later passed their own versions of the bill).[2]

Such hypocrisy didn't go unnoticed by the state's blacks, and by the mid-1960s, aggressive activism became a regular occurrence—particularly in the once-bucolic Eastern Shore town of Cambridge, a culturally southern locale that was racked by repeated outbursts of racial violence. Local civil rights leaders took a hard-edged approach to desegregation, and the city's whites refused to budge. In June 1963, the city experienced a night of stone-throwing and physical harassment of whites by a crowd of several hundred blacks; Tawes quickly declared martial law and sent in the National Guard to enforce it. Tensions remained high, and in July 1967 another riot broke out after SNCC chair H. Rap Brown gave a fiery speech urging a crowd to "take over them stores. The streets are yours. Take 'em." The ensuing violence resulted in the burning of two square blocks in the black area of town.[3]

The key to understanding the racial tensions in Baltimore and its environs—and, to varying degrees, in industrial cities across the East—was the dynamics of the declining white working class. Like other industrial cities, Baltimore had recently seen a boom in its black population; thirty-three thousand moved to the city between 1940 and 1942, mostly on the word that Baltimore had well-paying industrial jobs that needed filling to meet the demands of the war effort. But the job rush also brought in tens of thousands of rural whites from the Appalachians and the South, who didn't mix well with their black coworkers. Even during the war, blacks were kept to menial tasks, and as soon as the war was over, white-dominated unions agitated to push them out of the factory altogether. The problem, as historian Kenneth Durr noted, was in part economic—jobs were disappearing—and in part political—anticommunism was a deeply held sentiment among the city's working-class whites (fueled in part by the treason case of Baltimore native Alger Hiss), and it easily slid into a generalized distrust of liberals and whatever causes they might be pushing, including integration.[4]

Even more galling to Baltimore whites was the idea that they should be forced to live side by side with blacks. As was the case among working-class white ethnics in other cities, they did not perceive such segregation as racism per se: after all, they figured, Poles have their neighborhoods, as do the Italians and the Irish. So why shouldn't blacks?

By the mid-1950s, white Baltimore, divided into its various ethnicities, was a solid bloc that both reveled in its own traditions and perceived, on the horizon, growing threats to those very same ways of life. As one native Baltimorean later told interviewers, "Life was great. It was about being white. It was about being Catholic. It was about living in a neighborhood, going to the church that was five minutes away. It was about going to the school that was five minutes away, surrounded by my friends and my family."[5] Square mile after square mile of two-story row houses, each with concrete stoops and formstone facades, blanketed the inverted U of residential Baltimore that spreads out from the port at its center. For a fleeting time that soon became stretched into generations by myth and memory, working-class white Baltimore lived in its ethnic cocoon, ignorant of the changing world around them.

But the influx of black residents was already pushing against that cocoon. Between 1950 and 1955, thirty-two thousand more blacks moved to the city, even as the local steel mills and shipyards began shrinking—meaning more people were competing for fewer jobs. And the newly arrived blacks had every reason to complain. Not only were the job opportunities less than they expected, but also the everyday racism was worse, and the houses they were forced to live in were abysmal: in 1955 a full 75 percent of housing in black neighborhoods was officially blighted. Not surprisingly, they began agitating for change.[6]

When their way of life began to be disrupted by economic changes and black activism as early as the late 1940s, Baltimore's whites—along with whites across the state—reacted angrily. One white Baltimorean foresaw the city's coming decline in a 1966 letter to McKeldin. "What are people to do?" he asked after a large riot took place in the city. "When I say people I mean decent citizens, colored and white, that go to work every day . . . it is bad enough the way things are now in Baltimore . . . now we can look forward to riots, picketing, and the possibility of everything we have worked for being destroyed."[7]

By 1964 that anger was reaching national polls. In the Democratic primary, the state's white voters almost gave Maryland to Alabama governor George Wallace, the segregationist Democrat who had been barnstorming through the nation's white working classes, stirring up resentment against civil rights progress. Wallace understood, as his biographer Dan T. Carter wrote, that "once past the racial boundaries of public accommodations and voting rights, whites North and South shared the same deep and visceral apprehensions"—particularly when it came to things like housing, schools, and union membership, the pillars of their communal existence but also the gates to which many blacks demanded to be allowed access.[8] Wallace made ten visits to the state in the run-up to the primary, and his narrow loss—47 percent— to Senator Daniel Brewster, the Democrats' favorite-son candidate, was secured only by last-minute get-out-the-vote efforts among blacks by the state NAACP.[9]

Wallace wasn't the only politician to benefit from the white working-class backlash. Two years later, George Mahoney, a conservative Democrat, nearly won the governor's mansion on an anti-civil rights platform, built around the scare-tactic slogan "Your Home Is Your Castle." In the general election, 71 percent of white Baltimoreans voted for him. But the real benefactor of the backlash was Mahoney's opponent, the man who later came to embody white-middle-class political backlash on the national stage: Spiro Agnew.[10]

The lanky son of a Greek shopkeeper, Agnew was a little-known, mildly successful suburban Baltimore lawyer until the late 1950s, when he was appointed to the Baltimore County Board of Zoning Appeals. He didn't win an election until 1962, as county executive. Four years later, against Mahoney, he managed to convince enough prointegration Democrats to cross party lines and vote Republican, giving him the governorship by eighty-two thousand votes.

Agnew would be remembered for the tough stand he took during the Baltimore riots, and in the following months he buttressed that image with enough get-tough, law-and-order rhetoric to power him right into the vice presidency. But he also claimed, to many pundits' surprise, that he was and always had been a civil rights supporter, and he regularly trotted out appointments and legislation to prove it. In a way he was both, at least partly. He was both a conservative reactionary and a civil rights adherent, a feat achieved only because his vision of civil rights was so narrow as to cover only the most accommodating, take-it-slow desegregation strategies.

Luckily for Agnew, the civil rights movement in the state remained sufficiently in line with his own vision of racial progress just long enough for him to rise to the governor's office with a liberal reputation intact. He always eschewed, for example, the race-baiting politics of Wallace and Mahoney—in a 1964 speech he urged, "Please, my Democratic friends, do not encourage hatred and bigotry by supporting Mr. Wallace," even though it wasn't even his party's primary.[11]

But as with his tepid support for his party's presidential nominee that year, Arizona senator Barry Goldwater, Agnew's opposition was more temperamental than principled. He avoided extremists of all types, because to be extreme violated the consensus-centered politics he had imbibed as a middle-class suburbanite: In a November 1963 speech, he decried both "the hatreds of segregationist dogma on the one hand and the unreasonable ultimatums of some power-crazed integrationist leaders on the other."[12] Given the mood of the moment, his audience only paid attention to his attack on the former.

To his credit, Agnew never wavered from his position that, as he said in the 1963 speech, "The Negro is entitled as a matter of moral right to have his civil equality legislated and enforced," even after the April riots. What no one examined until then was what he meant, exactly, by that support. Sitting in his home in suburban Loch Haven,

Agnew had no sense of what it meant to actually be black in America, nor did he ever try to find out. For him, expunging the country of racism was a simple matter of striking down obviously discriminatory laws, and nothing more.

What it decidedly did not mean was support of anything that smacked of special treatment or incurred a cost to the rest of the community, such as open-housing legislation. As he explained in a 1966 TV statement, "It is unconscionable that a family compatible with the social and economic structure of a particular community should be denied entrance to that community by reason of race or creed . . . [but] I am against the type of fair housing legislation which attempts to regulate or restrict in any way the right of the owner of a private dwelling, who is not in the business of buying or selling homes, to sell his residence to whomever he pleases."[13]

Agnew could get behind civil rights as long as he saw it as an affirmation of a status quo he already enjoyed. But as soon as it implied changes in his own way of life and challenges to his own values—in the case of open housing, the absolute right to control one's property—he turned sourly against it.

Ultimately, Agnew's values were decidedly conservative from day one. He prized moderation over change, even when that change was morally necessary. Progress was acceptable only as it reinforced, rather than challenged, consensus. "Meaningful change can only come within the mainstream and with the establishment," he told a group of Greek Orthodox youth in New York. "Nothing can be gained from without."[14]

For men like Agnew, the civil rights movement was a wonderful thing as long as it focused on racist caricatures in the South, and as long as it sought access for southern blacks to abstract rights such as voting. As soon as it came north, as soon as it took on prickly issues such as open housing, as soon as more radical leaders came to the fore, he was opposed. But in Agnew's own mind, it was never he that changed—what changed was the movement, and the country. Through the course of the 1960s, he told an ecumenical conference in May 1968, "Civil disobedience fell prey to civil disorder; passive resistance gave way to erosive force. Logical leadership was obscured by the demagogue's harangue."[15]

So with Spiro, so with the nation. Agnew represented a new, fast-growing category in American politics: the suburban middle class.

That voting bloc, in Baltimore as in the rest of the country, was steadily replacing white ethnic voters as the pivotal electoral category at every level. Agnew understood and gave voice to their interests, their concerns, their fears. "He early grasped and overcame what white suburbanites take to be their main city problem—how to escape the city," wrote Garry Wills.[16] Well educated, usually white-collar, these families saw themselves as having successfully achieved the American dream, rising from urban ethnic ghettos or rural poverty to become, at middle age, comfortably situated amid a sprawling green lawn, a two-car garage, and maybe even a country club membership. They had leisure time and money to spend. They believed in political consensus, rejecting extreme candidates such as Wallace and Goldwater even as they became skeptical of the radical turn in the civil rights movement. Whether or not every stereotype was true—some families could afford only one car—the important thing is that they believed them to be true. They weren't just building a way of life; they were building a mythology. And they latched onto Agnew as an early god in their pantheon.

It would be hard, in fact, to find a more self-satisfied suburbanite than Spiro Agnew. What drove him, politically, was never clear, nor was his politics. Had he begun his ascent earlier, and more gradually, it is possible he would have moved on to other things well before his rise to national fame, settling for a nice county-level sinecure or deciding he would rather spend his free time at the bowling alley than on the hustings. But he proved the right man for the right time and the right place.

Even as Baltimore's urban ethnics stewed, their suburban neighbors prospered as their ranks grew. In 1954, according to Durr, two hundred separate subdivisions were rising outside Baltimore, and by 1960 nearly half the metropolitan population was suburban.[17] This was the mirror of the corroding ethnic inner city, the place where the successful sons and daughters of the corner shopkeepers and upstairs pieceworkers moved with their families. It was, noted historian Rafael Cortada, an era of "euphoric homogenization."[18]

What happened in Maryland during the second half of the 1960s was nothing less than a tightly turning microcosm of the country writ large. Combined with the prosperous suburbs in Prince George's and Montgomery counties, east and north of Washington, Maryland was going through a subtle but potent demographic and political sea change, from an urban white ethnic class powerful enough to nearly give Wallace the state in 1964 to vaulting suburbanite extraordinaire Spiro Agnew onto the national stage in 1968. The rapid changes of white America were butting up against an equally rapid set of changes across the racial divide, and scores of right-of-center politicians stood to benefit. Agnew was their archetype.

All he needed to make manifest his potential was a press spectacle. In April 1968, it arrived.

If Agnew represented the ascendant suburbs and a new politics of exclusionary consensus, Thomas D'Alesandro III, the great boy mayor, stood for the last of the old order. His father had been one of the country's prototypical New Deal mayors, so committed to the thirty-second president that he named one of his sons Franklin Delano Roosevelt D'Alesandro. The elder D'Alesandro served three terms as mayor of Baltimore after three terms in the U.S. House. In 1967 his son swept into office with more than 80 percent of the vote.

D'Alesandro III was just thirty-eight years old, and his youthful mien and beefy build made him look even younger. But by his surname as well as his rhetoric, he promised a fresh return to an idyllic Baltimore past that, somehow, was also taken to mean the city's future. "Seldom if ever in city history has a new mayor been installed with less political bitterness, or with more popular unanimity, or with a faster running start on his job," enthused the *Baltimore Sun* upon his inauguration in December. "This man . . . has a rendezvous with destiny."[19] D'Alesandro offered as much in his inaugural address: "There are many among us who despair of the future of our city. Some flee. Others are despondent and feel that this is a time of hopelessness. I do not share these views." Baltimore, he said, was "the city of our hope."[20]

But D'Alesandro soon found the going a lot harder than it had been for his old man. With the suburbs open and the industries leaving, it was proving nearly impossible to keep good workers in the city. Those who stayed were the elderly, the poor, and the bitter few who still had jobs but resented what they saw as abandonment by the establishment. For them the New Deal had not been about change, but about reinforcing their current way of life. Now it had brought change, after all, and there was little they could do about it. By the 1960s they were coming under a one-two punch: not only was that old way of life dying out, but the system they had stood behind now appeared to be helping everyone—blacks, the poor, criminals—except themselves. In short, the traditional consensus politics that had guided the liberal order seemed to stop working.

Black leaders were understandably suspicious of the rump white community and its motives, while the younger, more radical activists eschewed the sort of panracial compromise that D'Alesandro needed to push the city forward. "Suddenly the old ways didn't work anymore," wrote Baltimore journalist Peter Jay. "People screamed at you; they wouldn't listen to reasonable talk."[21]

Many men were broken on the rocks of the April riots, and D'Alesandro was one of them. It was his first major test as a mayor, and it was rigged for him to fail. The world he found himself commanding was much different from the one his father navigated. The city's population dropped 3.5 percent between 1960 and 1970, while its nonwhite population went from 35 percent to 47 percent. The employment base, already shrinking, was about to shrivel—in the decade after D'Alesandro's election, the city would lose almost thirty-four thousand jobs, a drop of more than 31 percent.

At the same time, the city was in the midst of a massive crime surge: between 1965 and 1970, burglaries tripled and robberies quintupled. Between 1961 and 1968, the murder rate rose 106 percent, more than double the national average. By the summer of 1968, Baltimore had the fifth-highest murder rate among major American cities.[22]

When King was killed, D'Alesandro nevertheless held out hope that his city could avoid the riots that were wrecking its southerly neighbor. As he told radio host Fraser Smith in 2007, "My hope, at that time, was that we could have made it to Sunday morning when the Ministerial Alliance and the black churches would be opened for services."[23]

Friday had passed tensely but without incident; as one cabbie told police, "Anything can happen now—and I do mean anything." A few scattered fires were reported Saturday morning, including a firebomb thrown a little after midnight into Hoffman's Liquor in the Denmore Park neighborhood, near the Pimlico racetrack on the city's northwest side. The bomb landed on a pool table, setting off the burglar alarm. But the owner arrived before the police and put out the fire.[24]

Then, a little after 5:00 P.M. on Saturday, someone pitched a firebomb through the window of a house on West Baltimore Street. Within minutes rampant looting had started along Gay Street on the near North Side. By 7:00 P.M. the National Guard had been alerted and all off-duty cops called in. Soon after, reports came in about a stolen army truck careening around the city, with people in back throwing bricks at windows and pedestrians. Sporadic but increasing reports of looting began to arrive at police headquarters.

The mayor immediately went to the city's emergency operations center, even as he continued to tell Agnew that things were "holding on." D'Alesandro later maintained that the riots were caused by rioters fleeing the D.C. clampdown, and indeed all during Saturday unconfirmed reports came into the Pentagon and the Baltimore police of cars full of young black men headed north on the interstate.

But those reports were never confirmed, and no Washingtonians were found among the arrestees. Not that D'Alesandro had time to muddle through the causes of the incipient riot. By 10:00 P.M. Saturday, he admitted to Governor Spiro Agnew that "things are getting worse," and he recommended sending in the Guard. Agnew wasted no time—within the hour two thousand troops were patrolling the city streets.[25] By midnight the National Guard was on patrol, the Pentagon had alerted the XVIII Airborne Corps of possible deployment to Baltimore, and the anxious city faced a grim Sunday morning just a few hours away.[26]

Saturday evening Richard Daley and his fire chief, Robert Quinn, had climbed into a helicopter for a forty-five-minute tour of the riot damage in Chicago. They flew up and down the West Side, maneuvering around billowing smoke from still-burning fires and lingering over the occasional looters. As they went, Quinn pointed his finger at looters, then at his firemen. His men had been attacked by looters, forcing some to abandon fires. They couldn't work under this kind of threat, Quinn said. He told Daley to get tough. Looters, he said, should be shot.[27]

They landed at Meigs Field, on Lake Michigan, and a scrum of reporters met them as they returned to City Hall. "I never believed it could happen here," Daley said. "I hope it will not happen again."[28] Then he called his police superintendent, Richard Conlisk, and dressed him down for not issuing shoot-to-kill orders. "Mr. Mayor, you issued no such orders," Conlisk replied, astounded. "You are the superintendent of police," Daley said simply.[29]

Something, it seemed, was cracking inside the mayor of the Windy City.

A week later, on April 15, after the riots in Chicago had died down and the looters gone home, Daley would hold a press conference. It would last only fifteen minutes, and he would refuse to discuss any other topic than the riots. He announced the appointment of a nine-member riot study committee headed by federal judge Richard Austin. Then, his anger barely under control behind his thick-rimmed glasses, he explained that the riots were the result of a breakdown in order among the city's black population, particularly in the schools.

"The conditions of April 5 in the schools were indescribable," he told the reporters. "The beating of girls, the slashing of teachers and the general turmoil and the payoffs and the extortions. We have to face up to this situation with discipline. Principals tell us what's happening, and they are told to forget it."

The crowd was shocked; reporters furiously scribbled. What was he talking about? There had been no reports of school violence, and the study committee, which dedicated an entire chapter to schools in its final report, could find no instances of teachers or female students being attacked.[30]

But Daley didn't stop. "I have conferred with the superintendent of police this morning and I gave him the following instructions," he said in measured words. "I said to him very emphatically and very definitely that an order be issued by him immediately and under his signature to shoot to kill any arsonist or anyone with a Molotov cocktail in his hand because they're potential murderers, and to issue a police order to shoot to maim or cripple anyone looting any stores in our city. Above all, the crime of arson is to me the most hideous and worst crime of any and should be dealt with in this fashion.

"I was most disappointed to know that every policeman out on his beat was supposed to use his own discretion and this decision was his [Conlisk's]. In my opinion, policemen should have had instructions to shoot arsonists and looters—arsonists to kill and looters to main and detain. I assumed the instructions were given, but the instructions to the police were to use their own judgment. I assumed any superintendent would issue instructions to shoot arsonists on sight and to main the looters, but I found out this morning that this wasn't so, and therefore gave him specific instructions."

The reporters took it all in. "What about children?" one asked.

"You wouldn't want to shoot them," the mayor said calmly, "but with Mace you could detain youngsters."[31]

It wasn't Daley's first suggestion of using violent means to suppress looting. Nine months prior, when asked soon after Detroit how Chicago would respond to such a riot, the mayor told a TV reporter, "I can assure you there won't be any blank ammunition [in the National Guard rifles]. The ammunition will be live."[32]

But those comments were soon forgotten. This time, they garnered a national response. The next day, April 16, with the riots still fresh in the national consciousness, the press conference was on the front page of almost every major paper in the country. The *Chicago Tribune* ran a page-one banner headline reading "Shoot Arsonists: Daley."

Many in the press criticized him, as did many liberals. John Lindsay called his remarks "unfortunate," while Ramsey Clark, speaking at a meeting of the American Society of Newspaper Editors, condemned the order and said that any police officer who shot someone for looting or arson would be prosecuted.[33] Daley himself backtracked, saying he had been misunderstood, while his press aide, Earl Bush, said, "It was damn bad reporting. They should have printed what he meant, not what he said." (This despite the fact that on April 17 the mayor had read a three-hundred-word statement to the City Council reaffirming his statement.[34])

But even as he was taking the defensive, Daley had an aide tabulate the letters and telegrams coming in on his comments. A week later he proudly reported that he had received ten thousand letters and a thousand telegrams, and they were running fifteen to one in his favor. Daley, it turns out, was just giving voice to what many already felt.

As one letter writer told the *Chicago Tribune* well before his speech, the anger of Chicago's urban whites went deeper than the April riots, even as those events brought it to a rolling boil. "Guilty men, even murderers, are freed if not 'advised of their rights,'" wrote Daniel Sobieski. "Rioters and lawbreakers are not punished, but psychoanalyzed and given government grants. We forget about brutality to police and society. You may not yell fire in a crowded theater but you can freely advocate burning a city down. Is it no wonder that sick minds, seeing this, feel free to act?"[35] Another reported that "the white community waits apprehensively, fearfully anticipating violence led by black militants." Yet another asked, "What are people to do? Put up with this sort of thing or run from the neighborhood we worked so hard to maintain?"[36] Chicago alderman Thomas Keane gave voice to many when he said, "I don't know why we are disturbed about the mayor's statements. . . . Instead of criticizing actions of police, I feel it's time to use brass knuckles and get down to telling those committing crimes to stop."[37]

Clark saw the same reaction, albeit from a different angle: Over the following weeks he bore the brunt of American anger against those they felt had facilitated the riots through a policy of permissiveness. Today anyone can go to the archives of the Lyndon Johnson Library and Museum and pore through the mounds of letters sent to Clark attacking him for his comments to the ASNE—and the meager handful in his defense.

"I feel you are as idiotic as some of our other leaders there in Washington who are taking the 'go easy' attitude and are making it difficult for our police and law enforcement officers!" read one. A correspondent from Burlington, Vermont—hardly a reactionary hotbed—wrote, "I was shocked to read how the Attorney General of the United States, the highest ranking legal officer in this country, would in effect, coddle these animals." Yet another, from Culver City, in Southern California, said, "I am not a racist but in the past year I am beginning to think the country is in a dangerous state because of over sympathy to Negroes who break the law and know they will not be punished." On Capitol Hill, conservatives, led by Texas Republican senator John Tower, called for his resignation.

A letter from Dallas concurred, with a tone that should have raised flags for liberals nationwide: "I am a borned [sic] Demo but I'm most heartily agreeing with our Republican senator and, no doubt, will vote Republican this year."[38]

13

April 7

PALM SUNDAY

Early Sunday morning found Robert Kennedy back in Washington, D.C., riding through the city in a green Mustang convertible. The car belonged to Peter Edelman, his campaign issues director. Kennedy had come back from his abbreviated midwestern tour after visiting Cleveland on Friday, and over the weekend he had told Edelman he wanted to visit a local church service on Sunday.

Why not Walter Fauntroy's New Bethel Baptist? his aide replied.[1] New Bethel sat on Ninth Street, a few blocks south of U Street—directly between two of the major riot zones.

Kennedy thought it was a great idea, and he had Edelman and his fiancée, Marian Wright, pick up him and Ethel at Hickory Hill, their northern Virginia home. The four drove across town, unaccompanied and unnoticed.

By that morning the city had calmed significantly. It was Palm Sunday, and congregants headed to services in their church best, passing by smoking rubble and picking their way around debris strewn across the sidewalks. Soldiers stood at each corner, rifles held high, with bored looks plastered across their faces. In some areas their

biggest problem wasn't rioters, but tourists. Thousands of suburbanites
had already had plans to attend the Cherry Blossom Festival that weekend; when it was canceled, the would-be attendees changed their plans
accordingly. Under the aegis of some 12,500 soldiers, they felt sufficiently safe to drive through town with their windows up and doors
locked, like vacationers on a safari. (Also driving around the city that
morning was Bill Clinton, then a senior at Georgetown University,
who was ferrying supplies to relief centers, having slapped a big red
cross on his white convertible.[2])

In that day's edition of the *Washington Star*, Haynes Johnson
reported on his tour of the riot-scarred areas the previous night. He
found a steel cable strung between concrete posts around Lafayette
Square, just north of the White House, presumably to prevent cars
from rushing the grounds. A sign on the White House East Gate read
"Closed to Visitors." A police barrier had been set up at Fourteenth
and R streets, at the northern edge of downtown; half a block north,
firefighters were pouring water on a still-burning building. With the
curfew on since 4:00 P.M., there was no one on the streets save firemen, soldiers, cops, and an occasional reporter. The marquee at the
shuttered Lincoln Theater, along U Street, still promoted its current
film, *Guess Who's Coming to Dinner?* The burglar alarm at the Snappy
Dress Shop, near Fourteenth Street, still blared. Another storefront
window was plastered with a picture of Robert Kennedy, imploring
people to register to vote in the upcoming D.C. primary. The buildings on either side of it were in ruins.[3]

The Kennedys, Edelman, and Wright arrived at New Bethel for the
8:00 A.M. service. They hadn't told the press of their plans; this was
not a campaign stop or a photo op. A few reporters were there anyway,
probably to hear what the city's leading civil rights moderate had to say
that morning, and perhaps because Stokely Carmichael was reportedly
in attendance (though Edelman did not remember him being there).
Once Fauntroy was finished with his sermon, he asked the senator to
deliver a few remarks.

As he did Thursday night in Indianapolis, Kennedy addressed the
crowd impromptu. His speech followed a line of thinking that had
been a hallmark of his campaign, but that he had been pressing even
harder in recent days.

Picking up notes of King's Riverside Church address a year before, Kennedy had been telling audiences something many Americans felt but didn't want to hear: the nation was in the depths of a spiritual crisis. With a war at home and abroad, it was mired in violence and unable to see a way forward.

King's death, and the ensuing riots, were proof that "we of our generation obviously have not done as well as we should, as we could. . . . We must leave a heritage far better to the younger generation." But can we? he asked. The critical question now was "which direction are we as Americans going to move—are we going to move forward together, or are we going to move toward extremism?" He could only hope, in the face of all countervailing evidence, that the nation would choose the former route.[4]

After the service, Edelman, Wright, and the Kennedys went out to the car. But at the last minute, Kennedy said he wanted to walk a little. Hands dug into his suit pocket, he and his wife headed north on Ninth Street, Edelman and Wright following in the convertible. Like his visit to New Bethel, Kennedy's walk was unplanned, and as he moved up the street bystanders and soldiers turned in amazement to see the boyish senator, a candidate for president, walking by as if taking a morning constitutional.

At U Street he turned left, heading toward Fourteenth Street. Soon he was joined by Fauntroy, and as word got around that he was in the area, a few, then dozens, then scores of people joined him. At one point Marion Barry trotted by Edelman's convertible and said hello. "A crowd gathered behind us, following Bobby Kennedy," Fauntroy said. "The troops saw us coming at a distance, and they put on gas masks and got the guns at ready, waiting for this horde of blacks coming up the street. When they saw it was Bobby Kennedy, they took off their masks and let us through. They looked awfully relieved."[5]

It was slow going. Kennedy stopped to talk with people along the way repeatedly; at other times he stopped to take in the expanse of damage. "I burned out my clutch that day," Edelman recalled. The spontaneous parade turned north at Fourteenth. Children in their Sunday outfits ran in and out of the crowd. At one point an elderly woman approached Kennedy. "Is that you?" she asked, grabbing his hand. He nodded. "I knew you'd be the first to come here, darling."[6]

Kennedy got as far as Fourteenth and Park Road, half a block from the site of his rally Wednesday night.[7] Then he and Ethel got into Edelman's car and drove off.

After breakfast with Vance and Westmoreland in his bedroom, President Johnson headed out to the noon service at St. Dominic's, where he could once again find comfort in his "little monks." It was an important outing: Not only was it Palm Sunday, but it also was the official day of mourning for King. He took with him Califano, his secretary Marie Fehmer, his aide Jim Jones, Luci, and her husband, Pat, all Catholics. Along with the Secret Service detachment came the White House doctor, Admiral George Buckley, who carried his medical bags into the service.[8]

More than eight hundred other congregants joined the president at the Mass, led by Reverend Norman Haddad. "I saw a reflection of Christ's passion in Martin Luther King accepting his cross. Let us reflect how we stand in our attitude toward this crucifixion," Haddad intoned. He then prayed that "the president and leaders of our country be given the wisdom and guidance to help bring about a responsible peace and that those who are filled with anarchy and the psychology of mob rule be brought to the realization that the way to violence is not the way to peace."[9]

After the final hymn, the president and his party rose to leave. Everyone else, as if by unspoken agreement, stayed seated as he departed the church. "Smiles and warm eyes seemed to reach out to the president, and a feeling of love and understanding was on each face," noted Juanita Roberts in the president's daily diary.[10]

Upon his return, Johnson dove back into meetings on Vietnam, occasionally stepping out to get updates on the various civil disorders. Baltimore, he learned, was falling apart fast, and the Department of Justice had sent a representative, Fred Vinson, to scope out the situation. At 4:00 P.M. the president and Westmoreland went before the cameras in the lobby (there was no dedicated press room at the time) to give statements.

A reporter asked offhandedly whether Johnson had gotten any sleep. "There's no sleep for the weary," the president retorted.[11] Another journalist joked drily that "we have an iron triangle of our own" in Washington, a reference to the dangerous warren of Viet Cong tunnels north of Saigon. Westmoreland, in contrast, was all good news—Tet was a failure for the North Vietnamese, the South Vietnam Army was high on victory, Khe Sanh was a success. "Militarily, we have never been in better relative position in South Vietnam," the general said. And then, without taking any questions, he left.[12]

At the last second, Johnson decided he wanted to come along on the general's helicopter ride to Andrews Air Force Base, so that on the return he could get a quick tour of the riot damage. Along with George Christian and Tom Johnson, the president flew up and down the center of the city, taking in the ruins and smoke. Tom Johnson reported later that he could still see buildings on fire, even though arson activity had been close to zero since the previous night.[13] The president took it all in, silently.

While Johnson was gone, Califano was getting updates on the rest of the country. Early that morning two thousand students at the Tuskegee Institute had trapped members of the board of directors—including retired general Lucius Clay—in an administration building. Six hundred Alabama National Guardsmen were sent out in response.[14] Disorders were popping up or reigniting across the country; in North Carolina alone, violence was reported in Wilmington, Goldsboro, Durham, Greensboro, and Raleigh.

But Baltimore was descending into anarchy the fastest. Despite the curfew and National Guard patrols, overnight the city had reported 250 fires, 273 arrests, and 3 dead—1 shot by the night manager of a bar, 2 found dead in a burned-out building. Sunday morning the Pentagon sent the commanding officer of the XVIII Airborne Corps, Lieutenant General Robert York, to the city to make contact with local officials and prepare for a possible deployment.

York arrived just before 10:00 A.M. and sat down with Agnew, D'Alesandro, Gelston, and local police and fire officials.[15] The rioters, they told him, were proving to be too much for the National Guard presence. Just before noon a crowd at Preston and Greenmont streets engaged in a pitched battle with Guard troops, trading stones and bottles for tear gas grenades and flying-wedge formations. But no matter how many crowds the Guard broke up or how many rioters the police arrested, there were always more to take their place.

One Guardsman, John Darlington, recalled, "We'd just go down one street after another in a line formation and just push people, herd 'em in to the areas where police would pick them up." Though Darlington and his men were carrying ammunition in their pockets, they marched with their bayonets fixed and unsheathed on their rifles. Regulation bayonets come with bluing on the metal to reduce glare and protect the blade. To make themselves more frightening, the soldiers used steel wool to scrape the blades clean, so that the bayonets glinted in the sun. "It was just a phalanx of bayonets, and that moved everybody out," Darlington said. But most of the looters just scattered and regrouped elsewhere.[16]

Gelston, the state's top Guard official, was getting frustrated with the conventional tactics—and that was a dangerous thing. Garry Wills described him as "a natty dresser, a gracious Southerner with the Tidewater diphthong 'aoot' for 'out,' lean and military yet convivial, a bon vivant." He smoked a pipe and smiled a lot. But he was also already on record in favor of using violent force against looters. Just a few months before the riots Wills had published *The Second Civil War*, in which Gelston expounded at length on his approach to civil disorder: "Riots like that in Detroit are not conventional police actions. This is guerrilla warfare; these people have been learning the lesson on Vietnam," he said. "The tactics against these actions are more like city-clearing operations than the old-style 'crowd control'—except that when clearing an enemy city you don't worry much abaoot who gets killed on the other side. We have to use all the weapons of combat, yet protect the rights of innocent civilians."[17]

Gelston's view was actually pretty typical for a state adjutant general, perhaps even relatively mild. Another, General Almerin O'Hara of New York, had told *New York* magazine that modern civil disorders had to be countered with lethal weapons, including bazookas and hand grenades.[18] National Guard units nationwide had received extensive riot-control training after Detroit—a thirty-two-hour training program for all units and sixteen additional hours for officers—but comments such as Gelston's and O'Hara's left the Pentagon brass and the civilian leadership wary of their role in putting down riots.[19]

Rain had tamped down violence that morning. But by noon the riot was back in swing, and at 1:30 State's Attorney Charles Moylan Jr. reported, "The looting in the eastern half of Baltimore has reached terrible proportions."[20] At 2:00 P.M. Agnew set a 4:00 P.M. curfew, but there was little sense among his advisers that it could have much effect. The riot area was simply too large and the police and troop numbers too small. "There was destruction everywhere," recalled Darlington. "Goods from the stores were thrown in the street, trash cans over-turned, I mean you name it, it was there."[21]

The violence, eventually spread over a thousand square blocks, was intense but random; some streets would be full of looters and arsonists, while others would be completely empty. Downtown had cleared out. The only restaurant open for business was the café in the Greyhound bus station.

Much of the early riot took place in the eastern sections of the city, with Gay Street as their rough axis. Late Saturday night, local busi-nessman Gerard Gassinger, known to his customers as Dynamo Jerry, got a call from a clerk at his enormous furniture store at 1752 Gay. The neighborhood, once German, was now almost entirely black, and it was riddled with poverty and crime. But while other stores had by then mostly decamped for the suburbs or other parts of the city, Gassinger's Furniture had stuck it out.

It proved Gassinger's undoing. There were 350 people swarming all over the store, the clerk told him, while 15 cops were standing across the street doing nothing. Gassinger said he'd be right there, but the clerk told him not to come. It was too dangerous, and besides, there was nothing he could do. When he arrived the next day at 6:00 A.M., everything was gone. "It was an empty warehouse," he said. The show-room windows were all broken—$10,000 worth of glass. He tried to scrounge up some plywood to cover them, but there wasn't enough in the city for all the shop owners looking to cover smashed windows. "Every looted store wanted plywood," he recalled.[22]

As men like Gassinger returned home that afternoon and evening, they brought horror stories of looted stores and still-rampaging crowds to their nervous neighbors. Word went around that the riots were spreading and that not even the National Guard could contain them, and many Baltimore whites decided to take matters into their own hands. In Little Italy, to the east of downtown and just south of the major rioting, residents were seen squatting on rooftops with weap-ons. "As far as they were concerned," said one East Baltimorean, "law and order had to be maintained even if it had to be maintained by the individual."[23]

Others took it farther; unique among the major riot cities, Baltimore saw numerous gangs of white vigilantes roaming the streets. At one point Jack Bowden, a local TV reporter, was out walking the streets when a car full of white men offered him a ride. As he climbed in, he asked where they were headed. "We're gonna go shoot some niggers," one of the passengers offered, matter-of-factly.[24] At one point a group of white men stopped a black businessman and his family as they drove across town, pulled him from his car, and began beating him until he managed to slip away, get in his car, and drive off.

Nerves ran especially high in Park Heights, at the time a predominantly Jewish and Russian neighborhood in northwestern Baltimore. There men such as Frank Bressler, who owned a nearby dry cleaning shop, listened nervously as reports came in about the rioting spreading out from the East Side. Eventually the neighborhood business leaders met and agreed to arm themselves. "We decided since most of us, or many of us, were ex-military people, we were going to set up a military type of defense in Baltimore to protect this type of area, to keep this from happening out here."

They got in touch with attorneys to make clear what counted as justifiable homicide. They even drew up a constitution. Then they collected funds and sent Bressler into town to buy weapons. "I bought sixteen double-barrel shotguns and three thousand rounds of ammunition. The man says you got enough to go to war. I says if we have to, we will." When he got back Bressler distributed the weapons among his fellow shop owners, who set about fortifying their stores. "I sat all night with a shotgun pointed at the door in case anyone came through to try to loot or burn my place," he said. But they also set up communal defenses at the main entryways to the neighborhood. There were "three lines of defense around the Pimlico Hotel area. We had short-wave radios and we were able to communicate with each other." Then they sent out word that they "were armed to the teeth."[25] Park Heights remained calm throughout the riots.

The vigilantes and the armed neighborhoods weren't redneck whites taking matters into their own hands. They were expressing what most whites nationwide were feeling as they watched the riots unfold on the TV screens: the nation's blacks were a problem, a collective threat. No longer a moral problem, they were now a domestic security concern. And if in the years ahead the nation didn't turn to vigilantism per se, it did see these same reactions—of Bressler, of the white gangs—transform at the ballot box into a thorough repudiation of liberal government and an embrace of get-tough conservatism.

It was getting late on Sunday, and Agnew had to make a decision. All day he had been conferring with D'Alesandro, Gelston, and his aides. By nightfall incident reports were beginning to come in from West Baltimore, previously a peaceful area. So many people had been burned out of their homes that the city established a refugee center on Dolphin Street, just northwest of downtown.[26]

By now Gelston was clamoring for more troops. But York was skeptical. He and other federal officers on the scene didn't think much of the Maryland National Guard; they found them disorganized and poorly controlled. As Major General Melvin Zais, the Pentagon's liaison, put it in an after-action report, "It is important to recognize the degree of confusion which existed in the early stages. . . . Information concerning the location of National Guard units was generalized and boundaries were not clearly defined, and it was difficult to ascertain the real strength of forces available. The police had the best information available on activities within the riot-torn city, but it had not been pieced together and reflected on some form of a situation map."[27]

After an afternoon tour, Agnew conceded. Just before 5:00 P.M., he called Attorney General Clark, who relayed the request to the White House. At 5:01 P.M. York got word that the president had authorized troops for Baltimore.[28]

Most of the troops deployed to Baltimore were already nearby. Though two brigades of the Eighty-second Airborne, which made up most of the XVIII Airborne Corps, along with the corps' provisional artillery brigade, had been flown up to Washington Saturday morning, the artillery brigade and the Eighty-second Airborne's First Brigade were being held in reserve at Andrews Air Force Base. With violence under control in Washington, it was an easy call to repurpose the artillery brigade's mission and send it up the highway. That unit, in addition to two federalized Maryland National Guard brigades, comprised the bulk of the military force in the city.[29]

As he did for Chicago, Johnson waited until the last minute to sign the papers for Baltimore. It came almost as an afterthought, in the middle of a lengthy Sunday repast with his daughters, Pat Nugent, Califano, Representative Jack Brooks and his wife, and George Christian and his wife. Johnson was in a surprisingly jovial mood; maybe it was the good news from Vietnam, maybe he was just punch-drunk. In the middle of a light dinner table conversation, he took a piece of candy out of a dish and popped it in his mouth, despite the fact that since his 1955 heart attack his doctors had forbidden all sweets. His aides took notice; the president's sweet tooth was usually held in check by Lady Bird's watchful eye, but she had left that morning for Texas. Johnson kept right on talking as if nothing had happened.[30]

At 10:15, Califano brought the proclamation and executive order to him. Johnson turned for a moment, signed his name, and continued eating.

14

April 8

BLUFF CITY ON EDGE

By Monday morning, Chicago was slowly coming back to order. Though fewer than a thousand people were left homeless, huge amounts of clothing and food poured in, as did offers from suburban church congregations and private homes for temporary housing, arriving from as far away as Rockford, seventy miles away. (At the same time, many displaced black families seeking apartments in the suburbs found rental offices suddenly closed and rents inexplicably raised.[1]) The Yellow and Checker cab companies announced that food donations could be left at their dispatch stations.[2]

Sunday night a thousand gang members met in the middle of the Midway, a grassy mall bisecting the University of Chicago, to declare a truce among rival factions and a common commitment to restore order. While hardly decisive, their efforts were substantial enough to merit army recognition, at least in confidential reports: "Cooperation of the Blackstone Rangers and the Disciples . . . may have helped in achieving the relative quiet."[3]

As it had in Washington, the massive troop presence had given the police room to do their job. Arrests, mostly for curfew violations, poured into the city and county jails. Chicago parks had been turned into military camps. On the South Side, the massive green lawn of Jackson Park was striated by neat rows of tents for twelve hundred soldiers, with guards posted at hundred-yard intervals; the four southernmost guards, in the heart of the South Side, were black.[4]

Along Sixty-third Street, a major South Side retail thoroughfare, all two hundred stores were shuttered, while police and army sound trucks plied the roads blasting, "Stay inside. Don't come out. No one is permitted on the streets." Armored personnel carriers coursed through the streets, their treads cutting shallow rivulets into the asphalt.[5]

The troops meant business; many of them Vietnam veterans, they took a no-nonsense approach to their task. As one lieutenant colonel told a *Tribune* reporter, "If anyone gives us trouble, they'll know right off the bat they're dealing with a tough outfit . . . we didn't relish getting shot at in the Mekong delta, and we won't like getting shot at here."[6] As the smoke cleared, the damage proved substantial. The rioting had ripped apart some 300 square blocks on the West Side, along with isolated pockets spread around the rest of the city. Twelve deaths were reported. Arrests totaled 893. Monday morning, the *Tribune* headlined a front-page story, "Madison St. a Blackened Scar in Heart of Chicago." In colorful but accurate prose, the article declared, "It was the crucifixion of a city, with Madison St. the blackened, still smoldering nail that had been driven into its heart. . . . It was as tho [sic] a flamethrower had played up and down the street, burning our roofs and crumpling walls until they arched inward to meet the heat-blackened, twisted steel structural members that hung into the ruins."[7]

Things weren't going quite so smoothly in Baltimore. The National Guard and army split the city in half, one patrolling each, with separate headquarters (though York retained ultimate control of the total force). The Fifth Regiment Armory, where the National Guard ran its operations, was a scene of "organized confusion," an "elbow-to-elbow operation" in which there was "incessant chattering of radios . . . constant shrilling of telephones . . . and [a] continuous flow of discussion and decision as reports were received and acted upon."[8] Hotlines connected the staff to the White House, the Pentagon, and York's own headquarters nearby. York emphasized close cooperation with local law enforcement, and he spent inordinate amounts of time huddled with Donald Pomerlau, the Baltimore police chief.

Monday saw another uptick in violence. Despite an early get-tough approach consisting of saturation patrols and liberal use of tear gas, crowds numbering in the hundreds began accumulating by 8:00 A.M., particularly in the western half of town, throwing bottles and obscenities at the troops. By late afternoon the violence had spread to encompass a full quarter of the city, including parts that had so far been assumed untouchable, such as the Edmondson Village shopping mall in the southwestern section. Calls for help, including a 2:00 P.M. report of looting at Provident Hospital, threatened to overwhelm the troops, and York accepted the Pentagon's offer of another infantry brigade as reinforcements.[9]

Incredibly, that afternoon Fred Vinson, from Justice, held a press conference to report his optimistic assessment of the situation. Baltimore, he said, had peaked, and the scene on the streets was comparable with Washington on Saturday. "The streets are relatively calm, the law-abiding citizens want to go about their business again, which they should do," he told reporters. "I'm told that reported incidents of looting are scattered, fires are down, and I assume arrests are down, because as I hear, the curfew is being well observed. I think that if you were graphing it, the curve is definitely down."[10]

Reporters didn't need to look far to find contradictory assessments. D'Alesandro and the City Council concluded that the police and National Guard would soon "be ordered to start shooting looters," a news item that swirled through the city despite the fact that, at least in the Guard's case, the decision was no longer up to either the city or the state to make. In any case, it didn't tamp down the violence; by nightfall, concluded army historian Paul Schieps: "The troops in Baltimore saw action as vigorous as anything that had yet occurred"— including gunfire that almost hit a battalion commander.[11]

But by midnight the violence had finally begun to ebb. Incident rates dropped steadily after 11:00 P.M., and by the next morning they were on a level with that of Sunday morning. Schools opened Tuesday, as did many businesses. At the peak on Tuesday morning, 11,570 troops were in the city. Seven were dead and 5,504 arrested, while 1,208 fires were reported. No troops were injured (though 1 died in a truck accident).[12]

Nevertheless, York later indicated that he was much more in line with Gelston's thinking than that of his superiors. While he didn't call for deadly force, he wrote in his after-action report that "more stress could be placed on the use of a weapon as a club to prevent looting and other criminal acts, or for crowd control purposes."[13]

Monday found Memphis on edge yet again. The massive violence feared in the immediate wake of King's death had failed to materialize, in part because of a crackdown by police and National Guard. Within an hour after the shooting, Mayor Loeb had set a strict curfew and called for troops and state police; by midnight thirty-eight hundred Guardsmen were on the streets.[14] Even as Loeb declared three days of mourning and went on TV to express the city's horror over the act, he armed himself with a pearl-handled revolver given to him by the police (and not without cause; in the following days he received numerous death threats). When he met with a biracial coalition of religious leaders urging a compromise on the strike, he did so with a shotgun hidden in his desk foot well, an image captured by a Memphis *Commercial Appeal* photographer.

The police, many of whom removed their badges to avoid identification, were particularly brutal. They set upon looters with their batons. One black lawyer visiting a police station recalled that many of the arrestees being processed were bandaged and bruised. Even innocent people caught out after the curfew were often beaten. The weekend brought one fatality: Friday night police shot and killed a twenty-six-year-old looter, Ellis Tate.[15]

But it's unlikely that the show of force alone halted rioting; it certainly didn't work in other cities. Instead, union members and King's SCLC staffers likely had the biggest impact. In the hours after his assassination, they rushed from youth group to radical outfit, trying to calm people down and convince them to stay off the streets. As one ACLU attorney on the scene later said, "They were having a terrific argument with a bunch of young Negroes . . . trying to talk them out of burning the town down. . . . And they did a fairly good job of it."[16]

The violence, scattered as it was, almost brought federal intervention. On Sunday, Major General Kelsie Reaves of the 101st Airborne Division flew to the city from Fort Campbell to confer with

Stephen Pollack, the assistant attorney general for civil rights and the head of the Justice Department's Memphis liaison team. Pollack recommended that the Tennessee Guard be federalized, though he didn't push for regular army troops yet. (In all likelihood, he was more concerned about the Guard's discipline than its ability to prevent a riot.)

But Reaves, along with Governor Ellington, strongly disagreed. Pollack backed off, but state officials smelled a trick when they learned that an air force tactical control team had landed at the airport in preparation for troop-transport sorties. Federal officials quickly claimed it was an accident and that no troops were coming, and they withdrew the team on April 9.[17]

There were, nevertheless, scattered incidents of violence over the weekend. A fire consumed the O. W. Ferrell Lumber Company.[18] Several stores were ransacked, while bands of rioters threw Molotov cocktails at storefronts. Rioters pelted city buses with rocks until the transit authority decided to shut down service. But the expected cataclysm never came.

Nevertheless, the city sat on edge all weekend. Just because riots hadn't erupted immediately didn't mean they couldn't emerge at any moment; Friday saw Chicago go up, Saturday saw Baltimore descend into chaos. Rumors spread about a plot to destroy Memphis State University. People blockaded themselves inside their homes, armed and ready to kill anyone who set foot in their part of town. "Our neighborhood was like a tomb," City Council member Wyeth Chandler recalled. "We were armed, ready for anything. I think this was generally true throughout our community. . . . If a Negro had stopped to change a tire I don't know whether he'd be left alive or not."[19]

A *Washington Star* reporter on the scene wrote that Memphis "gave the impression of a ghost city. At one point, not a single human being—not even a stray pedestrian, policeman, soldier, or Guardsman—could be spotted anywhere in the entire downtown section."[20]

Many whites expressed private glee over King's killing. Off-color jokes swirled through the city. "What's black and slower than a speeding bullet?" "I hear there's to be a spider march in Memphis tomorrow. What's a spider march? It's going to be led by a black widow." Others called radio stations requesting the song "Bye, Bye Blackbird."[21] If they expressed remorse, it was only over the fact that it had happened in their city, further inconveniencing their daily lives. A Sunday biracial memorial service at the city's Crump Stadium, organized by a group of Memphis businessmen, failed to bridge the gap—many blacks stayed away, while James Lawson and other black speakers refused to bend to the group's insistence on a collective "best face forward" approach to the city's troubles. "We have witnessed a crucifixion here in Memphis," Lawson told the crowd.

Once the immediate threat of disorder passed, the city turned its attention to Monday. King had already planned another march that day, and the SCLC quickly announced that plans were still on. Public safety director Holloman, arguing for a temporary restraining order, predicted that the violence the march would cause would "be worse than Watts or worse than Detroit," and he talked about classified tips that "Negroes are buying guns wholesale in our neighboring state of Arkansas."[22]

To prevent a repeat of the March 28 disaster, Lawson, the local leader of the strike, called in Bayard Rustin from New York, who arrived Friday afternoon—after his detour through the White House—to help coordinate it. Rustin was a master planner; it was he who had put together the nuts and bolts of the 1963 March on Washington, he who knew better than anyone how to make King's vision for nonviolent protest actually work.

All weekend Rustin worked with the SCLC and the strike leaders to train marshals in nonviolence techniques, plan the march route, and keep the police and FBI up to speed. He walked the route himself several times, noting vulnerable spots and ordering workers to place semitrailers at strategic points to keep marchers in line. Portable toilets went up along the way, and at the end a ten-foot-high platform for speakers was erected.[23]

The march, Rustin told the *New York Times*, was not just a way of honoring King. It heralded a "totally new stage" in the civil rights movement, "the beginning of the entry into economic justice" for black Americans.[24] Rather than a memorial for its slain leader, the movement was declaring its intention to move forward unabated.

The marchers set out that morning at 11:16 from Clayborn Temple under a steel-gray sky. Police estimated that nineteen thousand walked the route. Rustin put the number closer to forty-two thousand. "There were people from all over the country," recalled Steven Ober, a Texas college student who drove in with several friends from Waco.[25] Planes brought members of the American Federation of Teachers from New York, and trains brought union workers from Chicago. Harry Belafonte, Ossie Davis, and Rosa Parks walked, as did United Auto Workers president Walter Reuther.

Fog delayed Coretta Scott King's plane from Atlanta; a police escort brought her to the front of the march as it neared the city's commercial district. Holloman and Assistant Police Chief Henry Lux walked ahead of the pack, scoping rooflines for snipers. The entire march was almost completely silent, save for the clomping of shoes on the pavement. "The streets were lined with armed National Guardsmen," Ober said. "There was the pale of violence, somber and tense." But the peace held.

The march came to a close at City Hall, where the speakers' platform stood in front of its white marble columns. Thousands filled the plaza. Many others climbed nearby buildings and scaffolding for a better look. The ceremony started with a rendition of "Lord, Hold My Hand while I Run This Race." Then Reuther, picking up a theme from King's last sermons, told the crowd, "We have a nation poor in spirit—that's where our poverty is," handing the strike leaders a check for $50,000 from his union. A long list of speakers followed: Belafonte, Dr. Benjamin Spock, Ralph Abernathy. Then Mrs. King, wearing a black dress, rose to the microphone.[26]

"I come here today because I was impelled to come," she began, with three of her four children standing beside her. "I came because whenever it was impossible for my husband to be in a place where he wanted to be and felt that he needed to be, he would occasionally send me to stand in for him. And so today I felt that he would have wanted me to be here."

She thanked everyone who had sent her condolences, and she thanked those who had just marched with her. But the real way to memorialize him, she said, was to "carry on, because this is the way he would have wanted it to have been. We are not going to get bogged down, I hope, and this moment when we are going to go forward, we are going to continue his work to make all people truly free and to make every person feel that he is a human being."

The Poor People's Campaign, as well as the garbage workers' strike, were vital to his vision and must go on, she said. "Every man deserves a right to a job or an income so that he can pursue liberty, life, and happiness. Our great nation, as he often said, has the resources, but his question was: do we have the will? Somehow I hope in this resurrection experience the will will be created within the hearts, and minds, and the soul of those who have the power to make these changes come about."

If it can, then his soul will be redeemed, she went on. And so will the nation's. "If we can catch the spirit, which I believe, and the true meaning of this experience, I believe that this nation can be transformed into a society of love, of justice, peace and brotherhood where all men can really be brothers." And with that she stepped away from the microphone, her voice having held steady and measured for the entire duration.[27]

The crowd soon left; they all had to be home by the 5:00 P.M. curfew. That evening King flew back to Atlanta with her family and several of the SCLC workers to get ready for her husband's funeral the next day.

Back at the White House, Johnson had begun to sour on his planned speech to Congress. He had already postponed it a night, until Tuesday, supposedly to avoid overshadowing that morning's funeral in Atlanta.[28] Sunday he had finally seen the damage up close, by helicopter, but all weekend he had been hearing angry words from the Hill. "Neither Congress nor the Administration appeared in a mood to plunge headlong into massive new urban spending now," noted the *Washington Post*.[29]

His staffers felt it, too. "It was extraordinary that there should have been such a vast difference between the conversations in the White House and attitudes on the Hill," McPherson wrote in his memoirs. "On the Hill and probably for the majority in this country, [new social spending] seemed dangerously like a protection racket." [30]

By Monday the president was waxing philosophical over the recent turn in his—and the nation's—fortunes. That morning George Christian met with Johnson in the presidential bedroom to report the latest riot statistics. At the time, forty-six were dead, twenty-six hundred were injured, and twenty-one thousand were under arrest. "What did you expect?" Johnson replied. "I don't know why we're so surprised. When you put your foot on a man's neck and hold him down for three hundred years, and then you let him up, what's he going to do? He's going to knock your block off."[31]

With America on fire, Johnson realized that he would do better to focus his efforts on a single piece of legislation, one with preferably few costs attached. Naturally, he chose the fair housing bill, which had sat in Congress for years. The bill would ban racial discrimination in housing sales for some 80 percent of the real estate market by 1970, starting with federally funded homes before expanding to include all real estate bought or sold through a broker.[32]

Fair housing bills had failed in each of the past two years, and the latest iteration of the bill appeared to be facing a similar fate. It had passed the Senate in March when Illinois Republican Everett Dirksen had switched positions and endorsed the bill. It took a long list of promises from Johnson—including an effort to get Daley off the senator's back in his next election—for him to do so. "I do remember distinctly the president saying, 'We're gonna get them, Everett Dirksen's coming out in favor of us and don't ever ask me what I had to give him,'" recalled Jim Gaither.[33]

But it wasn't clear that Johnson's favors could do much in the House, where it languished for weeks in the Rules Committee. Its supporters were running up against the same sort of obstruction that had confronted earlier bills—endless amendments, threats of filibuster—though this time opposition came from outside the South as well, and from even moderate politicians. Many hoped that if they could delay the vote until after the Poor People's Campaign—which they assumed would be a disaster—public revulsion against the civil rights movement would be strong enough to give them cover to kill it.

"By that time," Johnson wrote in his memoirs, "the open housing issue had become a Democratic liability. More and more Republicans tried to base their 1968 campaigns on promises to protect the individual from 'LBJ's bureaucrats,' who, they said, would be swarming over every neighborhood setting up Negro-white quotas, forcing homeowners to sell their property, and encouraging vicious gangs of rioters and looters to destroy neighborhoods which dared to resist."[34] In Johnson's eyes, going against this new, suburban, security-based racism made him brave. It certainly did. But in going forward on this and nothing else, it also showed that he knew he was out of cards.

King's assassination gave the bill new life. Johnson had already sent a letter urging its passage to the House and Senate leaders, and he spent whatever free time he could find over the weekend jawboning congressional leaders. At the same time, he had Califano and Sanders working their own connections in the Capitol. They all knew it was going to be a tough fight, even with the new emotional momentum.

Its backers had initially hoped for passage on April 5; after a moment of silence for King, Pennsylvania Democratic senator Joseph Clark called on the House to pass the bill immediately (he also urged Congress to pass an emergency jobs bill, federal gun control, and more funds for ghetto education and the War on Poverty).[35] But a curious lack of quorum in the Rules Committee, where it currently sat, prevented action that week. By the end of the day its backers counted two hundred members in support, with fifty, from both parties, still up in the air.[36] Under the leadership of House minority leader Gerald Ford, Republicans tried to divert the bill to conference, where it could sit for weeks. Others tried to use the emotion of the moment against the bill; Ohio Republican representative Delbert Latta warned against the "enactment of legislation on the basis of emotion."[37]

But the tide began to turn over the weekend, even as riots swept across the country. The bill got a major boost when one of the Rules Committee Republicans who had previously supported sending the bill to conference, Illinois' John Anderson, announced Saturday that instead he would vote to send the bill directly to the House floor.[38] At about the same time, twenty-one moderate Republicans came out in support, including William McCulloch, ranking member of the Judiciary Committee. It also helped that GOP presidential candidate Richard Nixon had spent the weekend calling House Republicans, asking them to back the bill so as to remove civil rights from the campaign table.[39]

Nevertheless, the fight over the bill had been going on for so long that by Monday its supporters were still skeptical of its passage. Congressmen who might have voted for the bill on Friday, riding the wave of emotion after King's death, might switch sides again over disgust at seeing Washington burning and troops patrolling its streets. At an afternoon meeting of the bill's House backers, White House representatives, and members of the Leadership Council on Civil Rights,

Speaker McCormack expressed pessimism, saying, "I'm not sure we are going to accomplish anything."[40]

They ran through a list of every House member and realized they still needed fifteen to twenty votes. They picked their targets and went to work. One potential convert was Jake Pickle, a friend of the president who represented Johnson's former congressional district. The White House had just given its approval to a $1.4 million housing grant in his district, and they hoped that would persuade him to switch his position. But that was just one; they needed fourteen more. As House majority leader Carl Albert told the *New York Times* that day, "I think we can pass it. But it's going to be very, very close."[41]

With troops deployed to three cities and violence on the ebb in each, Monday was the first day that the White House felt the situation was coming under some control. Johnson left that night for Camp David, taking with him a sheaf of blank proclamations and executive orders in case he needed to send in the army to any more cities.[42]

It wasn't a hypothetical concern. Pittsburgh, on a low boil since Saturday, had begun to roil overnight. Rioting, for a time stanched in the Hill District, had spread to the nearby Homewood-Brushton ghettos. "The tempo of fires, looting and assaults seemed to be increasing in early evening," wrote a federal observer on the scene.[43]

By nightfall there were two more Guard battalions deployed, for a total of four thousand Pennsylvania National Guardsmen in the city. But local commanders feared more would be needed, particularly given the possibility of riots in other major cities in the state. "They do not believe they have sufficient reserves," read a Department of Justice intelligence report sent to the White House that evening. "They have not yet asked for federal troops but are thinking about it."[44]

A complicating issue was transportation: Even though the 197th Infantry Brigade, in reserve at Andrews Air Force Base, was available to move on to Pittsburgh, the army didn't have enough trucks to take them there, and the air force's transport fleet was already committed, ferrying troops into Baltimore and Chicago. The AOC contacted a private bus company, but it said it would need a three-hour notification to get the buses to Andrews. All told, once the decision to commit was made, it would take some nine hours to get the troops into the city.[45]

Johnson told Califano to keep regular contact with officials in Pittsburgh but to make no mention of troops, let alone an offer.[46] Word passed down the ranks to do the same. In one testy exchange, Major General Francis Greenlief, the deputy chief of the National Guard Office at the Pentagon, dressed down a Pennsylvania National Guard colonel for even implying that they might need federal troops. "I suspect by this time that [Pennsylvania Deputy Adjutant] General [Richard] Snyder thinks we are being pretty damn pushy here because we have been so concerned about Pittsburgh. We have generally felt your mobilizations have been pretty minimal. . . . We are very concerned about it there. . . . This is going on all over, you know, and I would hope that he and the governor are not thinking about federal troops rescuing him. Our reaction time is even slower. Plus, we have commitments all over the country now."[47]

That seemed to do the trick. Pennsylvania never requested troops, and by Tuesday afternoon it had most of the rioting under control.

15

April 9

A COUNTRY RENT ASUNDER

T he next morning 120 million Americans tuned in to watch the funeral for Martin Luther King Jr. in Atlanta.[1] All three TV networks, which had broadcast most or all of the Memphis march the day before, carried hours of live feed from Atlanta. Around the country, stores, schools, movie theaters, museums, and banks shuttered in respect (and, in some cases, fear of renewed violence). The New York and American stock exchanges closed for the day, their first time in honor of a private citizen. The International Longshoremen's Union closed down ports along the coasts and the Great Lakes. The New York Yankees even postponed their season opener, against the California Angels.

In Central Park the New York Philharmonic played a memorial concert for five thousand people; the Westminster Choir and the Camerata Singers performed "Nobody Knows the Trouble I've Seen," "Go Down, Moses," and "Swing Low, Sweet Chariot"; the orchestra played Bach and Verdi. Hundreds gathered in Chicago's Grant Park for a hushed service, ringed by still-present army soldiers. Where offices did stay open, many black employees simply didn't show up for work, a response to Floyd McKissick's call for a national "black Tuesday."

At 9:30 A.M. Central Time, workers around the country took a moment of silence as the funeral service in Atlanta began. "Empty classrooms, lowered flags, stopped trains, pealing bells, and flag-draped photographs of Dr. King in store windows, all attested to [New York City's] formal posture of grief," wrote the *New York Times*.[2]

Urban America ground to a halt.

The service took place at Ebenezer Baptist Church, where King had been copastor with his father. Its enormous sanctuary could hold only thirteen hundred people, a fraction of the hundreds of thousands who descended on Atlanta in mourning. Those seats went first to friends and families, then movement figures, dignitaries, and celebrities. Between fifty thousand and a hundred thousand people were expected to participate in the march from the service to Morehouse College, where King had been an undergraduate. Eastern Airlines alone reported that thirty-three of its planes had been chartered to Atlanta, while Greyhound said a hundred of its buses were now en route. Governor Nelson Rockefeller of New York rented fourteen limousines to ferry him and his friends to and from the church.[3]

It was yet another day of nerves—would Atlanta, already on edge, follow other cities into violence? And what about Washington, Chicago, Memphis, Baltimore, or even some other city that had so far escaped the riots? Gary mayor Richard Hatcher, one of the nation's leading black politicians, had to cancel his plans to attend because of renewed rioting in his city Monday night.[4] Chicago and federal authorities announced they had uncovered a plot to "cause more chaos" in the city by gathering troublemakers under the guise of an SCLC-sponsored memorial service.[5] And bomb threats came into the FBI against Rich's Department Store, First National Bank, and other Atlanta area buildings, though police officers swept each and found nothing.[6] Atlanta was "hot, about to snap," Roger Wilkins said. "People were in a rage. Only their grief kept them in check, but no one knew for how long."[7]

At the Pentagon, officers readied equipment and several thousand more men for deployment, crossing their fingers that none would be needed. Officials from the Atlanta Police Department, the FBI, the Department of Justice, and the Secret Service met all weekend to plan for the march, while more than half of the APD's nine hundred men were tasked with maintaining order around the march. Several thousand Georgia National Guardsmen were kept in reserve at a nearby, undisclosed location. Students from traditionally black Clark University launched "Operation Respect," asking fellow area students to avoid "all violence, looting, and rioting during the mourning period." It was likely no comfort to Atlantans that they had to ask in the first place.[8]

Wilkins, tired and grieving, had spent part of the weekend in Washington, catatonically going through the motions of directing his CRS staff in riot-hit cities. On Saturday, Clark directed him to Atlanta to help run federal efforts and to liaise with various black leaders expected to show up. Wilkins's first problem upon arrival was what to do about the tens of thousands of people in town for the funeral, many of whom either couldn't find or couldn't afford a hotel room. It had rained Monday. What if it picked up again Tuesday night?

"We didn't want people sleeping on the streets, especially with all the riots," he said. "So I called Joe Califano, told him what we needed. There were lot of cots in the National Guard armory, but in order to use them, we had to have presidential dispensation. I said, 'Joe, listen, if it rains, it'll be a disaster. We've got to have something.' He said, 'I'll talk to the president.' Then he called back, said, 'I don't know. Just don't know.' So I pressed him a little harder. He called back and said, 'Okay, you've got your authorization, I'll call the [National Guard] commissioner now. But don't tell Johnson.'"[9]

The president had more or less checked out of the King ceremonies. The King family had requested a personal liaison between them and the White House, but Johnson turned them down.[10] He later claimed that he had initially planned to go to the funeral himself, but that numerous tips about assassination threats—some through the FBI, but also through black comedian and activist Dick Gregory—had led him to send Humphrey instead. In his memoirs, Johnson claims that he badly wanted to thank King's father in person for his telegram and to express his condolences to the family. "As president of the United States I had to heed the unanimous judgment of the Secret Service and the FBI," he wrote. "The situation in Atlanta was tense and dangerous; they recommended in the strongest terms that I not attend the funeral."[11] This is likely a case of gilding the past for future generations, though—there is no evidence that Johnson made any preparations for attending, nor did he put up much of a fight when the various security arms, on thin reeds of evidence, recommended that he stay away.

Johnson was one of the few national politicians not to attend the funeral; so many showed up that black militants carped to the media about "vote-getting" and "crocodile tears." According to Wilkins, the family had requested that only the president or vice president come as a representative of the federal government, but the White House had refused to cooperate.[12] Almost all the major presidential candidates from both sides of the aisle were there (Ronald Reagan, then a serious contender for the GOP nomination, decided to sit it out). Fifty House members and thirty senators made the trip. John Lindsay and Nelson Rockefeller were there, as was Michigan governor George Romney.

Jacqueline Kennedy was there, too. Early that morning she had paid a visit to Coretta Scott King at her home before driving to the church. A guest book, which she signed, sat by the front door. The house was full of people, so the two widows spoke in the bedroom for five minutes, seeking privacy and consolation. When Kennedy arrived at the church, there was such a rush of press and admirers that she couldn't get through the door. Eventually marshals grabbed her hand and squeezed her through.[13]

Stokely Carmichael arrived soon after. More or less in hiding since his appearance at Howard on Friday, he had gotten to Atlanta at eleven the night before, greeted like a rock star as he pulled up in his car to the Paschal's Motor Hotel and Restaurant, a motel popular with black activists. As the crowd huddled around him, they asked what was going on. He reportedly muttered, "Brother, tomorrow night we gonna burn them."[14]

But the next morning he was looking anything but the radical; even undercover FBI observers reported he was "neatly dressed" in a black mock-Nehru jacket. He got to Ebenezer at 10:20, trailing behind him a cortege of bodyguards. All of them, Carmichael included, repeatedly raised their fists as they approached the entrance, chanting "black power, black power." At the door he was told he couldn't enter with his associates. "You better let him in," said one, "he's a black man." At the risk of making a scene, the doormen let them all pass inside.[15]

Much of white Atlanta ignored the funeral; in the suburbs, the day went on as usual. Governor Lester Maddox, a prosegregation reactionary who told reporters King had arranged his own death, holed up in his office at the state capitol behind a swarm of 180 Guardsmen and state police. While several downtown stores closed (reportedly for security reasons), Maddox refused to close the schools, and many offices remained open.[16]

Still, some fifty thousand blacks and whites turned out for the event. The doors opened sometime before 9:00 A.M., and the sanctuary quickly filled to standing-room-only capacity. The famous included more than just politicians: Stevie Wonder, Diana Ross, Bill Cosby, Floyd Patterson, and Jackie Robinson brushed shoulders with Richard Nixon, Jacob Javits, and Eugene McCarthy.[17] Romney and Rockefeller gave up their seats to women, joining Lindsay standing along the side of the sanctuary. People anxiously jostled for seats. There was so much hubbub that it looked for a moment like the family, which was arriving late, wouldn't get seated.

At one point King's brother (and successor as Ebenezer's copastor), A.D., mounted the black hearse at the front of the sanctuary used to carry flowers and boomed, "At this hour our hearts are very heavy. Please let the family through. You would want Dr. King's wife, children, mother, and father to have an opportunity of seeing this service. Please don't make Mrs. King have to fight her way in." But no one moved. "If we can't receive your cooperation, we have but one choice: to remove the body and bury it privately."

Eventually enough people grudgingly gave way, and Mrs. King, draped in a black veil, and nearly a hundred other family members entered the sanctuary and took their places at the front. King's youngest child, Bernice, sat in her mother's lap. At the last minute, Humphrey entered from a side door, passing slowly by the coffin and greeting the King family before taking his seat in the front left pew, beside Senator Edward Kennedy.

In his final sermon at Ebenezer, on February 4, King had spoken at length about the type of funeral he wanted and the message he hoped it would convey, and a recording of those words played before the services began.

If any of you are around when I have to meet my day, I don't want a long funeral. And if you get somebody to deliver the eulogy, tell him not to talk too long . . . tell him not to mention that I have a Nobel Peace Prize—that isn't important. Tell him not to mention that I have three hundred or four hundred other awards—that's not important. Tell him not to mention where I went to school. . . . I'd like somebody to mention that day that Martin Luther King Jr. tried to give his life serving others. I'd like for somebody to say that Martin Luther King Jr. tried to love somebody.

King's coffin, made from African mahogany, had been lying in at Sisters Chapel at Spelman College since Saturday, where some sixty thousand people had filed by in respect. The casket had a glass top. "Martin's body seemed small," Wilkins said.[18]

Monday night the coffin had been moved to Ebenezer. Two hundred onlookers stood by in the rain, flanked by an all-black detachment of Atlanta police officers. Eight pallbearers had carried the coffin inside the church, where a long line of dignitaries filed by, including Robert Kennedy and Ethel, who were cheered as they left the church. The coffin now sat at the front of the sanctuary, topped with a large cross of white chrysanthemums and flanked by arrangements of more chrysanthemums, along with lilies and roses.

The service began at 10:43 with a sermon by Ralph Abernathy, King's aide de camp and his successor at the head of the SCLC. His friend's death, Abernathy said, was "one of the darkest hours of mankind." King's closest friend and one of the men with him when he died, Abernathy told the audience he had not eaten since the assassination. "I am seeking to purify my soul," he said, in preparation for taking on King's job. "I will continue my fast until I am satisfied and thoroughly convinced that I am ready for the task at hand." Fasting, he noted, was a common practice between him and King; they never ate during their first twenty-four hours in jail, the better to prepare themselves for their stay.

One of King's fellow Atlanta pastors, Rev. Ronald English, then offered a prayer, for comfort and wisdom. "We raise the perennial question of Job: Why?" he said. "Like a wild, carnivorous beast, history has turned upon our own because it could not bear the truth." He concluded by praying that "this country will not be rent asunder by the black masses."[19]

Joining them at the podium was Wesley Theological Seminary dean Harold DeWolfe, who had worked with King on his doctorate at Boston University. "Dr. King sought to relieve the slavery of the oppressors as well as that of the oppressed," he intoned. "It is now for us, all the millions of the living who care, to take up his torch of love. It is for us to finish his work, to end the awful destruction in Vietnam, to root out every trace of race prejudice from our lives, to bring the massive powers of the nation to aid the oppressed, and to heal the hate-scarred world." His words rang true inside the sanctuary, but few could have much hope that they could stand up in Chicago or Baltimore—or their vast suburbs. More than a few people inside Ebenezer that day must have wondered if they were burying King, or the movement he had led.

At the end, Martin Luther King Sr. read his son's April 3 speech at Mason Temple. "Free at last, free at last, thank God almighty I am free at last," the father said, standing over the body of his son. Muffled sobs wafted through the cavernous sanctuary. The service, planned for thirty minutes, went until noon.

Many of the gathered dignitaries left right afterward; only a few joined the three-and-a-half-mile march, including Rockefeller and Robert Kennedy (though Rockefeller eventually gave in and drove part of the way). The others were hardly missed—some fifty thousand people, who had waited patiently outside the church until the service concluded, walked silently down Auburn Avenue, past bars and honky-tonks, small businesses and law offices, all closed. The marchers stretched from one side of the road to the other, and went on for thirty blocks. At their head marched Mrs. King and her children, her face still veiled. King's coffin traveled on a crude wooden farm wagon pulled by two mules, symbolizing his plans for the Poor People's Campaign, now cut short. Marchers joined Aretha Franklin in singing "We Shall Overcome."[20]

Kennedy walked with his sleeves rolled up and his jacket slung over his shoulder. The crowds, otherwise somber, cheered as he strode past them. People ran from the sides to offer him Cokes and water. The well-wishers were almost all black. The columnist Jimmy Breslin, walking beside him, said, "You'd think even a few of them [whites] would come out and just look, even for curiosity."

"You'd think so," Kennedy replied.

"Then maybe this thing won't change anything at all?"

"Oh, I don't think this will mean anything," Kennedy said. Charles Evers was on his other side. "Charles," he asked, "do you think this will mean anything?"

"Nothing," his comarcher said. "Didn't mean nothing when my brother was killed."

"I know."[21]

The weather was clear and bright, eighty degrees with light winds that cooled the marchers as they went. Nevertheless, dozens fainted from the heat and the press of the crowd; aid stations set up along the way treated hundreds. An estimated hundred thousand people stood quietly along the route as the marchers passed. The crowd wound past the state capitol, where Maddox sat. As it moved over the Hunter Street Viaduct and into the black West Side, several pockets began to sing "We Shall Overcome" and "This Little Light of Mine."

The SCLC and the APD had worked out an agreement in which the conference would handle the actual march while the police watched from afar, and hundreds of SCLC workers acted as parade marshals. In white armbands, they stood on the side of the route, saying politely, "Move back just a little, please" and "We'd like just a little more room on this side, if you don't mind."[22]

The marchers reached Morehouse shortly before 3:00 P.M., settling at a corner of the campus surrounded by thousands of flower bouquets and azalea bushes sent by well-wishers from around the country. By then some 150,000 people had joined the procession. In an open-air general service at King's alma mater, Benjamin Mays, one of his many mentors and now president emeritus of the school, once again invoked King's memory and the new mission he had taken up at the end of his life.

"I make bold to assert that it took more courage for King to practice nonviolence than it took his assassin to fire the fatal shot," Mays said. "He believed especially that he was sent to champion the cause of the man farthest down. He would probably say that, if death had to come, I'm sure there was no greater cause to die for than fighting to get a just wage for garbage collectors."

Mahalia Jackson sang "Precious Lord, Take My Hand" as hundreds wept and shouted. Abernathy then rose and called on a series of dignitaries to come speak—Nixon, Humphrey—most likely knowing that none of them had stuck around. Kennedy was there, though, and he rose to give a few words, his third impromptu eulogy for King in five days. Then others rose to join him, including his fellow New York senator, Javits. The ceremony had to be cut short, though, because by then so many out of towners in the crowd, not used to such sultry weather so early in the year, were falling from heatstroke and exhaustion; an address by Rosa Parks, among others, went undelivered.

The funeral cortege moved on again, another four miles to South View Cemetery. There King would be buried next to his maternal grandparents, Adam and Jenny Williams. Under the blooming dogwoods of early spring, Abernathy said, "The cemetery is too small for his spirit but we submit his body to the ground. The grave is too narrow for his soul, but we commit his body to the ground. No coffin, no crypt, no stone can hold his greatness. But we submit his body to the ground."

The doors to the family crypt were closed shortly before 5:30. Mrs. King, having retained her quiet composure throughout, lowered her veiled face and wept gently. King's epitaph read, "Free at last; free at last; thank God Almighty I'm free at last."

Violence did not erupt in Atlanta that day, nor did it spike in Chicago, Baltimore, or Washington. Kansas City wasn't so lucky. Monday afternoon hundreds of high school students converged on Civic Plaza, in front of City Hall, where a series of speakers from the black community were holding a rally. Mayor Ilus Davis, bullhorn in hand and standing atop a nearby car, pleaded in vain for them to go home. Finally, a minister from Holy Name Church announced he would sponsor a dance that evening, the better to vent frustrations. That seemed to cool people off, and they began to disperse.

As they did, though, a few nervous police officers set off tear gas. That got other cops going, and soon twenty-four grenades were spewing gas through the crowd. People began running, some for home, but many to nearby shopping streets, where they began smashing windows. "An elderly lady stepped out from First National Bank onto the Tenth Street sidewalk and was knocked down by a gang of three or four who grabbed her purse and ran," recalled one eyewitness.[23]

Davis issued an emergency proclamation ordering rioters to desist, set an 8:00 P.M. curfew, and banned all liquor, gun, and gasoline sales. Nevertheless, mobs of rioters tore apart the black sections of the city that night, as well as Country Club Plaza, a fashionable shopping district. Arsonists set fires, looters ransacked stores. They threw rocks and bottles and even took potshots at police and firemen. Police shot and killed one looter before finally bringing order back to the city by midnight.[24]

But the violence continued the next night, after a late-afternoon rally of several hundred students at Municipal Stadium. Because the rally went peacefully, the city assumed the worst was over, and Davis didn't issue a curfew. But as night fell, violence broke out on the predominantly black East Side of the city, much worse than on the previous night. Five people were killed, and a fireman was shot and wounded. The police and the three thousand National Guardsmen who had been rushed in could do little to stanch the rioting. Rioters were even seen tossing Molotov cocktails from moving cars as passersby.

Kansas City didn't come under full control until Thursday. In the end, six people were dead and six hundred arrested.[25]

There was some good news that day, though. In Washington, the Rules Committee in the House finally met to vote on the fair housing bill. But along the way the bill had also been sweetened, for conservatives at least, with a strong antiriot provision, something they had been proposing for several years. The bill made it a federal crime to cross, or broadcast across, state lines with the intent to incite a riot; it also made it a crime to teach the construction or use of firearms, bombs, and other weapons to be used in a riot. Though the White House and congressional liberals blanched at the vagueness of these planks—what constituted intent? If someone merely gave a fiery speech that happened to lead to a riot, would that count?—they accepted it as the price to pay for fair housing.

Nevertheless, the vote was razor-close, 8 to 7. Anderson's conversion was, it turned out, the key to passage. With the bill out of committee, it proceeded to the floor. On Wednesday opponents made a stormy last-minute effort to send it to a joint House-Senate conference, which was defeated 220 to 195. "This is spineless capitulation to those with nothing but contempt for law and order," said Iowa republican H. R. Gross. "The flag should be at half staff for this once-great nation."[26] But he failed to persuade enough of his colleagues. The bill passed soon after, 250 to 171. It was, Johnson said in a statement immediately after, "a victory for all Americans." The bill then went to the White House for his signature the next day.[27]

Passage of the Civil Rights Act of 1968, the bill's formal title, was a real achievement. By reaching into the buying and selling of individual homes, in essence setting rules for what people were allowed to do with their own property, it represented a new step in federal activism. But it also took King's death to make it happen, hardly a positive reflection on the moral courage of American politicians.

And if it stood out as a symbol, the act was something less so in substance. Congress later refused to fund its antihousing discrimination planks, making it, for the time being, toothless. Moreover, two months later the Supreme Court obviated much of the bill's utility in *Jones v. Alfred H. Mayer Co.*, in which it ruled that the 1866 Civil Rights Act forbade housing discrimination. Arguably the bill did a lot less than the wave of state- and local-level bans, which were better enforced and better targeted to regional particularities, that swept the nation in the coming years. And in cold political terms, the bill's passage gave a leg up to Republicans, many of whom, at Nixon's behest, ended up supporting it to get civil rights out of the 1968 campaign.

Even as its House and Senate supporters were celebrating its passage, they publicly recognized that it was likely the last hurrah of Johnsonian liberalism, and, worse, that it was likely the most they could hope from in a political climate quickly turning to the right. It was now all but admitted that Johnson wouldn't deliver his promised address to Congress, and that there wouldn't be any more new social legislation coming to either chamber's floor in the coming months. "This is no time to sit tight," pleaded Connecticut Democratic senator Abraham Ribicoff. "We know what we have to do. Will the crisis be set aside until every know-nothing has had his say? The immediate need is money."[28]

But no one, likely not even Ribicoff, thought that would happen. Johnson was giving up; he had felt such hope, such momentum, right up until the moment his aide handed him the note about King's assassination. He had thought that by withdrawing he could regain some sort of control. As an ardent New Dealer, he truly believed in the power of the government—and, at its head, the president—to shape the nation's destiny. But in the course of a week, history had taught him otherwise.

At times, he privately lashed out at black America. "I asked so little in return," he later lamented. "Just a little thanks. Just a little appreciation. That's all. But look what I got instead. Riots in 175 cities. Looting. Burning. Shooting. It ruined everything."[29]

In one telling memo, Califano confronted his boss, writing, "You are publicly on record promising a message. Failure to deliver will be considered a breach of faith by the entire Negro community and a good deal of the influential white community." Johnson angrily scribbled in reply, "I promised nothing. Stated my intentions only. Since changed by riots."[30]

He had naively hoped that a massive assault of federal spending would change the ghetto overnight; when 120 ghettos erupted over a single weekend, he had to confront the fact that nothing he had done seemed to have had an effect. Over time, Johnson turned from bitterness to ironic reflection. As he later told Doris Kearns Goodwin, "God knows how little we've really moved on this issue, despite all the fanfare. As I see it, I've moved the Negro from D+ to C−. He's still nowhere. He knows it. And that's why he's out in the streets.

"Hell," he said, "I'd be there, too."[31]

16

April 10 and 11
TWO SPEECHES

Wednesday was a day for picking up pieces. Early that morning all but one battalion of the Tennessee National Guard withdrew from Memphis, and the remaining unit pulled out at midnight. The army officers who had been sent to Pittsburgh for potential deployment were called home. Squadrons of insurance adjusters descended on Chicago, Washington, and Baltimore to assess the damage. Chicago even set up an office for them near the heart of the West Side damage. Califano and Clark talked that night and agreed that the attorney general would call Daley, D'Alesandro, and Washington; if they felt safe, then he would recommend that the troops be redeployed and the National Guard defederalized.

The Oscars, postponed from Monday, went on that night (it was a great year for film: *In the Heat of the Night* beat out *The Graduate* and *Bonnie and Clyde* for best picture, while Rod Steiger and Katharine Hepburn snagged the lead acting awards). In Washington, the Senators baseball team finally played their season opener, the first game of a double-header against the Minnesota Twins that they had twice delayed (the Senators lost both games, 2 to 0 and 5 to 4). Thirty-two thousand people attended the game, and they left without incident.

Demolition and rubble clearance began, and the city lobbied the Small Business Administration for disaster loans to help the hundreds of shop owners and other small businesspeople affected by the riots.

Troops still patrolled the streets, but they also got to relax: several hundred received tickets to the baseball game, while others were treated to a magnificent seafood dinner at Hogart's, a fancy restaurant on the city's Southwest waterfront. They bivouacked at three colleges, three parks, and fourteen junior and senior high schools, and as a show of thanks, divisional bands gave concerts for students. But the troop presence didn't make everyone happy. Mayor Washington, for one, was grating under the added requirements that a federal presence brought, as well as the gifts and plaudits heaped on the regular soldiers instead of his police and firemen. "These guys were being paraded around and feted and partied, and we had a serious matter," he said later.[1]

It was also the first day of near-normalcy in the White House. With the rioting under control and the fair-housing bill headed to passage, they could all relax a bit. Lady Bird returned from her Texas trip that afternoon, landing at Dulles and taking a White House limousine into town. "I drove home," she wrote in her diary, "with that sense of expectancy that you might have on a battlefield looking for trenches and gutted buildings and, of course, saw nothing except very silent and deserted streets." No one apparently informed her that the rioting mostly occurred in the "other" Washington, the part that first ladies and other dignitaries rarely see.[2]

Johnson returned from Camp David, and that evening he and Lady Bird played host to the first formal event since King's death, a state dinner with Austrian chancellor Josef Klaus. "We welcome you to this beautiful Washington spring," Johnson said as the two leaders stood before the press on the South Lawn of the White House that morning. "There is turbulence today in America—and in Eastern Europe—and in Southeast Asia—and there is hope in all these places." Notedly, he spoke of the need for "self-discipline" between the races—a far cry down from his earlier admonitions for understanding and cooperation.[3]

The evening was a fine affair. Klaus, just beginning a nationwide tour of the United States, showered Johnson with gifts, including a Bulova clock and a black lizard-skin traveling case. Along with the administration's top officials, present at the 140-person dinner were Douglas MacArthur Jr., ambassador to Austria; Kurt Waldheim,

Austrian minister of foreign affairs; and perhaps the most famous living Austrian in America, Maria von Trapp. After the meal Sarah Vaughan sang, while Van Cliburn played Beethoven's Sonata in E-flat Major and several Chopin pieces.[4]

Normal was relative, of course. For many the new normal would be much harsher. Approximately 90 percent of the stores within a one-block radius of Fourteenth and U had been looted or burned; in most cases, both. Up Fourteenth, only one store between Irving and Park had been left untouched. A Secret Service survey team, weaving its way through sightseers now teeming around the riot area, reported that there was "not much left to loot on Fourteenth Street NW and Seventh Street NW except in the downtown area."[5] In the eyes of many who later analyzed the riots, that was the only reason the disorder had ended.

The next afternoon, April 11, some one hundred of Baltimore's leading black figures gathered at the State Office Building downtown, at Governor Agnew's request. On April 6, his office had issued a press release citing the need to "consolidate gains that have already been made in the civil rights field and to chart a positive course for the future" and inviting "prominent leaders of the Negro community" to "a frank and far-reaching discussion of the problems that have faced this State and nation."[6] Almost all the invitees came, curious about how the governor would lead the state back from the riots.

Agnew had always seemed like a person the state civil rights establishment could work with—not necessarily an ally, but not an enemy, either. He had run on a racially moderate platform, after all, and he appeared to understand the root causes of ghetto violence. After the riots in Newark and Detroit, he had said, "It is evident that there is ample cause for unrest in our cities. There is still discrimination and, in too many cases, there are deplorable slum conditions"—a far cry from the law-and-order-at-all-costs rhetoric coming from many of his fellow Republicans.[7] Best of all, despite his early opposition, he was slowly coming around to support for thorough open-housing legislation. On the same day he issued his invitation to black leaders, he called on the state's congressional representatives to back the federal fair housing bill.[8]

But recently, away from the public, Agnew had been hardening his stance on race relations. It started with Cambridge. The governor had a tape recording of H. Rap Brown's incendiary speech from earlier in the year, the speech that purportedly led to a night of rioting. The tape obsessed him: Agnew played it over and over, for guests, staffers, anyone who would listen. "He paced up and down as it played," recalled one visitor, "in great distress, and said, 'How can we put up with agitators like this?'" Guests tried to tell him that Brown was more a symptom than a cause, that cities rioted with or without "agitators." And views like Brown's were hardly news to anyone who paid attention to the real black community. But Agnew wouldn't listen. He demanded regular intelligence reports on militant activity. Black radicals, he seemed to believe, were the answer to everything. This, here, was why blacks were rioting. It was militancy that kept blacks from being happy with what the white majority gave them. It was ruining the cities and, to hear his neighbors tell it, even threatening his beloved suburbs. "For Agnew," wrote Garry Wills in *Nixon Agonistes*, "it was a time of lurid revelation."[9]

The week leading up to King's assassination and the riots provided more fodder for Agnew's obsession. On Wednesday, April 3, an undercover cop reported that he had overheard Stokely Carmichael in a Baltimore café telling an unidentified local civil rights figure, "The only way to deal with the white man is across the barrel of a gun." It was over this exchange that Agnew had first conceived his meeting with the black leaders. Here was the world-famous black militant fomenting violence in Agnew's hometown! And worse, no one in the black community seemed to care. "This perturbed him to no end," recalled Colonel Robert Lally, the superintendent of the Maryland state police.[10]

Nor did it help that for weeks Agnew had been dealing with a simmering crisis at Bowie State, a black college halfway between Washington and Annapolis. Since late March the students had been protesting poor dormitory and classroom conditions, as well as the denial of tenure for a popular professor. On March 27, the student body president, Roland Smith, led two hundred students in a series of boycotts and sit-ins; overnight, class attendance dropped 90 percent.

Things came to a head the morning of April 4, when Smith and other leaders heard erroneous reports that Agnew was planning to visit a student protest at white-majority Towson State, in suburban

Baltimore. Smith organized chartered buses, and hundreds of students headed to Annapolis, where that afternoon they launched a sit-in at the State House. Agnew was incensed; such disruption violated his sense of orderly progress. He ordered the protesters arrested and the school closed. The police hauled 227 to jail.

The news of King's assassination came as they were being processed. Several began to cry. Finally, a sympathetic Bowie State professor arrived and convinced the police to release the students into his custody. It was raining outside, and all the students wanted to do was go back to their dorm rooms. But Agnew hadn't just closed the school. Fearing violence, he had evacuated the campus. State police descended on Bowie State, rousting students from their bedrooms. Many had nowhere to go. Most eventually found transportation and housing, and a few were finally let back onto the campus. Agnew, who had handled the crisis personally, certainly knew of their plight. But in his mind he had already done enough—they were, after all, agitators.[11]

By April 11, then, Agnew had already spent two weeks stewing in his own self-righteousness. That morning he sent copies of his speech to local news outlets, knowing that once they read it they would flock to the steps of the State Office Building. One of the TV stations called D'Alesandro for comment; it was the first he had heard about it. The speech was, he learned, indeed "frank and far-reaching," just as the governor had promised. Whether it would lead to a "discussion" was unclear. It was nothing less than a bomb, an attack on the black establishment at precisely the moment when blacks and whites needed to step back from the rhetorical weaponry.

D'Alesandro hurriedly called Agnew. "Governor, can you, can you either not make the statement or redo the statement or not call for a declaration of war with the black community?" he pleaded. "Smoke is still present in the city; let's just have a cooling-off period." "Sorry," Agnew replied coldly. "Tommy, I'll tell you, Tommy, that's how I feel and I am going to say it and I'm going to stick by my statement."[12]

Agnew knew he was taking a big risk. He told his aides he was "committing political suicide." But he had to make a stand—the day before he had received a death threat. That, if nothing else, flipped his switch. He had orchestrated his own Marathon—or his Waterloo. For hours before the meeting, he met in his office upstairs with Lally, Pomerlau, and Gelston. In the middle of their talk he sent Herb Thompson, his press aide, to find Gil Ware, his only black adviser and supposedly his expert on race relations. But by the time Ware got to the room, they were getting ready to head down. Thompson grabbed a copy of the speech and handed it to Ware. "Gil, you won't like it." Ware didn't even know there were prepared remarks in the first place. He, like everyone else outside Agnew's circle, thought this was supposed to be a discussion.

Meanwhile, the assembled black leaders were being lectured to by Charles Bressler, the governor's real estate expert and another of his inner circle. They were on edge since walking in—state police had frisked them as they came through the door, as if they might be carrying Molotov cocktails in their briefcases and purses. The topic of Bressler's impromptu speech was minority advancement. "Charlie gave us a little talk on how his people had worked their way up in the world by industry and thrift," recalled Parren Mitchell, who ran the city's poverty program. "I didn't think we needed that lesson in the history of minorities." Clarence Mitchell III, who had heard a very different take on black-white relations from President Johnson six days earlier, said, "Bressler's speech about 'all his father wanted was a little place to open a business' irritated us before the governor even arrived. We were ready to walk out then."[13] Several reporters and news cameras were there, too. One *Baltimore Sun* reporter characterized Bressler's speech as "the most offensive thing I had ever heard north of Mississippi."[14]

At 2:00 P.M. the doors at the back of the room suddenly swung open and Agnew strode in, with state troopers in front of and behind him. Switching course in midsentence, Bressler introduce his boss. "Ladies and gentlemen, the governor of Maryland." Behind Agnew came Ware, Pomerlau, Lally, and Gelston—the martial Gelston in a taut uniform and paratrooper boots, a riding crop under his arm. Even Bressler was taken aback. "It looked like the Gestapo was ready to interrogate you," he said later. Lally, who was not supposed to be there, took a seat at the dais alongside Pomerlau, Gelston, and Agnew. Ware, left chairless, stood in the corner.

Agnew immediately began his speech. "Hard on the heels of tragedy comes the assignment of blame and the excuses. I did not invite you here for either purpose," he said. At the same time, he went on, "I did not request your presence to bid for peace with the public dollar." He noted the moderation of the assembled leaders. "If you'll observe, the ready-mix, instantaneous type of leader is not present. The circuit-riding, Hanoi-visiting type of leader is missing from this assembly."

But when militants such as local bomb-thrower Bob Moore—a name he couldn't even bring himself to speak—criticized them, "You ran." Gasps went up around the room.

Even worse, he said, "You met in secret with that demagogue and others like him—and you agreed, according to published reports that have not been denied"—and here he waved around a newspaper article that described a recent meeting with Moore—"that you would not openly criticize any black spokesman, regardless of the content of his remarks." The remarks were completely unfair. Many of those assembled had just spent the past several days pushing back against the riots, and the article described a completely different meeting, a realistic attempt to bridge a yawning gap in the black leadership, not a capitulation.

People began getting up to leave. "Nobody calls me a coward," Parren Mitchell said of the moment. "I had gone forty-eight hours without sleep, walking streets at war, trying to calm them." As they exited the building, the departing leaders were met by reporters and camera crews. The Reverend Frank Bascom, one of the first, told reporters, "He is as sick as any bigot in America. He is as sick as anything I have seen in America."[15]

About twenty of the hundred stayed to hear Agnew dive into conspiratorial thoughts about the riots. "The looting and rioting which has engulfed out city during the past several days did not occur by chance," he charged. "It is no mere coincidence that a national disciple of violence, Stokely Carmichael, was observed meeting with local black-power advocates and known criminals on April 3, 1968, three days before the Baltimore riots began"—a conspiracy theory with no basis in fact and, as Wills notes, a theory that works only if an even larger conspiracy was at work, one that would have coordinated Carmichael's April 3 visit with King's assassination a day later.[16]

Agnew continued his harangue. "I publicly repudiate, condemn, and reject all white racists. I call upon you to publicly repudiate, condemn, and reject all black racists. This, so far, you have not been willing to do." Again, untrue. Clarence Mitchell had recently denounced the "bigotry" of black militants on the floor of the State Senate.

At one point NAACP activist Juanita Jackson Mitchell rose to respond. Agnew cut her off. "Do you repudiate black racists?" he demanded. "Are you willing, as I am willing to repudiate the white racists, are you willing to repudiate the Carmichaels and the Browns?"

Mitchell was momentarily flustered. "We have already done so. Didn't you read our—"

"Answer me!" he screamed, his face reddening. "Answer me! Do you repudiate Stokely Carmichael and Rap Brown? Do you? Do you?"

Mitchell left, along with several others. As she got up, one of the attendees said, "If you want to talk to us like ladies and gentlemen, Mr. Governor, we'll stay and listen."

Those who walked out met at a church across the street. There they quickly drafted a statement in response, which they rushed out to the reporters. "We are shocked at the gall of the governor, suggesting that only he can define the nature of the leadership of the black community," it read. "Agnew's actions are more in keeping with the slave system of a bygone era. At a time when the chief executive should be calling for unity, he deliberately sought to divide us."

But Agnew didn't care. To him, the line in the sand he had just drawn was an indelible one; those who came to his side were in the right, while those who didn't were no different from militants. It mattered little that he delivered his ultimatum in a blunt and insulting manner at a highly tense moment. When someone later asked him what he'd have done if everyone had walked out, he merely replied, "I would have simply have been faced with a situation where I would have to find other Negro leaders."[17]

The story of Agnew's ambush made national news immediately, and Agnew became a national figure almost overnight. Many figured that fame was precisely what he'd been looking for. It soon became public that Agnew, who had been courting the Nelson Rockefeller presidential campaign, had been snubbed by the New York liberal; in response, people theorized, he was tacking to the right in order to appeal to the Nixon people. "You go with the breeze," Clarence Mitchell III said later.

But Agnew's rise was never about political scheming. He was almost instinctively unable to change his political tack in midcourse. In fact, what makes Agnew significant is that in his mind he never changed tack at all—it was the rest of the country that did.

Agnew spoke as much for as to the white suburbs, and it showed in the reception following the speech. He was condemned by black newspapers and civil rights leaders, along with many liberals. Even his "friend" D'Alesandro told the *Baltimore Sun* that the governor's words were "somewhat inflammatory" and that "this is a bad time to say what he said."[18] But Agnew played pretty well where it counted. The suburban Maryland papers loved him. The editorial board of the *Bethesda-Chevy Chase Tribune* said, "He was blunt but he was honest."[19] The *Catoctin Enterprise* of Frederick County, Maryland, castigated the black leaders for walking out. "They could," it said, "with much more grace, admit the Governor's indictment and confess that in this crisis their expected leadership in time of tension failed to develop."[20] The *Suburban Record*, a Montgomery County paper, was even more enthusiastic. "Governor Agnew is to be commended for his forthright remarks," it wrote. "A white person's fear of having integration come too close to his door has become a wholly understandable fear."[21] The next day Agnew's office released some of the correspondence it had received in support. One said via telegram, "I would like to congratulate you for standing up for the average middle-class American." Another said, "Thank you for telling them off."[22]

Nor was his appeal limited to the city and its environs. By the end of the month his staff reported that it had received 7,588 pieces of correspondence supporting his position from around the country and only 1,042 opposed.[23] His position as a "liberal Republican" who dared to go against the ideological grain was endorsed by *Human Events*, a national conservative weekly, as well as, more disturbingly, the racist National States Rights Party. In the minds of many, Agnew and Daley were speaking the same language. "Both men spoke the truth if ever the truth has been spoken," wrote one reader to the *Washington Post*. "Governor Agnew is that type of man who is needed in the White House."[24]

If Agnew's April 11 speech and ensuing jump to the national stage foreshadowed a dark time for urban, big-government liberalism, a speech given that same day, just down the Baltimore-to-Washington parkway, was its swan song.

The mood in the White House was on the upswing. The riots were over, Lady Bird was back from Texas, and the president had yet another historic civil rights bill on his desk in the East Room, waiting for his signature. Some two hundred people attended the signing—civil rights leaders, congressmen, cabinet secretaries, key aides.

Johnson sat at the desk, beaming. As tradition holds, he used hundreds of pens to ink his name to the bill, one of which would go to each of the attendees. Dozens of men, black and white, jostled behind him, trying to get a good view of those historic pen strokes.

When he finished, Johnson rose to a lectern. Two years ago to the month, he said, he had convened a meeting in the Cabinet Room, where he had signed a message to Congress calling for a fair housing bill. "Few in the nation, and the record will show that very few in that room that afternoon, believed that fair housing would in our time become the unchallenged law of this land," he said. "And indeed this bill has had a long and stormy trip."

But finally it had arrived, and its passage was a historic occasion. Johnson often compared himself to Abraham Lincoln, and he often thought of his administration's work as a Second Reconstruction, a completion of what his Republican predecessor had begun. He carried that theme into his speech. The Emancipation Proclamation, he said, was just that—"a proclamation. It was not a fact." To realize its promise took Reconstruction, the Supreme Court in 1954, the Civil Rights Act of 1964, and the Voting Rights Act. "Now with this bill the voice of justice speaks again. It proclaims that fair housing for all—all human beings who live in this country—is now a part of the American way of life."

But he couldn't avoid discussing the riots. "We all know that the roots of injustice run deep, but violence cannot redress a solitary wrong or remedy a single unfairness," he said. Looting and rioting could never be justified. To stop them, though, America needed to make further progress on social and economic justice. "And so I urge the Congress to enact the measures for social justice that I have recommended in some twenty messages. These messages went to the Congress in January and February of this year," he said. "These measures provide more than $78 billion that I have urged the Congress to enact for major domestic programs for all Americans." The fair housing bill, he said, was a good start—"we can all take some heart that democracy's work is being done. In the Civil Rights Act of 1968 America does move forward and the bell of freedom rings out a little louder"—but it wasn't enough. "We have come some of the way, not nearly all of it," he said. "There is much yet to do."[25]

When he was done, Lady Bird, in a bright green dress, took his arm and led him to the receiving line. He shook hands with each of the attendees. Then he walked slowly back to the Oval Office. It had been a long week.

17

A Summer Postscript

Unlike Tolstoy's unhappy families, in the months following the riots every postriot city seemed to follow a similar pattern: Pleas for federal aid, followed by furious planning efforts to rebuild, followed by little or no financial backing to make it happen. These were not small efforts, either. In Washington alone, the riot resulted in $57.6 million in property damage ($354.1 million in 2007 dollars).

A survey of business owners found that 97 percent of those affected were white, resulting in the shuttering of 510 businesses. The destruction of local businesses resulted in nearly 5,000 lost jobs, 57 percent of which were held by blacks; many more were lost as the riots' impact coursed through the local economy. Part of the reason was laid to insurance companies, which, as happened across the country, paid at best 40 percent of the damage. And 2,115 people were permanently displaced from their homes.

The federal government refused to step in with any large-scale aid. The Small Business Association denied disaster grants to District businesses until the city came up with a comprehensive rebuilding plan—a ridiculous condition when the disaster was man-made and the underlying causes were still very much in evidence. And federal and local job-training programs were intermittently successful at best—and in any case, training meant little if the jobs didn't exist in the first place.[1]

Without political impetus, even Washington, the nation's capital, was left to fester. The city government actually charged owners for cleaning up riot damage, with the obvious result that some damage was simply not cleaned up. Promised urban renewal schemes had the perverse effect of stymieing development, as owners refused to invest in areas that were slated for bulldozing anyway. A year after the riots, of the three hundred commercial buildings completely destroyed in the District, only two had been replaced, both by liquor stores.[2]

As one witness at a May 1969 congressional hearing put it, "Walking along Fourteenth, Seventh, and H streets, you will see very little progress in physical improvements beyond the removal of the debris of the civil disorders, the demolition of those building shells which were a menace to the public health and safety, the start of con-struction of a small park, and some buildings that have been repaired or rebuilt by the property owners. No large-scale public or private rebuilding has yet begun."[3]

The problem was not just at the federal level. The Washington government wasn't getting much done, either. The city had announced at the outset that it would involve community organizations in every step of the rebuilding. The problem was, it left the offer open-ended—and, not surprisingly, within weeks scores of community groups sprung up representing all aspects of D.C. life, legitimate or not, all demanding an equal seat at the planning board. No framework other than town-hall-style meetings existed, and as a result the loudest and most radical groups and coalitions got heard. As one report concluded about a 1968 town-hall planning meeting, "The more militant voices spoke for a 'no white' policy, suggesting that unless all planning and rebuilding by white people be stopped, another burning would occur. There was anger in the talk of many black witnesses—suspicion of white motives and purpose."[4]

At the very worst moment, the relationship between the civic body politic and the civic leadership became inverted. What should have been a process for informed community participation became, for lack of a better term, a hostage situation. Marion Barry, then the head of PRIDE, Inc., demanded that all rebuilding aid go to black-owned businesses, and that all white-owned businesses cede at least 51 percent of their operations within black parts of the city to black ownership. "When the city rebuilds the riot corridors, if you don't let my black brothers control the process—and I mean all the way to owning the property—it might just get burned down again," he said.[5] He didn't get his wish, but he wasn't contravened, either. When existing business owners called for the city government to improve security and help guard against future riots, the City Council simply stated, "Absolute assurance cannot, of course, be given."[6]

Not surprisingly, many property owners weren't interested in rebuilding. In the wake of the riots, violent crime of all sorts—from muggings to store holdups to arson to murder—skyrocketed; by May 894 major crimes were taking place each week. Store owners reported threats from local militants—often common criminals posing as militants—to "pay or burn." In late April, after shopkeeper Ben Brown was murdered in his store, an ad appeared in the *Washington Post* that read, "Where will the tragedy strike next? Today, the Inner City. Tomorrow, the residential areas, the suburbs. Today, Ben Brown. Tomorrow???"[7] On May 17 the *Post* ran an open letter to Johnson and Washington from the Greater Washington Division of the Maryland-Delaware-District of Columbia Jewelers' Association, which declared, "The District of Columbia has become a disaster area and a battleground."[8]

The exodus of inner-city business owners would have mattered less if there had been enough qualified black business owners to take over. But, as Lyndon Johnson noted in his famous 1965 Howard University address, you cannot remove the chains from a man after two hundred years and expect him to win a race. Likewise, it was simply unrealistic to expect that people with little to no business training, in some cases little to no effective formal education, could take over from the fleeing business establishment. Some could, but most couldn't. Generic job training didn't prepare people to balance books, maintain inventory, or deal with customers (some community-minded business owners did, however, volunteer to train would-be businessmen, to great effect).

As Senator Abraham Ribicoff noted during a 1969 hearing, the city was essentially planning an entirely new town of forty thousand people—new commercial centers, new housing, new community leaders. "Now you have a period, as I see it, for at least two or three years before these businesses open," he said dejectedly. The city simply couldn't wait that long and remain viable.

Washington wasn't alone that summer. Baltimore, Chicago, Pittsburgh, Kansas City, and other cities hit hard by riots were lucky to just pick up the pieces; in no place did significant rebuilding get under way. And those cities that suffered only mild unrest—or, somehow, managed to escape it at all—spent the summer shivering in fear at the possibility of new violence. The white, middle-class public was disgusted with what they saw as an overly soft approach to rioters. In a CBS poll that summer, 70 percent of respondents felt the police "should have been tougher in their handling of riots."[9] A September Harris poll found that 81 percent of Americans felt law and order in the country had "broken down." Fifty-four percent said they felt uneasy on the streets, and 53 percent said that their unease was due to fear of racial violence.[10]

The April riots led to a near arms race among suburban whites. If the police, National Guard, even the army couldn't prevent riots, then men like Frank Bressler were going to take matters into their own hands. Between King's assassination and mid-May, gun sales went up 44 percent in Maryland, and through the end of April 11,275 new gun permits were issued in the state, double the number during the first four months of 1967.[11] In June the gun lobby defeated strong gun control provisions in the Safe Streets crime legislation through, according to the *Washington Post*, "a whispering campaign that the gun control bill would prevent white people from buying weapons to guard their homes against Negro rioters."[12] The gun craze got so bad in Detroit that Mayor Jerry Cavanaugh went on TV to declare, "This arms race must be stopped. We must return to sanity."[13]

And it wasn't just guns that people were buying—the home and commercial security industry, heretofore a relatively niche sector, exploded in 1968. As one president of a security firm told the *New York Times* in mid-April, "Naturally a great deal of fear psychology has developed during the last week's period. Our industrial plants are hollering for more manpower to supplement what we do for them."[14] *Chain Store Age*, a trade magazine, ran an article in May 1968 that asked, "If Rioters Come, Are You Ready for Them?"[15] The next month *Modern Manufacturing* ran a long article explaining how to "get your plant ready for riots."[16] And these weren't aimed only, or even primarily, at inner-city firms; as the latter article made clear, urban guerrillas might well seek out suburban stores and plants as targets. "Distance alone from 'riot areas' offers little or no protection from arson," it warned readers.

The Pentagon went into high gear as well. By mid-1968 the army had largely eclipsed the Department of Justice in the realm of riot preparation and domestic surveillance, thanks to its enormous resources. "There was a tendency at the Department of Defense to see us as a ma and pa operation with them as a national chain," said Attorney General Clark. "I think they were too busy with the Vietnam War to consider adequately the risk of militarizing domestic riot control and prevention."[17] Clark's impression wasn't unwarranted; as one later internal Defense report remarked, "It may be that the army got involved in collecting intelligence because subconsciously we did not feel we could rely on the Department of Justice intelligence collection and prediction efforts and we wanted our own independent sources."[18]

Plans for more intelligence went forward as well. It was the Department of Defense, not Justice, that in May 1968 gave $100,000 to the Washington government to beef up its undercover antimilitant efforts; the money went to equipment, training, and informant payments. The 116th Military Intelligence Group, based at Fort McNair in Southwest D.C., flooded the city with undercover agents; reports forwarded to City Hall reveal that they attended rallies, activist sessions, and even church services. Army agents infiltrated the caravans converging on Washington for the Poor People's Campaign. And an August 1968 memo indicates that the army even performed wiretapping operations, which it knew to be illegal.[19] A black agent registered at New York University in 1968 to spy on students in black studies courses.[20] The army even had agents posing as news cameramen—for "Mid-West Video"—at the Democratic National Convention.

The idea, it became clear, was to move beyond targeted infiltration to continuous monitoring nationwide. As General William Yarborough, the head of domestic intelligence, said at a meeting in April, "This has to do not with penetration of subversive groups but with widespread deployment of fingers on the pulse of the community—guys who listen in the barber shops, etcetera. Maybe we can discover some of the new radicals and find out what the hell is going on. They are writing up the plan now which will be fully coordinated."[21]

Likewise, after April 1968 the army boosted its operational preparedness. A domestic corollary of the DEFCON preparedness metric, "Civil Disturbance Readiness Condition" (CIDCON), was introduced. On the heels of the April riots the army established the 176-person Directorate for Civil Disturbances and Planning Operations, led by General George Mather (who had overseen the Chicago deployment), and in May it moved forward with plans to build a massive operations center, the Civil Disturbance Command Center (CDCC) within the Pentagon, dedicated to riot prevention and control. Its goal was to have the capacity to deploy 250,000 soldiers to 25 cities simultaneously, an amazingly ambitious plan for a military already involved in a major war.

"The approximately $13 million to $15 million [$80 million to $90 million in 2008 dollars] required would be a small price to pay for the possible savings of hundreds of millions of dollars in damages that might be suffered if the decisions to employ federal forces in riot-torn cities when needed are not made in a sound and timely manner," wrote Mather in a June 1968 memo.[22] Milton Hyman, who worked in the secretary of defense's office in the late 1960s, later concluded, "The April disturbances had a marked impact on all those military planners who were involved in it. The magnitude and multiplicity of the disturbances worried us greatly . . . the emphasis after the April disorders was on detailed planning at the headquarters level and the development of techniques to control multiple disturbances."[23]

Justice couldn't afford to match those kinds of resources, and tensions between the two departments grew. To make things worse, interdepartmental relations were further eroded by J. Edgar Hoover's zealous sense of political turfdom, and he consistently rejected army efforts at cooperation. A February 1968 Defense plan to run joint domestic spying operations into "designated organizations of civil disturbance interest," with FBI approval, was nixed by Hoover because it "did not provide for adequate FBI control."[24] In March 1968 the Pentagon had requested that the FBI assign a liaison officer to the Defense Department to help coordinate antiriot intelligence and planning; Hoover initially agreed but then quickly recanted, saying it was "too dangerous"—though he left Pentagon planners baffled as to what he meant.[25]

In short, it appeared by mid-1968 that the country was seeing the emergence of not one but two separate domestic intelligence operations—both of which had little concern for civil liberties and an overriding interest in monitoring and suppressing domestic dissent.

The riots also played a major role in the passage of the Omnibus Crime Control and Safe Streets Act that summer. While some sort of crime control package was inevitable—Johnson had promised as much in the 1968 State of the Union—the eventual legislation certainly gained political momentum from the destruction of the riots and the urban decay they uncovered. The final act gave $400 million in block grants to states, in effect a blank check, which many quickly began putting toward equipment and riot training. It established the Law Enforcement Assistance Administration, which, while certainly helping to improve professionalism at the local level, also served as a conduit for massive amounts of military and paramilitary equipment to flow into local and state police departments; it also created a reciprocity that tied local policymaking into a federal structure.

By laying the groundwork for future national crime policies—the War on Crime, the War on Drugs—the Safe Streets Act was, in the words of law professor Jonathan Simon, "the mother of all contemporary crime legislation."[26] The act presented significant civil liberties concerns as well: Title II lowered the standards for admissibility of confessions—a blatant pushback against the Supreme Court's *Miranda* ruling, the scourge of law-and-order conservatives—while Title III allowed for federal and local wiretapping, at times without court approval. Both Johnson and Clark promised not to utilize this latter plank, but they could do nothing about future administrations.

While there were no more riots of any significance in 1968—no repeat of the long, hot summer—the months following the April disorders were not entirely peaceful. Beginning in early May, the nation was treated to the civil rights Waterloo that was the Poor People's Campaign. For six weeks, several hundred poor whites, blacks, Hispanics, and Native Americans camped out in East Potomac Park, south of the Washington Monument. Many arrived by mule train. They set up a tent city and spread through the town, holding sit-ins, protest marches, and rallies. But they also suffered through torrential rains that turned the paths in their camp into rivers of mud—one punishing shower lasted seventeen hours.[27] Concerned local residents turned out to cook them food.

Many protesters, nevertheless, ended up leaving the camp before the police eventually tore it down. Nor did it help the campaign's image when the media reported that Ralph Abernathy and other leaders were staying warm and dry in local hotels. Their efforts were not totally in vain; Marian Wright (by then Marian Wright Edelman) and other activists used the occasion to push a bill to expand the food stamps program, which Congress soon passed. But the leadership's demand for an "economic bill of rights," including $30 billion in aid to the poor and a guaranteed national income, was a nonstarter. And the cost of any gains was high indeed—after the Poor People's Campaign, the civil rights movement was effectively dead as a political force, depriving the riot-torn ghetto of perhaps the only quarter of American society that could still militate for substantial public monies to help them revive.

There were, as well, a series of smaller riots that summer: Cleveland, Miami, and, of course, at the Chicago convention. But while this last incident was hardly a race riot, and while it took place far from the ghetto, such distinctions meant little to the millions who watched it on television. Nor did it make a difference to many of those who participated, on either side—a fact driven home by Haskell Wexler's 1969 pseudo-documentary account of the convention riots, *Medium Cool.* The film begins with live footage of Illinois National Guardsmen practicing riot tactics, bookended by comments from General Richard Dunn about the Guard's preparedness this time around. Of course, it didn't take a movie director to tell millions of Americans what they were seeing on TV. Watching students and leftists involved in the same riotous violence they had seen explode in the ghetto a few months earlier (even though postriot investigations roundly blamed the Chicago Police Department for inciting it), it was easy for the "silent majority" to decide that the entire spectrum of liberal America was hopelessly debased.

The campaign and the summer's "bumper" riots were only part of the reason for the movement's senescence. Though King never held anything like an official position atop the movement, his death left the remaining factions, already pushing against each other, to spin out of control. Like the Macedonian Empire after Alexander's death, the movement devolved into regional and ideological fiefdoms, often in competition with each other. Some leaders, such as Carmichael, simply gave up and left (in his case, for Ghana). Others, such as Barry, moved to solidify local control, while others, such as Jesse Jackson, tried to convert the centrist momentum of King's biracial movement into a national political power base.

This was not as bad as it sounded. The movement had arguably run its course. Local activism had always been an underexposed aspect of civil rights, and now it moved to the fore—and how. In Washington, for example, a newfound energy emerged around community issues such as education and policing; if some of the rhetoric was harshly critical of the white and middle-class black establishment, it also could be read as the birth pangs of a new era in black leadership, the actualization of the black power dream. Many of these young leaders—Barry most notably—began a long march through their local institutions, culminating, by the late 1970s, in their takeover of city councils, mayors' offices, and state house delegations.

And, oddly, the riots proved a major impetus in this movement. Rebuilding, no matter from what, can do that. "I think there was more hope that [city life] would get better," said Adrienne Israel, a 1968 Howard graduate who went on to be a local journalist and activist. "Did it actually get better? No. But I think there was more hope that there would be opportunities for poor people to improve themselves, for communities to get better, for polarization to lessen."[28] What followed, of course, was the dashing of that hope—shrinking federal funds, increasingly oppressive police action, rising crime, welfare dependency, and the crack epidemic.

Thus an irony: only in the wake of white retreat were black activists able to take the reins of local power. But the very mechanisms that gave them that power—a white withdrawal and a laserlike ideological focus on race—made it nearly impossible, at least for the next generation, to build a better life for their communities.

Perhaps the biggest short-term beneficiary of the April riots was Richard Nixon. The leading candidate for the GOP nomination by late spring, Nixon could hardly have asked for a more perfect event to encapsulate his evolving economic, political, and social critique of liberal America. The April riots seemed to vindicate a line of attack that the GOP had been building upon since Detroit, seven months prior: liberals had coddled the ghetto with welfare programs, and in doing so both prevented residents from taking opportunities to improve themselves and increased frustrations to the point of violence.

It was a message that began to emerge well before the riots. "Widespread rioting and violent civil disorder have grown to a national crisis since the present Administration took office," read a Republican National Committee press release in late July 1967.[29] Likewise, Nixon and his allies made dark predictions about the coming summer. "In Watts and Harlem and Detroit and Newark, we have a foretaste of what the organizers of insurrection are planning for the summers ahead," he said in a March 1968 address on NBC. "The violence being threatened for this summer is more in the nature of a war than a riot."[30] At the same time, though, he explicitly held back from making riots a full-bore issue, lest he repeat the racial-demagoguery trap into which Goldwater had fallen.

Nevertheless, when the riots did break out, Nixon was perfectly poised to pick up the pieces of a broken liberalism. He spoke of efforts to renew cities—"The fact is that all the money in the world wouldn't solve the problems in our cities today," he told *Time*. "We won't get at the real problems unless and until we rescue the people in the ghetto from despair and dependency."[31] He demanded more job training. He called for massive private investment in the cities. And it seemed to work. *Time* praised him by writing, "No candidate has addressed himself more realistically to the plight of the Negro slum dweller thus far in the 1968 campaign."[32]

But as the spring passed into summer, Nixon's tone began to change. One of his most noteworthy achievements was to realize, early on, that 1968 would be a seminal year politically, the first presidential election in which suburban voters represented the plurality of the electorate. There were now forty-three million voters in the sixty-one largest central cities, while there were eighty-seven million in the suburbs and smaller (often commuter) cities.[33] Speak to them, he realized—not the urban ethnics, not the rural reactionaries—and you will win the election. Nixon was already the candidate of the suburbs, having carried them easily in the 1960 race. If he merely carried the same counties this time around, he had a huge built-in advantage.

Nixon knew he could do even better. After the riots, his pollsters found a dramatic increase in antiliberal, antigovernment sentiment among suburban voters. With April fresh on their minds, they didn't want to hear more about improving the ghetto. They wanted to know how the federal government would protect them from the ghetto. This was the real white backlash: secluded in their de facto-segregated suburbs, whites could revel in their racial innocence while at the same time lying awake at night fantasizing about black hordes tearing down the barriers of their new Eden. They were not antiblack—at least not explicitly, and most would be offended if so accused—but they were prosecurity, and ambivalent at best about government spending on the inner cities. By the summer, an amalgamation of tightly interrelated issues—riots, crime, race, welfare, law and order—dominated polls. "Soundings across the country point to another kind of uprising that may be in the making—a big protest vote at the polls in November," noted *U.S. News & World Report*. "Some politicians are beginning to call it 'the revolt of the middle class.'"[34]

Nixon responded in kind. As he said at one point during the campaign, "I am not going to campaign for the black vote at the risk of alienating the suburban vote."[35] By the convention, he had largely thrown out his talk of a new approach to improving the ghetto in favor of appeals to the new suburban angst. In his nomination acceptance speech at the Miami Republican National Convention, Nixon claimed to hear "the voice of the great majority of Americans, the forgotten Americans—the nonshouters; the nondemonstrators. They are not racists or sick; they are not guilty of the crime that plagues this land." This was the great silent majority, and he played on their own sense of victimhood. "Let them also recognize that the first civil right of every American is to be free from domestic violence," he proclaimed.[36]

In his post-April strategy, Nixon was drawing up nothing less than "a suburban blueprint," in the words of historian Matthew Lassiter, one "that ultimately resonated from the 'conservative' subdivisions of Southern California to the 'liberal' townships of New England: a bipartisan political language of private property values, individual taxpayer rights, children's education privileges, family residential security, and white racial innocence."[37] Nixon promised more money for police departments, harsher penalties for rioters, and an end to forced school busing, already a reality in the South and a looming possibility in the North (busing outside the South began in 1971). In other words, what the suburbs demanded, and what Nixon promised, was that a line of separation be drawn between the two halves of the post-war metropolis, the urban core and the suburban ring.

The strategy paid off in November: Nixon swept the suburbs and the white middle class, only a third of which supported Hubert Humphrey (versus half of the white working class). And he picked up those states that had gone to Kennedy and Johnson in the previous two elections but, during the past decade, also had exploded in suburban populations: Tennessee, Virginia, and North Carolina, among others.

Nixon's turn to the theme of suburban security was highlighted most of all by his selection of Spiro Agnew as his running mate. In the wake of his April 11 harangue and the press that followed, Agnew had at first tried to reconnect with the black leaders he had shunned. But faced with a poor response from them and a terrific response from the white suburbs, he canceled his plans for a second meeting. And even as he asserted his pro-integration bona fides—citing, at an April 18 press conference, his "record of unprecedented action through executive appointments" of blacks—he pressed further with his law-and-order theme. He made May 15 "Law Day" in Maryland. At a mid-May speech to the American Society for Industrial Security, he endorsed harsher measures against rioters, saying, "If we decide not to act against looters in a stern way, can we muster the manpower needed to contain the increased volume of such criminal behavior which would come about when the threat—the deterrent—of serious consequences to the criminal is removed?"[38] He even backed shooting looters: when "a fugitive runs in the face of an order to halt, I think the policeman is justified in using the severest means to stop him . . . and if that includes shooting him, he has to shoot him."[39]

Serious people began to take notice. One of them was Pat Buchanan, then a speechwriter and adviser on the Nixon campaign. Nixon had always kept law and order as a minor theme in his speeches, but since April, with concern of racial violence making national headlines, it had moved to the center of his stump speech. Agnew, Buchanan realized, was the avatar for an entire subnation, a massive voting bloc that could propel Nixon to the White House. Agnew was not your father's race-baiter, or even a race-baiter at all. He spoke in terms that seemed to many moderate, considered. A suburbanite, just like Nixon's base, who was sick and tired of it all, who'd had the guts to speak up.

Best of all, the men had already met and hit it off, at a chance encounter in New York City in January 1968. Now Agnew was being feted as a rising star by politicians around the party—a travel fund had even been set up for him to make speeches across the country—and the Nixon folks warmed to him further. The two met again in June at Nixon's New York apartment, then yet again for dinner in Annapolis.

Nixon's eventual selection of Agnew was by no means a sure thing, at least as far as the lead candidate let on. At the Republican National Convention in Miami, Nixon and his close advisers ran through a long list of possibilities, from George H. W. Bush to Ronald Reagan. But the arguments that put Agnew over the top derived largely from his April 11 performance and what came after. The southern bloc, led by Republican senator Strom Thurmond, liked him for his strong stand on law and order. At the same time, he was moderate-seeming enough not to scare off the liberals and centrists—and, in any case, appealing to them was Nixon's bag.

Agnew the vice-presidential candidate did not fare well in the media that fall. The man remembered for later denouncing the press as "nattering nabobs of negativity" also called an Asian American reporter a "fat Jap" and referred to Polish Americans as "Polocks." He called Humphrey "soft on communism," then swore that he didn't realize such name-calling reeked of McCarthyism. "Agnew," wrote journalist Theodore White, "made a fool of himself—not so much out of malice or stupidity as, simply, by a coarseness of fiber."[40]

But even as editorialists strained to make him look like an anchor around Nixon's neck, Agnew was tearing it up with the suburbanites. After all, he wasn't hired for his foreign policy sophistication, and if he dropped an occasional racial epithet, the uncomfortable truth was that so did many in the white middle class. More importantly, he exuded an unbridled, unashamedly pro-American spirit at a time when many in the center and on the right felt under attack for those same views. As one letter writer from Norristown, Pennsylvania, told *Time* in late August, "After listening to the acceptance speeches of Nixon and

Agnew, I can only comment: thank God—we have two candidates who are speaking for the forgotten middle class. May they find the strength and courage to carry out the power of their convictions and, once again, make America a proud nation."[41]

Perceptive journalists saw it, too. "Agnew has managed to project himself as a firm, forceful advocate of the traditional American virtues," wrote *Newsweek*, calling him the "apotheosis of the new suburban man." He bowled. He wore white pants and cardigans. He loved Lawrence Welk. He had a bar in his basement. Most importantly, "What Agnew has got is a reflexive feel for how millions of fellow Americans view the world—many of them through suburban windows."

"Feel" might be the wrong word. This wasn't a worldview Agnew could adopt or discard to fit the moment. Unlike Nixon, who could put on the mask of the forgotten man if need be, Agnew couldn't take off the mask if he wanted, because for him it wasn't a mask. If some in the party began to see him as a liability, they held their tongues—polls found him hitting high marks with the white middle class, and that's all he had to do to earn his keep.

When it came down to Election Day, Agnew clearly didn't hurt Nixon, and he may even have put him in the winner's circle. Veteran political journalist Jules Witcover, who followed Agnew's rise at the *Baltimore Sun*, noted in his 1972 biography that Agnew's strength in the suburbs was key to Nixon's winning Tennessee, North Carolina, South Carolina, and Kentucky—states that, with forty-one electoral votes, were enough to give him the margin of victory.[42]

Whether or not that was the case, Agnew's selection represented the arrival of the suburban, middle-class voter as the key constituency in nationwide elections. And the reasons behind his selection, and his popularity—namely, riots, crime, antiliberalism, and racial conservatism—mark the rise of a new paradigm in American voting patterns. For generations afterward, the political center would be dictated by the concerns and desires of the white suburban middle class. And, from the beginning, the issues that mattered most centered on law and order, the relationships between black and white, the city versus the suburb—all issues crystallized by the April 1968 riots.

18

1969 and After

Richard Nixon took the presidential oath of office under a concrete sky on January 20, 1969. Some sixty-five thousand people huddled below the Capitol podium, bundled against the near-zero-degree temperatures. It was a dour morning, "a day out of Edgar Allen Poe," wrote *New York Times* reporter Russell Baker, "dun and drear, with a chilling northeast wind that cut to the marrow." Even Nixon's just-married daughter Julie Nixon Eisenhower barely cracked a smile. Lyndon Johnson, seated nearby, certainly didn't.[1]

Nixon's speech was, given the moment, extremely optimistic. "Because our strengths are so great," he told the audience, "we can afford to appraise our weaknesses with candor and to approach them with hope." Invoking none other than Franklin Roosevelt, he challenged the country, racked by war abroad and unrest at home, to join him in listening to "the better angels of our nature," to "celebrate the simple things, and the basic things—such as goodness, decency, love, kindness."

This meant, above all, putting aside the harsh rhetoric of the past five years. "America has suffered from a fever of words," he said, "from inflated rhetoric that promises more than it can possibly deliver;

from angry rhetoric that fans discontents into hatreds; from bombastic rhetoric that postures instead of persuading." When the public does so, he promised, the government would listen. "Those who have been left out, we will try to bring in; those left behind, we will help to catch up." One could be forgiven for thinking that Johnson (or McPherson, or Califano) himself had written the speech.

Nixon even addressed the question of race. "No man can be fully free while his neighbor is not. To go forward at all is to go forward together. This means black and white together, as one nation, not two. The laws have caught up with our conscience. What remains is to give life to what is in the law: to ensure at last that as all are born equal in dignity before God, all are born equal in dignity before man."[2]

For the victims of the April unrest, there was reason to find hope in Nixon's words, which sounded so much like those of the liberal Democrats who preceded him. Then, less than two weeks later, he took a walking tour of the riot-torn Washington streets with Mayor Washington and the new secretary of housing and urban development, George Romney. The trio coursed along Seventh Street, examining the cleanup efforts and chatting about plans for a new park. One of the hundreds of bystanders shouted, "Soul brother!" Nixon smiled and began shaking hands with the crowd. "You help the mayor now," he said. The crowd cheered.[3]

But whatever people thought Nixon's speech and brief ghetto tour promised, it didn't arrive. His inauguration, far from offering renewed hope for the inner city, signaled its relegation to pariah status in American politics. Connecticut Democratic senator Abraham Ribicoff said as much at a May 1969 Senate hearing in which federal and Washington city officials testified on rebuilding efforts. While cross-examining National Capital Planning Commission assistant director Robert Gold, Ribicoff asked, "What happened with all this fanfare? I remember seeing a big hullabaloo with the president visiting the area personally with [Romney], with the admonition of, 'Let's get the money together and let's get this job done.' What has happened?"

Gold: The planning has moved forward. We had the initial item after the riot, the mayor's one hundred days for planning. That sort of went by the board. The preliminary plans were prepared at that time, but there was then a lapse of time until the president and Mr. Romney went down there. Then the instructions were given to the agencies to move.

Ribicoff: What has happened since the president and Mr. Romney went into this area?

Gold: Renewal areas are in the process of being established.

Ribicoff: But nothing has actually been done? No renewal has actually taken place?

Gold: No, sir. There has been cleanup.

Ribicoff: Have any businesses been rebuilt since then?

Gold: We know about the businesses which incurred damage or loss. No one has surveyed new businesses in this area. There have been reports that several have located in these areas, but we have no overall counts that suggest any magnitude.

Ribicoff: Isn't this one of the basic problems we have in all of these areas? There is a big fanfare, people get their pictures in the newspapers, plans are announced of what is to be achieved, and then it lapses back to where it had been before and nothing really takes place. I got the impression at the time that all systems were "go."

Gold: Yes, sir; they are.

Ribicoff: All systems are "go," but nothing has happened. In other words, we will be walking on the Moon, we hope, by July 21. It shouldn't be so hard to get some building started here on Earth. We are going to be walking on the Moon a lot sooner than we are going to get some of these properties rebuilt.[4]

What Ribicoff highlighted, but what most people were only beginning to realize, was that the massive federal and local funds promised for ghetto rebuilding were not, in fact, on their way. The war was sapping the budget, and while there was still a slight federal surplus, there was hardly the political will to break into a deficit just to rebuild from the riots. After all, many Americans had long since concluded, the residents would just burn them down again. "Rural and small-town people resent vast sums being poured in cities," reported *U.S. News & World Report* in May 1968.[5]

Meanwhile, suburban whites were learning to avoid the District at all costs. Existing commuter suburbs such as Bethesda, Silver Spring, and Arlington became major commercial and business hubs, while new developments such as Tyson's Corner spread like kudzu across northern Virginia. Indeed, by 1969 the riots were already having a clear effect on racial interaction within the District—or lack thereof. The city, demographically dominated by blacks, was being permanently abandoned by whites. Shop owners and shoppers alike retreated to their suburbs and stayed there, shriveling the District's tax base.[6]

Whites weren't the only ones fleeing the inner city. Over the next two decades, many of the inner-ring suburbs of Maryland, particularly Prince George's County, would essentially flip racially; what had been one of the wealthiest white counties in the country became the wealthiest black county. Between 1970 and 1995, 1 percent of the city's black population left each year.[7] This was, of course, a sign of progress—it was only in the late 1960s that fair housing legislation made it possible for them to move anywhere. But their flight also left behind a *lumpenproletariat* disconnected from real job opportunities, a decent tax base to support their education, or the class and racial intermixing that is ultimately decisive in opening up life opportunities.

For another two generations, Washington would become and remain one of the nation's most crime- and poverty-ridden cities. The population would drop nearly in half, while every pathological social indicator—out-of-wedlock births, infant mortality, drug use, murder, school dropouts—would increase several-fold. Gains made in the late 1990s and early 2000s only obscured the ongoing social crisis that is Washington: according to 2007 statistics from the Bureau of Economic Analysis, Washington had the highest per capita income, at $61,092—more than $20,000 more than the national average.[8] But the city also had some of the highest rates of per capita HIV cases, unemployment, and income inequality.[9] According to a joint study by the Urban Institute, the Twenty-first Century School Fund, and the Brookings Institution, in 2006 white median household income in Washington, at $92,000, was nearly three times that of black households, at $34,000.[10] Strikingly, Washington has both one of the best- and worst-educated populations in the country—the most residents with advanced degrees and the highest level of adult illiteracy. And forty years after the riots, the city's black population had not seen an appreciable increase in income after adjusting for inflation, according to an analysis by the Fiscal Policy Institute.

The 1968 riots can't be blamed for all the factors in the city's malaise. Washington was a problem city beforehand, and with middle-class flight already an established fact, it was inevitably going to get worse. But the riots certainly took a bad situation and made it much worse. The riots destroyed a vast swath of the city's working-class section, leaving no place for social mixing. It sent a message to potential investors and residents alike that Washington was pathologically disturbed, and thus no place to relocate. And by scaring off middle-class residents (and thus a middle-class tax base) for decades, the riots arguably rendered it impossible for the city to get back on its feet.

What was happening in Washington, in the near and the long term, could be seen happening in city after city across the country. On April 10, 1968, Chicago mayor Daley promised that he would send Lewis Kill, his commissioner for development and planning, to deliver a comprehensive rebuilding plan to the City Council, including emergency urban renewal funds, reduced strip shopping centers, more zoning for corner shops, and subsidies to encourage middle-income housing. And yet, as in Washington, a year passed with no reconstruction. As the *Chicago Tribune* reported on March 30, 1969, "In a tour of the area hardest hit, a *Tribune* photography team found dozens of square blocks totally vacant. Even the smallest heaps of rubble had been taken away. Not one of the buildings that once filled these blocks has been replaced."[11]

It shouldn't have been surprising. A year after Watts, reporters found little if any rebuilding in Los Angeles.[12] The New Detroit Committee, a body of business and civic leaders formed to plan redevelopment after the 1967 riot, compiled three key recommendations for the City Council: open housing statewide, $5.3 million in state funds for Detroit schools, and a study of the Detroit Police Department. A relatively modest list, but not a single item passed. As the committee admitted in a 1968 report, "If anything, the conflict is in a more advanced state than it was in late July 1967." Black unemployment was estimated at

9 percent to 10 percent; federal education aid reached only 31 percent of eligible students, and the city was $16.8 million in debt.[13]

With commercial activity grinding to a halt, the middle class scared away to the suburbs, and federal and state aid not forthcoming, riot-hit cities descended into a climate of near-*Mad Max* lawlessness. In Baltimore, Jerry Gassinger, whose furniture store on Gay Street had been completely looted, was one of the few merchants who tried to recover (he finally closed shop in October 1972, a mark of stamina that earned him a write-up in the *Sun*). It wasn't easy—by December he had cut all but nine of thirty employees from his showroom and ware-house. Business was getting better, he wrote in a 1969 letter to his chil-dren, but he was just "waiting for another riot." As a sign of how little confidence he had in the area's stability, he left up the plywood boards, refusing to put down the thousands of dollars needed to replace his showroom windows. And he armed. "The office is a Viking fort," he wrote, with perhaps some hyperbole. "On the desks 9 of them all have rifles—12 gauge shotguns—Pistols—shark spears—and Mexican throwing knives. We are called the Vikings. When a suspicious nigger enters the store a cow bell rings overhead the door—I call out #10 and everyone goes to these battle stations. If he is clean we lower the bar-riers. Niggers are taking over the entire city." He wasn't the only one concerned. "All the whites carry guns when walking the streets—all the streets at night in the city are silent, empty, and deserted."[14]

And this from someone who actually stuck around. Most fled. Churches that were once the centers of community life shriveled. Fraternal organizations closed for lack of nearby membership. Even the architecture of Baltimore changed. Frank Bressler, the World War II vet who helped arm his white Baltimore neighborhood, told an interviewer in 2007, "If you ride through [East Baltimore] today, you're gonna find all the places have been bricked up, stoned up, the windows have been removed, the doors have been barred, there's bars, there's grates in front of the windows, grates in front of the doors, none of this existed before the riots."[15] In 1966 George Mahoney ran on the slogan "Your Home Is Your Castle." Now, postriot, homes—and stores, and apartments, and warehouses—were castles in the literal sense.

Perhaps the starkest impact of the riots was to draw an indelible line between the suburbs and the inner city. Before the 1968 riots, there had been a division between the two, but a permeable one. Many suburbanites, having moved from the urban core, still looked to it fondly, still visited to shop downtown, still saw at heart a continuum between the center and the periphery. Central cities were still able to annex suburbs, and in a few cases even entire counties. But through the 1960s, as "urban" became synonymous with "black," as the liberal-black coalition broke down, and as millions of whites fled urban riots and crime for the safety of the suburbs, that became harder to do. It's telling that in 1963 Nashville was able to absorb the entirety of sprawling Davidson County into a metropolitan government, but at the end of the decade and through the 1970s Atlanta, a supposedly more progressive city, was rebuffed again and again in its attempts to annex suburbs such as Sandy Springs. Historian Kevin Kruse calls it the "politics of suburban secession."[16] Few wanted to live near blacks, but it was getting difficult to say so. The riots allowed them to cover their prejudice behind concerns about civil disorder, crime, and poverty. (It didn't help that even many self-described liberals were turning against the civil rights movement; Norman Mailer himself professed in late 1968 that he was "getting tired of Negroes and their rights."[17])

But up until the April disorders, riots were still something that happened to other cities. A July 1967 Gallup poll (albeit on the eve of the Detroit riot) showed that 78 percent of Americans felt there was no risk of riots in their city. Perhaps this was simply residual faith in their hometown; perhaps it was an iteration of the racist "our nig" stereotype, that blacks in their city weren't the kind to cause trouble. In any case, it took the April 1968 riots, in 125 cities big and small across the country, to change white opinion.

U.S. News & World Report underscored the reality of this new divide in an April 22, 1968, article, "Where It's Still Pleasant in the U.S." As the magazine felt compelled to remind its readers, "The fact is that the great majority of Americans live in communities where it is safe to walk the streets at night, where one can enjoy life and trust his neighbors, where schools are not deteriorating, where traffic is not snarled endlessly, where air is breathable, where race war is not threatened, and where there is no talk of burning down the community."[18]

Secession and domestic armament had causes other than the riots; even without them, crime, along with the media's fascination with black militant rhetoric, might have been enough to scare many into well-defended suburban castles. And urban decline has causes other than white flight and racism. But each riot—Watts, Newark, Detroit, Washington—had a way of underlining for whites the proximity and concrete possibility of black violence hitting them or their families. Riots were not just crime on a larger scale. They represented the upending of social order that middle-class whites had been raised to expect. They occurred in parts of town that many suburban adults recognized as childhood homes, either literally or in spirit. Most of all, they vividly highlighted the vast gulf that separated one America from another.

The stark split between the urban core and suburban sprawl had a corollary in the local, state, and federal government approaches, post-1968, to the problems of the inner city. If the Great Society and the War on Poverty represent the apogee of the liberal state's efforts to integrate the ghetto into mainstream America, then the riots, and the April 1968 riots in particular, are the sharp breaking point after which a new paradigm took over. What was once a problem to be solved became a threat to be contained. Security for the suburbs replaced opportunity for blacks as the watchword.

The change was as swift as it was drastic. Millions who were, before King's death and the riots, hopeful for government-led social change turned away in droves post-April. This is why Johnson's initial plans for a new slate of social programs, followed by a postriot rejection of those very same plans, are so significant. Even the Great Legislator, the last of the true New Dealers, could be disheartened by mass civil disorder. What seemed, in those first few days after his withdrawal from the race, like a final opportunity to complete his legislative agenda was transformed by the riots into lame-duck status—not only for Johnson, but for his entire governing philosophy as well.

And despite his rhetoric on that cold January day, Nixon did in fact represent a stark break with the Johnson administration, if not the entire liberal era. Things didn't change overnight, of course. He kept the OEO open, and he increased funds for housing subsidies. That's partly because while Nixon the era might have represented a new paradigm, Nixon the man was a pragmatist at heart, and he understood the need to maintain a centrist stance until at least the 1972 election.

But such posturing wasn't to last. In 1973, he not only told his staff to "flush" the OEO, but he also announced a moratorium on federal subsidies for public housing.[19] His promises to support minority business went nowhere. While the number and total value of Small Business Association loans rose dramatically between 1968 and 1969 (1,676 loans for $29.9 million to 4,120 loans for $93.6 million), they plateaued under Nixon. Even the newly created Office of Minority Entrepreneurship, which he had touted as a model for his new, private-sector-driven social policy, was barely funded and went nowhere. "The Nixon administration has been charged with failure to support the very type of program it endorsed so eloquently in the campaign," wrote researcher Sar Levitan.[20]

Nixon ushered in a new era of suburban politics that dominated American political discourse well past the turn of the millennium. He announced his strict opposition to court-ordered busing. He named two suburban, law-and-order conservatives, Lewis Powell and William Rehnquist, as Supreme Court justices; their votes in turn helped decide three landmark, prosuburban cases: *San Antonio School District v. Rodriguez*, which held that using local property taxes to pay for schools was constitutional even if it causes interdistrict funding disparities; *Milliken v. Bradley*, which held that the 1954 *Brown* decision did not require busing; and *Warth v. Seldin*, which rejected a suit alleging that the Rochester, New York, suburb of Penfield had used zoning laws to exclude low-income residents from the city. "Together," writes Kruse, "these landmark decisions represented an abandonment of the integrationist ideal and a practical acceptance of the secession of the American suburbs."[21]

At the same time, despite the dramatic drop-off in urban disorder following 1968, Nixon ratcheted up funding for city law enforcement agencies through the Law Enforcement Assistance Administration, money that largely went to fund equipment and weapons purchases. LEAA's 1969 budget of $59 million ballooned within a year to $268 million. The Justice Department and the Pentagon offered weapons, interjurisdictional coordination assistance, and riot-control training aimed at the formation of elite antiriot squads. By 1970, thanks to LEAA, of 1,267 cities with more than 10,000 citizens, 585 had special riot-control units, the police departments in 957 had undergone riot training, and 640 had detailed riot contingency plans. Several received helicopter training.[22]

All of this was probably, at the time, prudent. But as the riot era receded, it left behind a superstructure ready to take on new, and

newly constructed, threats from the ghetto. When Nixon declared the
War on Drugs in 1971, creating a new, postmilitant racial demon to
threaten the suburbs—the black drug dealer and his clientele—the
militarized residue of the federal riot-control system was ready.

Nixon also greatly expanded the domestic intelligence apparatus that
had developed within the army and the FBI. Using the new wiretapping powers granted by the Safe Streets Act, Attorney General John
Mitchell immediately approved surveillance on Black Panther operations.[23] He opened up the taps on cooperation between police departments and the FBI, strengthening local intelligence efforts but also, in
the process, diluting the quality of federal intelligence collection with
a flood of subprofessional local input. Nevertheless, Mitchell quickly
built a tight intelligence web, with the result that, as the political
scientist John Eliff wrote, "Regular cooperation among law enforcement agencies had been transformed from a means for anticipating
and controlling civil disorders intro an instrument that threatened
oppression."[24]

But the real story was taking place across the Potomac River.
Already by fall 1968, the Pentagon was trying to cut back on the risk
that it would again have to intervene. After a summer of relative calm,
the Pentagon quietly ratcheted back some of its planning. The new
CDCC office was scrapped, and funds for antiriot R&D were cut
to below $1 million. With no end in sight in Vietnam, the Pentagon
needed all the resources it could muster overseas. And as several
memos indicate, the Department of Defense understood the political
poison that would result if the public learned that it was preparing for
future urban occupations.

The one thing that didn't change, though, was the extent of domestic spying. Even though Deputy Secretary of the Army McGiffert
ordered spying operations shuttered as he left office in January 1969,
they in fact increased dramatically that year, with agents making
twelve hundred spot reports a month, all fed into the army's database,
which was accessible by most local, state, and federal agencies, even
the CIA. Amazingly, this all happened even as the army top brass was
getting nervous about the extent of its intelligence activities. In August
1968 they had replaced General Yarborough with the much more

cautious Major General Joseph McChristian. But the operation had a momentum all its own, and because no one was willing to shut it down completely without another agency picking up the responsibility, it continued growing.

It has been suggested by more than a few commentators that one can draw a direct line between the Nixon administration's experiences with domestic intelligence and that of the George W. Bush administration, thirty years later.[25] And, indeed, there are striking parallels: Both were in the middle of a costly foreign war that, they believed, had a significant domestic component (antiwar activism in the former, terrorist cells in the latter). Both placed executive power, as a principle, at the center of their governing philosophy. And both claimed the right to monitor and investigate domestic activities by American civilians in the name of national security.

But the connections go farther. In early 1970 an army whistleblower exposed the military's spying activities, and under strong congressional pressure, the department unilaterally shut down its domestic intelligence operations. In response, Mitchell greatly expanded funding for the Justice Department's Interdivisional Intelligence Unit, to $274,000, with twelve full-time staff.[26] When pressed on the justification for such activities, Mitchell claimed "the inherent powers of the federal government to protect the internal security of the nation. We feel that's our job."[27] With domestic unrest still costing $31 million in 1969 (though this was mostly antiwar activism, not rioting), the department could claim a powerful mandate to step up observation of dissenters and activists.

The Nixon Justice Department proved to be made of heartier stuff than the Pentagon, at least when under fire from Congress. During the 1971 Ervin hearings, run by North Carolina senator Sam Ervin, Justice officials repeatedly refused to back down from the same sorts of activities that had so embarrassed their military counterparts. Then-Assistant Attorney General Rehnquist, testifying before the panel in a loud suit and thick muttonchops, said that Justice "will vigorously oppose any legislation" to limit government surveillance. "Self-discipline on the part of the executive branch will provide an answer to virtually all of the legitimate complaints against excesses of information gathering," he said, adding that limiting legislation would "obscure the fundamental necessity and importance of federal information gathering, or the generally high level of performance in this area by the organizations involved."[28]

What he did not reveal was that the Justice Department had also expanded the scope of its intelligence gathering to cover all sorts of dissent activity, whether or not it threatened violence, and that it had come under strict control of the White House itself, which was wary of allowing departments to run things. The previous July, Tom Charles Huston, Nixon's coordinator of security affairs, developed a plan to centralize all intelligence gathering under White House control, ostensibly because it was "fragmentary and unevaluated" but also because it was being developed and potentially mishandled by professionals in Defense, Justice, and other departments of unknown loyalty to Nixon. Though Nixon initially signed off on the plan, it was beaten back by Hoover, in one of his last bureaucratic victories. Not to be stymied, Nixon and his inner circle simply created their own intelligence arm inside the White House, the Special Investigations Unit, which they nicknamed the "Plumbers"—the same group that a few years later would bungle the Watergate break-in and precipitate Nixon's resignation.

While for most people the story of the Plumbers would be a cautionary tale against the risks of excessive executive secrecy, for many of the young staffers in the Nixon administration, the lesson ran the opposite way. As Congress tore down the imperial edifice that Nixon and his predecessors had built, these officials, including Dick Cheney and Donald Rumsfeld, decided that Nixon's problem was that he had too little power, not too much, that an antagonistic Congress was able to meddle in the executive's prerogatives. It is no coincidence that thirty years later, both Cheney and Rumsfeld became leaders of the Bush administration's efforts to reconstruct the imperial presidency, in part by using executive-controlled units—the Office of Special Plans under Rumsfeld, for example—to counter the influence of independent voices within the federal policymaking apparatus.

The desk where I am writing this conclusion is on the ninth floor of an apartment building less than a quarter mile from U and Fourteenth streets in Washington, the epicenter of the first of the King riots. I have lived in the immediate area for just over five years, but in that time

I have seen the area transform completely, from a mix of thriving local businesses and run-down lots to a breeding ground for high-priced condos and expensive, hip restaurants. Five years ago, the eastern side of Fourteenth, leading up to Columbia Heights, was a string of vacant lots. Now it's a canyon wall of high-priced condos. Parts of the neighborhood I considered too dangerous for me to live in are now too expensive for me to afford.

The corner where the riots started, the Peoples Drug through which the first brick was thrown, is now home to the enormous Frank Reeves Municipal Center, a massive city office building initiated by Marion Barry and designed, coincidentally, by the firm of Paul Devrouax—the black architect who as a young soldier had ridden at the front of the Sixth Armored Calvary Regiment column on the afternoon of April 5, 1968. When it opened in 1986, the building was hailed as the cornerstone of a yet-unforseeable future rebirth of the city's central districts. Now, twenty-two years later, the brick plaza out front plays host to a yuppie organic market every weekend. And Shaw, the neighborhood around it, is one of the trendiest hubs in the region. The success that Barry's rise had promised has now made it harder for working-class blacks to afford to live in the city.

Newcomers to the once predominantly black neighborhood are as likely to be white, Asian, or Hispanic; they are likely to be wealthy, or at least young and headed toward great wealth. And unless they stumble across an inconspicuous historic marker at U and Fourteenth, chances are they don't even know the riots happened. Virtually every physical trace has been obliterated.

That's Washington: a transient city with a bad memory. But such historical amnesia is also partly willed; we would rather not remember the bad parts. And yet history cannot simply be a retinue of the inspiring moments in our past; we do ourselves a disservice if we don't remember everything. As the poet Stanley Kunitz wrote, "We learn, as the thread plays out, that we belong/Less to what flatters us than to what scars." As we finally get around to rebuilding vast sections of our inner cities, we owe it to ourselves not to forget the scars that remain.

Notes

Prologue
1. Memo, Ray Price to Leonard Garment, June 18, 1968. Leonard Garment Papers, White House Central Files, Richard Nixon Library and Birthplace Foundation.
2. Jonathan Simon, *Governing through Crime: How the War on Crime Transformed American Democracy and Created a Culture of Fear* (Oxford: Oxford University Press, 2007), p. 3.
3. Richard Nixon, 1973 State of the Union address. http://janda.org/politxts/state%20of%20union%20addresses/1970-1974%20Nixon%20T/RMN73C.html. Accessed April 27, 2008.
4. Doris Kearns Goodwin, *Lyndon Johnson and the American Dream* (New York: Harper & Row, 1976), p. 305.
5. Newsletter, April 15, 1968. Box 14, Campaign 1968 Research Files, Richard Nixon Library and Birthplace Foundation.
6. Cited in John A. Andrew III, *Lyndon Johnson and the Great Society* (Chicago: Ivan R. Dee, 1998), p. 46.
7. Hazel Erskine, "The Polls: Demonstrations and Race Riots," *Public Opinion Quarterly* 31, no. 4 (1968): 658–659.
8. As recent scholarship by historians Peniel Joseph, Komozi Woodard, Jeanne Theoharis, and others demonstrates, the civil rights movement as usually understood encompassed only a fraction of black racial activism in the 1950s and 1960s, some of it radical and violent, but no less historically relevant for being so. See, for example, Peniel E. Joseph, *Waiting*

'Til the Midnight Hour: A Narrative History of Black Power (New York: Henry Holt, 2006); Jeanne F. Theoharis and Komozi Woodard, eds., *Freedom North: Black Freedom Struggles outside the South, 1940–1980* (New York: Palgrave Macmillan, 2003).

1. King, Johnson, and the Terrible, Glorious Thirty-first Day of March

1. *Washington Post*, April 1, 1968, p. A1. *New York Times*, April 1, 1968, p. 20. See also Taylor Branch, *At Canaan's Edge: America in the King Years 1965–68* (New York: Simon & Schuster, 2006), p. 745.
2. Ted Widmer, ed., *American Speeches, vol. 2, Political Oratory from Abraham Lincoln to Bill Clinton* (New York: Library of America, 2006), pp. 66–680.
3. Branch, *At Canaan's Edge*, p. 588.
4. Widmer, ed., *American Speeches*, pp. 651–667.
5. Branch, *At Canaan's Edge*, p. 595; David J. Garrow, *Bearing the Cross: Martin Luther King, Jr., and the Southern Christian Leadership Conference* (New York: HarperCollins Perennial Classics, 1986; reprint, 1999), pp. 553–555.
6. Branch, *At Canaan's Edge*, p. 659.
7. Adam Cohen and Elizabeth Taylor, *American Pharaoh: Mayor Richard J. Daley: His Battle for Chicago and the Nation* (Boston: Little, Brown, 2000), p. 444.
8. Gerald D. McKnight, *The Last Crusade: Martin Luther King, Jr., the FBI, and the Poor People's Campaign* (Boulder, Colo.; Westview Press, 1998), p. 18.
9. Michael K. Honey, *Going Down Jericho Road: The Memphis Strike, Martin Luther King's Last Campaign* (New York: W. W. Norton, 2007), p. 174.
10. Garrow, *Bearing the Cross*, p. 581.
11. McKnight, *The Last Crusade*, p. 21.
12. Honey, *Jericho Road*, p. 290.
13. Ben W. Gilbert, *Ten Blocks from the White House: Anatomy of the Washington Riots of 1968* (New York: Frederick A. Praeger, 1968), p. 11.
14. Crosby S. Noyes, *Washington Evening Star*, April 4, 1968, p. 10.
15. McKnight, *The Last Crusade*, passim.
16. Honey, *Jericho Road*, p. 3.
17. Ibid., p. 117.
18. *New York Times*, March 18, 1968, p. 28.
19. Honey, *Jericho Road*, pp. 296–303.
20. Ibid., p. 296.
21. Ibid., p. 352.
22. *St. Louis Globe-Democrat*, March 30, 1968, p. 6. *Memphis Commercial Appeal*, March 30, 1968, p. 6.
23. Honey, *Jericho Road*, pp. 364–367 and p. 377.
24. Theodore H. White, *The Making of the President 1968* (New York: Atheneum, 1969), p. 132.
25. Horace Busby, *The Thirty-first of March: An Intimate Portrait of Lyndon Johnson's Final Days in Office* (New York: Farrar, Straus, & Giraux, 2005), p. 181.
26. Lady Bird Johnson, *A White House Diary* (New York: Rinehart & Winston, 1970), p. 642.

27. Merle Miller, *Lyndon: An Oral Biography* (New York: Putnam, 1980), p. 508.

28. Johnson, *Diary*, p. 644.

29. Emmett S. Redford and Richard T. McCulley, *White House Operations: The Johnson Presidency* (Austin: University of Texas Press, 1986), p. 72.

30. Stanley Karnow, *Vietnam: A History* (New York: Viking, 1983), p. 564.

31. Johnson, *Diary*, p. 645.

32. http://www.lbjlib.utexas.edu/johnson/archives.hom/speeches.hom/680331.asp.

33. Busby, *The Thirty-first of March*, p. 187.

34. Johnson had contemplated stepping down as early as summer 1967. Nick Kotz, *Judgment Days: Lyndon Baines Johnson, Martin Luther King Jr., and the Laws That Changed America* (New York: Mariner, 2006), p. 281.

35. Busby, *The Thirty-first of March*, p. 176.

36. Richard Rovere, *New Yorker*, April 13, 1968, p. 146.

37. Author interview, Harry McPherson, November 7, 2007.

38. *Washington Post*, November 6, 1967, p. A1.

39. Branch, *At Canaan's Edge*, p. 552.

40. Doris Kearns Goodwin, *Lyndon Johnson and the American Dream* (New York: Harper & Row, 1976), p. 344.

41. Joseph A. Califano Jr., *The Triumph and Tragedy of Lyndon Johnson: The White House Years* (New York: Simon & Schuster, 1991), p. 260.

42. Karnow, *Vietnam*, p. 541.

43. Miller, *Lyndon*, p. 502.

44. Karnow, *Vietnam*, p. 547.

45. *Report of the National Advisory Commission on Civil Disorders* (New York: E. P. Dutton, 1968). Quotes appear on pages 2, 411, and 23, respectively.

46. Estimates from *U.S. News & World Report*, April 29, 1968, pp. 34–36.

47. Fred Harris and Roger Wilkins, *Quiet Riots: Race and Poverty in the United States* (New York: Pantheon, 1988), p. 13.

48. Text of speech in Box 36, Office Files of James Gaither, Lyndon Johnson Library and Museum.

49. Memo from Harry McPherson to Joe Califano, Box 32, Office Files of Harry McPherson, Lyndon Johnson Library and Museum.

50. *Chicago Tribune*, March 7, 1968, p. A6.

51. *Time*, March 15, 1968, pp. 16–17.

52. Robert Dallek, *Flawed Giant: Lyndon Johnson and His Times, 1961–1973* (Oxford: Oxford University Press, 1998), p. 506.

53. Goodwin, *Lyndon Johnson and the American Dream*, p. 347.

54. Joseph A. Califano, *The Triumph and Tragedy of Lyndon Johnson: The White House Years* (New York: Simon & Schuster, 1991), p. 265.

55. Interview, McPherson.

56. Ibid.

57. Ibid.

58. *New York Times*, April 16, 1988, p. 31.

59. Miller, *Lyndon*, p. 510.

60. Ibid., p. 513.

61. Interview, McPherson.

62. Johnson, *Diary*, p. 646.
63. Ibid.
64. Ibid., p. 647.
65. Busby, *The Thirty-first of March*, p. 230.

2. Before the Bullet
1. *New York Times*, April 5, 1968, p. 1.
2. Horace Busby, *The Thirty-first of March: An Intimate Portrait of Lyndon Johnson's Final Days in Office* (New York: Farrar, Straus, & Giroux, 2005), pp. 226–228.
3. Harry McPherson, *A Political Education: A Washington Memoir* (Boston: Houghton Mifflin, 1988), p. 264.
4. Robert Dallek, *Flawed Giant: Lyndon Johnson and His Times, 1961–1973* (Oxford: Oxford University Press, 1998), p. 530.
5. Joseph A. Califano Jr., *The Triumph and Tragedy of Lyndon Johnson: The White House Years* (New York: Simon & Schuster, 1991), p. 272.
6. Lyndon Baines Johnson, *The Vantage Point: Perspectives of the Presidency 1963–1969* (New York: Holt, Rinehart, & Winston, 1971), p. 174.
7. Johnson wrote in his memoirs, "I awakened in the morning feeling optimistic. Something very good had happened the day before, April 3, 1968." Ibid., p. 173.
8. *New York Times*, April 5, 1968, p. 1.
9. For chronological details of Johnson's trip, see President's Daily Diary, Lyndon Baines Johnson Archives and Museum, www.lbjlib.utexas.edu/johnson/archives .hom/diary/1968/680404.asp.
10. Johnson, *The Vantage Point*, p. 174.
11. Michael K. Honey, *Going Down Jericho Road: The Memphis Strike, Martin Luther King's Last Campaign* (New York: W. W. Norton, 2007), p. 408.
12. Cited in "Riot Data Review," JL 3 King Box 35, White House Confidential Files, Lyndon Johnson Library and Museum.
13. Daryl Gates, *Chief: My Life in the L.A.P.D.* (New York: Bantam, 1992), p. 110.
14. Ibid., p. 116.
15. Tracy Tullis, "A Vietnam at Home: Policing the Ghettos in the Counterinsurgency Era" (Dissertation, New York University, 1999), pp. 146–151 passim.
16. Michael Flamm, *Law and Order: Street Crime, Civil Unrest, and the Crisis of Liberalism in the 1960s* (New York: Columbia University Press, 2005), p. 47.
17. Ibid., p. 51.
18. Paul J. Scheips, *The Role of Federal Military Forces in Domestic Disorders, 1945–1992* (Washington, D.C.: Center of Military History, 2005), pp. 268–270.
19. Garry Wills, *The Second Civil War: Arming for Armageddon* (New York: New American Library, 1968).
20. Honey, *Going Down Jericho Road*, p. 402.
21. Author interview, Roger Wilkins, July 31, 2007.
22. Gerold Frank, *An American Death: The True Story of the Assassination of Dr. Martin Luther King Jr., and the Greatest Manhunt of Our Time* (Garden City: Doubleday, 1972), p. 44.
23. David J. Garrow, *Bearing the Cross: Martin Luther King Jr. and the Southern Christian Leadership Conference* (New York: HarperCollins Perennial Classics, 1986; reprint, 1999), p. 620.

24. Ted Widmer, ed., *American Speeches,* vol. 2, *Political Oratory from Abraham Lincoln to Bill Clinton* (New York: Library of America, 2006), pp. 681–692.

25. Taylor Branch, *At Canaan's Edge: America in the King Years 1965–68* (New York: Simon & Schuster, 2006), p. 766.

26. Frank, *An American Death,* pp. 34–38 and 58–64.

3. The News Arrives

1. Author interview, Ramsey Clark, September 18, 2007.

2. Joseph A. Califano Jr., *The Triumph and Tragedy of Lyndon Johnson: The White House Years* (New York: Simon & Schuster, 1991), p. 222.

3. Interview, Clark. Also see Gerold Frank, *An American Death: The True Story of the Assassination of Dr. Martin Luther King Jr. and the Greatest Manhunt of Our Time* (Garden City: Doubleday, 1972), p. 117, and Michael K. Honey, *Going Down Jericho Road: The Memphis Strike, Martin Luther King's Last Campaign* (New York: W. W. Norton, 2007), pp. 433–434. Like many of the minute details during the immediate aftermath of King's death, there are different accounts of how Clark got the news. Clark and Frank say it came from Laue, but in his memoirs Warren Christopher says a secretary brought a note. See Warren Christopher, *Chances of a Lifetime: A Memoir* (New York: Scribner, 2001), p. 56. I chose the above account based on Clark's memory and Frank's research, conducted soon after the events, but it is worth noting Christopher's own recollection.

4. Frank, *An American Death,* p. 117.

5. Merle Miller, *Lyndon: An Oral Biography* (New York: Putnam, 1980), p. 514. President's Daily Diary, April 4, 1968. http://www.lbjlib.utexas.edu/johnson/archives.hom/diary/1968/680404.asp. Accessed April 27, 2008.

6. President's Daily Diary, ibid.

7. Frank, *An American Death,* p. 93.

8. President's Daily Diary, Lyndon Baines Johnson Archives and Museum, www.lbjlib.utexas.edu/johnson/archives.hom/diary/1968/680404.asp.

9. Lyndon Baines Johnson, *The Vantage Point: Perspectives of the Presidency 1963–1969* (New York: Holt, Rinehart, & Winston, 1971), p. 174.

10. Honey, *Going Down Jericho Road,* p. 451.

11. For timing, see President's Daily Diary. See also Johnson, *The Vantage Point,* p. 174.

12. "Statement by the President on the Assassination of Dr. Martin Luther King, Jr.," The American Presidency Project, University of California, Santa Barbara, www.presidency.ucsb.edu/ws/?pid=28781.

13. *Washington Evening Star,* April 5, 1968, p. A9, and *Washington Evening Star,* April 5, 1968, p. B1.

14. *Washington Evening Star,* April 4, 1968, p. A4.

15. *New York Times,* April 5, 1967, p. 37.

16. Christopher Lasch, "A Special Supplement: The Trouble with Black Power," *New York Review of Books,* February 29, 1968, pp. 4–14.

17. Permanent Subcommittee on Investigations of the Committee on Government Operations, *Riots, Civil and Criminal Disorders,* 90th Cong., 1st sess., November 1–3 and 6, 1967, p. 302.

18. Clayborne Carson, *In Struggle: SNCC and the Black Awakening of the 1960s* (Cambridge, Mass: Harvard University Press, 1981), p. 215.

19. *New York Times*, November 5, 1967, p. 24.

20. *U.S. News & World Report*, January 18, 1968, p. 33.

21. Kwame Toure (Stokely Carmichael) with Ekwueme Michael Thelwell, *Ready for Revolution: The Life and Struggles of Stokely Carmichael* (New York: Scribner, 2003), p. 571.

22. *Washington Post*, February 11, 1968, p. C1.

23. Ben W. Gilbert, *Ten Blocks from the White House: Anatomy of the Washington Riots of 1968* (New York: Frederick A. Praeger, 1968), p. 13.

24. Sworn witness statement, April 8, 1968. FBI Carmichael File, Series 100-446080 (FBI Archives).

25. Harry Jaffe and Tom Sherwood, *Dream City: Race, Power, and the Decline of Washington, D.C.* (New York: Simon & Schuster, 1994), p. 68.

26. Taylor Branch, *At Canaan's Edge: America in the King Years 1965–68* (New York: Simon & Schuster, 2006), p. 640.

27. Jules Witcover, *The Year the Dream Died: Revisiting 1968 in America* (New York: Warner Books, 1997), p. 149.

28. *Washington Evening Star*, April 4, 1968, p. A1.

29. *Washington Afro-American*, April 6, 1968, p. 1.

30. *Washington Evening Star*, April 5, 1967, p. A7.

31. Arthur M. Schlesinger Jr., *Robert Kennedy and His Times* (New York: Houghton Mifflin, 1978), pp. 912–913.

32. Jean Stein and George Plimpton, eds., *American Journey: The Times of Robert Kennedy* (New York: Harcourt Brace Jovanovich, 1970), p. 255.

33. Schlesinger, *Robert Kennedy and His Times*, pp. 913–914. Also, Ted Widmer, ed., *American Speeches*, vol. 2, *Political Oratory from Abraham Lincoln to Bill Clinton* (New York: Library of America, 2006), pp. 693–694. Also, see footage of the speech at www.youtube.com/watch?v=OCg05pTYt0A.

34. Stein and Plimpton, eds., *American Journey*, p. 257.

35. Schlesinger, *Robert Kennedy and His Times*, p. 915.

36. Cited in Thurston Clarke, *The Last Campaign: Robert F. Kennedy and 82 Days that Inspired America* (New York: Henry Holt, 2008), p. 98.

4. U and Fourteenth

1. Author interview, Larry Levinson, December 21, 2007. See also Emmett S. Redford and Richard T. McCulley, *White House Operations: The Johnson Presidency* (Austin: University of Texas Press, 1986).

2. Horace Busby, *The Thirty-first of March: An Intimate Portrait of Lyndon Johnson's Final Days in Office* (New York: Farrar, Straus, & Giroux, 2005), pp. 234–236.

3. Ibid., p. 234.

4. See memo, April 4, 1968, Box 95, Appointment Files Diary Backup, Lyndon Johnson Library and Museum.

5. Gerold Frank, *An American Death: The True Story of the Assassination of Dr. Martin Luther King Jr. and the Greatest Manhunt of Our Time* (Garden City: Doubleday, 1972), p. 120.

6. Lady Bird Johnson, *A White House Diary* (New York: Holt, Rinehart, & Winston, 1970), p. 648.

7. President's Daily Diary, April 6, 1968.

8. "Events Involving Stokely Carmichael on Evening of April 4, 1968." FBI Carmichael Papers, Series 100–446080, File # WFO 62–9737 (FBI Archives).

9. Ben W. Gilbert, *Ten Blocks from the White House: Anatomy of the Washington Riots of 1968* (New York: Frederick A. Praeger, 1968), p. 17.

10. "Events Involving Stokely Carmichael on Evening of April 4, 1968."

11. Ibid.

12. Ibid.

13. Report, "Operation Band-Aid One," Office of Emergency Planning Papers, Box 1, District of Columbia Archives, Washington, D.C., p. 1.

14. Ibid., p. 4.

15. Gilbert, *Ten Blocks from the White House*, pp. 18–19.

16. Ibid., p. 22.

17. "Events Involving Stokely Carmichael on Evening of April 4, 1968."

18. Gilbert, *Ten Blocks from the White House*, p. 21.

19. "Events Involving Stokely Carmichael on Evening of April 4, 1968."

20. *Washington Post*, April 5, 1968, p. 1.

21. Thomas B. Morgan, "The King Assassination," *New York*, April 11, 1993, pp. 111–112.

22. Vincent Cannato, *The Ungovernable City: John Lindsay and His Struggle to Save New York* (New York: Basic Books, 2001), pp. 132–139.

23. "Voices of New York: The King Assassination," *New York*, April 11, 1988, p. 54.

24. Author interview, Harry McPherson, November 7, 2007.

25. Many of the details of Lindsay's trip to Harlem and his antiriot efforts can be found in Gloria and Lloyd Weaver Steinem, "Special Report: The City on the Eve of Destruction," *New York*, April 22, 1968.

26. Morgan, "The King Assassination," pp. 111–112.

27. John V. Lindsay, *The City* (New York: W.W. Norton, 1969), p. 103.

28. *New York Post*, April 8, 1968, p. 13.

29. Cannato, *The Ungovernable City*, p. 212.

30. *New York Times*, April 5, 1968, p. 1.

31. Gilbert, *Ten Blocks from the White House*, p. 22.

32. *New York Times*, April 5, 1968, p. 26.

33. "Events Involving Stokely Carmichael on Evening of April 14, 1968."

34. "Operation Band-Aid," p. 5.

35. Cited in Gilbert, *Ten Blocks from the White House*, pp. 31–32.

36. "Operation Band-Aid One," p. 6.

37. Gilbert, *Ten Blocks from the White House*, p. 36. This quotation, which originally appeared in the *Washington Post*, became a point of heated contention during later congressional hearings, at which Murphy defended himself against charges that he had gone easy on the rioters. He denied ever making the statement.

38. Ibid., p. 31.

39. Transcript, "Anonymous B" oral history interview, April 28, 1968, by James Mosby, Moreland–Spingarn Library Archives, Howard University, p. 36.

40. "Preliminary Action and Status Reports Relating to the Mayor, Director of Public Safety, and the Police Department Relative to April 1968 Disorders

in the District of Columbia," p. 3. Washington Historical Society Archives, Washington, D.C.

41. District of Columbia Fire Department's Role in the Civil Disturbances of April 4, 5, 6, 7, and 8, 1968, p. 1. Washington Historical Society. Also, Interview, Donald Mayhew, June 13, 2007.

42. Harry Jaffe and Tom Sherwood, *Dream City: Race, Power, and the Decline of Washington, D.C.* (New York: Simon & Schuster, 1994), p. 62.

43. *Washington Evening Star*, April 5, 1968, p. A1.

44. Gilbert, *Ten Blocks from the White House*, pp. 26–27.

45. *Washington Evening Star*, April 5, 1968, p. A1.

46. Gilbert, *Ten Blocks from the White House*. p. 40.

47. Ibid. For fire totals, see "District of Columbia Fire Department's Role in the Civil Disturbances of April 4, 5, 6, 7, and 8, 1968," p. 1.

48. President's Daily Diary, April 4, 1968.

49. Author interview, Ramsey Clark, September 18, 2007.

5. Midnight Interlude

1. "Army Operations Center Report on Events of April 4–17." Box 1, Entry 415, Record Group 319, National Archives.

2. For an excellent discussion of the military's changing domestic role during the 1960s, see James R. Gardner, "The Civil Disturbance Mission of the Department of the Army, 1963–1973: An Analysis of Perceptions, Policies and Programs" (Dissertation, Princeton University, 1977).

3. Paul J. Scheips, *The Role of Federal Military Forces in Domestic Disorders, 1945–1992* (Washington, D.C.: Center of Military History, 2005), p. 143.

4. Colonel Robert B. Riggs, "A Military Appraisal of the Threat to U.S. Cities," reprinted in *U.S. News & World Report*, January 15, 1968, pp. 68 and 71.

5. Scheips, *The Role of Federal Military Forces*, pp. 197–202.

6. Committee on the Armed Services, Hearings by the Special Subcommittee to Inquire into the Capability of the National Guard to Cope with Civil Disturbances, 90th Cong., 1st sess., August 10 and October 3, 1967, p. 5,805.

7. "Army Operations Center Report on Events of April 4–17."

8. Ibid. See also Scheips, *The Role of Federal Military Forces*, and Gardner, "The Civil Disturbance Mission of the Department of the Army."

9. Ibid.

10. "Army Operations Center Report on Events of April 4–17, 1968."

11. "The Role of the Army in the Civilian Arena, 1920–1970," Box 9, Entry 415, Record Group 319, National Archives.

12. Christopher Pyle, "Conus Intelligence: The Army Watches Civilian Politics," *Washington Monthly*, January 1970, pp. 4–16.

13. Memo from Director of Army Operations General Hollis to Acting Secretary of the Army, August 1, 1967, Box 27, Entry 415, Record Group 319, National Archives.

14. "ASCI TF Reference Chronicle and Topical Index," Box 1, Entry 415, Record Group 319, National Archives.

15. Cited in "Army Civil Disturbance Intelligence Activities," Box 27, Entry 415, Record Group 319, National Archives.

16. Pyle, "Conus Intelligence."

17. "Counterintelligence Research Report," April 1, 1968, Box 4, Entry 415, Record Group 319, National Archives.

18. *Memphis Commercial Appeal*, March 21, 1993. http://www.commercialap peal.com/news/1993/Mar/21/top-spy-feared-current-below-surface-unrest/. Retrieved March 25, 2008.

19. Ibid.

20. Scheips, *The Role of Federal Military Forces*, p. 281.

21. Patrick V. Murphy and Thomas Plate, *Commissioner: A View from the Top of American Law Enforcement* (New York: Simon & Schuster, 1977), p. 113. See also "Army Operations Center Report on Events of April 4–17."

22. Murphy, *Commissioner*, p. 99.

23. Ibid., p. 101.

24. Ibid., p. 102.

25. Ibid., pp. 105–108.

26. Ben W. Gilbert, *Ten Blocks from the White House: Anatomy of the Washington Riots of 1968* (New York: Frederick A. Praeger, 1968), p. 35.

27. Memo from Harry McPherson to Lyndon Johnson, April 5, 1968. Box 95, Appointment Files Diary Backup, Johnson Archives, Lyndon Johnson Library and Museum.

28. Memo from Jim Gaither to Lyndon Johnson, April 5, 1968. Box 95, Appointment Files Diary Backup, Johnson Archives, Lyndon Johnson Library and Museum.

29. Horace Busby, *The Thirty-first of March: An Intimate Portrait of Lyndon Johnson's Final Days in Office* (New York: Farrar, Straus, & Giroux, 2005), p. 237.

30. Nick Kotz, *Judgment Days: Lyndon Baines Johnson, Martin Luther King Jr., and the Laws That Changed America* (New York: Mariner Books, 2006), p. xii.

31. Joseph A. Califano Jr., *The Triumph and Tragedy of Lyndon Johnson: The White House Years* (New York: Simon & Schuster, 1991), pp. 51–52.

32. For an excellent account of King's radical vision see Thomas F. Jackson, *From Civil Rights to Human Rights: Martin Luther King, Jr. and the Struggle for Economic Justice* (Philadelphia: University of Pennsylvania Press, 2007).

33. Author interview, Ramsey Clark, September 18, 2007. Also see Kotz, *Judgment Days*, p. 195.

34. Clark interview.

35. Kotz, *Judgment Days*, p. 128.

36. W. Marvin Watson and Sherwin Markman, *Chief of Staff: Lyndon Johnson and His Presidency* (New York: Thomas Dunne Books, 2004), pp. 210 and 215.

37. Cited in Kotz, *Judgment Days*, p. 395.

38. Ibid., p. 375.

39. "The President's News Conference of March 30, 1968," *The Public Papers of the President*. http://www.presidency.ucsb.edu/ws/index.php?pid=28770. Accessed February 9, 2008.

40. Kotz, *Judgment Days*, p. 404.

6. "Any Man's Death Diminishes Me"

1. Seating chart, April 5, 1968, Box 95, Appointment Files Diary Backup, Lyndon Johnson Library and Museum.
2. See Alex Poinsett, *Walking with Presidents: Louis Martin and the Rise of Black Political Power* (New York: Rowman & Littlefield, 2000).
3. Harry McPherson, *A Political Education: A Washington Memoir* (Boston: Houghton Mifflin, 1988), p. 347.
4. Author interview, Joseph Califano, September 19, 2007. See also Poinsett, *Walking with Presidents*, p. 165.
5. Gunnar Myrdal, *An American Dilemma: The Negro Problem and Modern Democracy* (New York: Harper & Brothers, 1944), p. 763.
6. On SNCC's financial woes, see Peniel E. Joseph, *Waiting 'Til the Midnight Hour: A Narrative History of Black Power* (New York: Henry Holt, 2006), p. 179.
7. *U.S. News & World Report*, April 22, 1968, pp. 45–46.
8. Meeting notes, April 5, 1968, Box 95, Appointment Files Diary Backup, Lyndon Johnson Library and Museum.
9. Transcript, Warren Christopher oral history interview 3, December 2, 1968, by Thomas Baker, Lyndon Johnson Library and Museum, p. 4.
10. Warren Christopher, *Chances of a Lifetime: A Memoir* (New York: Scribner, 2001), p. 57.
11. Transcript of press conference with George Christian, 4:42 P.M., April 5, 1968. Box 95, Appointment Files Diary Backup, Lyndon Johnson Library and Museum.
12. Horace Busby, *The Thirty-first of March: An Intimate Portrait of Lyndon Johnson's Final Days in Office* (New York: Farrar, Straus, & Giroux, 2005), p. 238.
13. Interview, Califano.
14. Merle Miller, *Lyndon: An Oral Biography* (New York: Putnam, 1980), pp. 514–515.
15. Press conference with George Christian, April 5, 1968. Box 95, Appointment Files Diary Backup, Lyndon Johnson Library and Museum.
16. *New York Times*, November 4, 1988. http://query.nytimes.com/gst/fullpage.html?res=940DEEDA1038F937A35752C1A96E948260. Accessed March 26, 2008.
17. Transcript, Louis Martin oral history interview I, May 14, 1969, by David G. McComb, Internet copy, Lyndon Johnson Library and Museum. http://www.lbjlib.utexas.edu/johnson/archives.hom/oralhistory.hom/MartinL/martin.asp. Accessed April 19, 2008.
18. Poinsett, *Walking with Presidents*, pp. 166–167.
19. FBI Carmichael Papers, Series 100-446080 (FBI Archives).
20. *Washington Post*, April 6, 1968, p. A16.
21. *New York Times*, April 6, 1968, p. 25.
22. Walter Fauntroy, Letitia Woods Brown Memorial Lecture, Thirty-fourth Annual Washington Studies Conference, Washington Historical Society, November 1, 2007. Author transcript.
23. *New York Times*, April 6, 1968, p. 25.
24. Ibid.
25. Author interview, Ramsey Clark, September 18, 2007.

26. Transcript, Ramsey Clark Oral History Interview IV, April 16, 1969, by Harri Baker, Internet copy, LBJ Library. http://www.lbjlib.utexas.edu/johnson/archives.hom/oralhistory.hom/ClarkR/clark-r4.pdf. Accessed February 9, 2008. Also, author interview, Roger Wilkins, July 31, 2007.

27. Transcript of press conference, April 5, 1968, Box 61, Ramsey Clark Papers, Lyndon Johnson Library and Museum.

28. Ibid.

29. Interview, Wilkins.

30. Michael K. Honey, *Going Down Jericho Road: The Memphis Strike, Martin Luther King's Last Campaign* (New York: W. W. Norton, 2007), pp. 452–453.

31. Transcript of Ramsey Clark press conference, 2:30 P.M., April 5, 1968. Box 61, Personal Papers of Ramsey Clark, Lyndon Johnson Library and Museum.

7.   "Once That Line Has Been Crossed"

1. Thomas Fletcher, interview transcript, Brookings Institution Archives.

2. Ben W. Gilbert, *Ten Blocks from the White House: Anatomy of the Washington Riots of 1968* (New York: Frederick A. Praeger, 1968), p. 45.

3. Author interview, Edward Smith, December 3, 2007.

4. Author interview, Tony Gittens, January 30, 2007.

5. Transcript, Michael Harris oral history interview, June 26, 1968, by Robert Martin, Moreland-Spingarn Library Archives, Howard University, p. 33.

6. Sophia F. McDowell, Gilbert A. Lowe Jr. and Doris A. Dockett, "Howard University's Student Protest Movement," *Public Opinion Quarterly* 34, no. 3 (Autumn 1970): 383–388.

7. *Washington Evening Star*, April 6, 1968, p. A22.

8. Gilbert, *Ten Blocks from the White House*, p. 63.

9. Witness statement, April 8, 1968, FBI Carmichael File, Series 100-446080 (FBI Archives).

10. Transcript, "Anonymous B" oral history interview, April 28, 1968, by James Mosby, Moreland-Spingarn Library Archives, Howard University, p. 31.

11. Gerald Horne, *Fire This Time: The Watts Uprising and the 1960s* (New York: Da Capo Press, 1997), p. 183.

12. Nicholas Lemann, *The Promised Land: The Great Black Migration and How It Changed America* (New York: Alfred A. Knopf, 1991), p. 6.

13. Ibid., p. 75.

14. Thomas J. Sugrue, *The Origins of the Urban Crisis: Race and Inequality in Postwar Detroit* (Princeton: Princeton University Press, 1996). Sugrue's prize-winning book is only one of many histories that upend our conventional thinking about urban decline; even a cursory bibliography would have to include Kenneth T. Jackson, *Crabgrass Frontier: The Suburbanization of the United States* (Oxford: Oxford University Press, 1985); Arnold R. Hirsch, *Making the Second Ghetto: Race & Housing in Chicago 1940–1960* (Chicago: University of Chicago Press, 1998); Kenneth D. Durr, *Behind the Backlash: White Working-Class Politics in Baltimore, 1940–1980* (Chapel Hill: The University of North Carolina Press, 2003); and Jon C. Teaford, *The Rough Road to Renaissance: Urban Revitalization in America, 1940–1985* (Baltimore: Johns Hopkins University Press, 1990).

15. Teaford, *The Rough Road to Renaissance*, table 3, p. 24.
16. Transcript, "Anonymous B" oral history interview, April 28, 1968, by James Mosby, Moreland-Spingarn Library Archives, Howard University, p. 21.
17. Claude Brown, *Manchild in the Promised Land* (New York: Macmillan, 1965), p. viii.
18. Gilbert, *Ten Blocks from the White House*, p. 41.
19. Ibid., pp. 49–50.
20. Seymour Spilerman, "The Causes of Racial Disturbances: A Comparison of Alternative Explanations," *American Sociological Review* 35, no. 4 (1970): 645.
21. Stanley Milgram, "The Perils of Obedience," *Harper's*, December 1973, pp. 62–77.
22. Transcript, "Anonymous A" oral history interview, April 26, 1968, by James Mosby, Moreland-Spingarn Library Archives, Howard University, p. 4.
23. Gilbert, *Ten Blocks from the White House*, p. 49.
24. Alex Poinsett, *Walking with Presidents: Louis Martin and the Rise of Black Political Power* (New York: Rowman and Littlefield, 2000), p. 167.
25. Horace Busby, *The Thirty-First of March: An Intimate Portrait of Lyndon Johnson's Final Days in Office* (New York: Farrar, Straus & Giroux, 2005), p. 238.
26. "Address to the Nation upon Proclaiming a Day of Mourning Following the Death of Dr. King, April 5, 1968," The American Presidency Project, www .presidency.ucsb.edu/ws/?pid=28783.
27. Joseph A. Califano Jr., *The Triumph and Tragedy of Lyndon Johnson: The White House Years* (New York: Simon & Schuster, 1991), p. 276.
28. "Letter to the Speaker of the House Urging Enactment of the Fair Housing Bill, April 5, 1968," The American Presidency Project, www.presidency.ucsb .edu/ws/?pid=28785.
29. Busby, *The Thirty-first of March*, pp. 239–241.

8. "Official Disorder on Top of Civil Disorder"

1. Interim report and letter to Thomas Fletcher, May 6, 1968. "Records Concerning the Brookings Study of the Washington, D.C., Riot," Brookings Institution Archives, Washington, D.C.
2. "The District of Columbia Fire Department's Role in the Civil Disturbances of April 4, 5, 6, 7, and 8, 1968." Washington Historical Society Archives.
3. "Transportation—Traffic," City Council Riot Report, Washington Historical Society Archives.
4. "Army Operations Center Report on the Events of April 4–17, 1968," Box 1, Entry 415, Record Group 319, National Archives.
5. See Vance's bio at http://www.state.gov/secretary/former/40811.htm. Vance's fix-it duties didn't stop after Johnson left office. Later in 1968 he joined Averell Harriman as the lead negotiators in the U.S.–Vietnamese peace talks in Paris. Vance was secretary of state under Jimmy Carter (until he resigned over the failed hostage rescue effort in Iran) and later oversaw the United Nations' negotiating efforts during the Balkan wars. He died in 2002.
6. "Final Report of Cyrus Vance, Special Assistant to the Secretary of Defense, Concerning the Detroit Riots," 1967. Box 56 (2 of 2), HU 2 Equality of the Races, White House Confidential Files, Lyndon Johnson Library and Museum.

7. Transcript, Cyrus R. Vance oral history interview 1, November 3, 1969, by Paige E. Mulhollan, Internet copy, Lyndon Johnson Library and Museum. http://www.lbjlib.utexas.edu/johnson/archives.hom/oralhistory.hom/Vance-C/ Vance1.pdf. Accessed February 12, 2008.

8. Transcript, "Anonymous A" oral history interview, April 26, 1968, by James Mosby, Moreland-Spingarn Library Archives, Howard University, pp. 12–13.

9. David O. Sears and John B. McConahay, "Participation in the Los Angeles Riots," *Social Problems* 17, no. 1 (Summer 1969): 3–20.

10. Ben W. Gilbert, *Ten Blocks from the White House: Anatomy of the Washington Riots of 1968* (New York: Frederick A. Praeger, 1968), pp. 227–235.

11. Ibid., pp. 140–141.

12. Transcript, "Anonymous A," p. 6.

13. *Washington Star*, April 7, 1968, p. A1.

14. Gilbert, *Ten Blocks from the White House,* pp. 53–54.

15. Transcript, "Anonymous A," p. 4.

16. *U.S. News & World Report*, April 22, 1968, pp. 32–33.

17. Ibid.

18. Gilbert, *Ten Blocks from the White House*, pp. 72–73.

19. Transcript, "Anonymous B" oral history interview, April 28, 1968, by James Mosby, Moreland-Spingarn Library Archives, Howard University, p. 14.

20. Gilbert, *Ten Blocks from the White House*, p. 87.

21. Author interview, Donald Mayhew, June 13, 2007.

22. Author interview, Larry Levinson, December 22, 2007.

23. Michael Flamm, *Law and Order: Street Crime, Civil Unrest, and the Crisis of Liberalism in the 1960s* (New York: Columbia University Press, 2005), p. 146.

24. Transcript, Warren Christopher oral history interview 3, December 2, 1968, by Thomas Baker, Lyndon Johnson Library and Museum, p. 5.

25. Interview with General Ralph Haines by the staff of Senator John McClellan, April 28, 1968, Box 21, Entry 415, Record Group 319, National Archives.

26. Transcript, Christopher, p. 6.

27. Letter from Walter Washington, Patrick Murphy, and Thomas Layton to Lyndon Johnson, April 5, 1968, Box 96, Appointment Files Diary Backup, Lyndon Johnson Library and Museum.

28. Author interview, Leroy Rhode, February 2, 2007.

29. Author interview, Paul Devrouax, February 7, 2007.

30. "Army Operations Center Report on the Events of April 4–17," August 13, 1968, Box 1, Entry 415, Record Group 319, National Archives.

31. *Washington Star*, April 7, 1968, p. A4.

32. "Army Operations Center Report on the Events of April 4–17."

9. The Occupation of Washington

1. Kenneth T. Jackson, *Crabgrass Frontier: The Suburbanization of the United States* (Oxford: Oxford University Press, 1985), pp. 209–213.

2. Ben W. Gilbert, *Ten Blocks from the White House: Anatomy of the Washington Riots of 1968* (New York: Frederick A. Praeger, 1968), p. 72.

3. *Washington Post*, April 6, 1968, p. A14.

4.   *U.S. News & World Report*, April 15, 1968, p. 8.
5.   *Chicago Tribune*, April 5, 1968, p. 12.
6.   *Washington Post*, April 6, 1968, p. A14.
7.   "Action Reports, Baltimore Police Department, from 0600 Hours, Friday, April 5, 1968, to 0600 Hours, Friday, April 12, 1968," University of Baltimore Online Archives, http://archives.ubalt.edu/bsr/archival.htm.
8.   Garry Wills, *The Second Civil War: Arming for Armageddon* (New York: New American Library, 1968), p. 41.
9.   Gilbert, *Ten Blocks from the White House*, pp. 109–110.
10. Ibid., pp. 83–85.
11. Ibid., pp. 84–85.
12. Ibid., p. 106.
13. Author interview, Leroy Rhode, February 2, 2007.
14. "Notes on Interview with Thomas Fletcher, Deputy Mayor, by Gilbert Steiner, April 13, 1968," Brookings Institution Archives.
15. Author interview, Roger Wilkins, July 31, 2007.
16. Author interview, Larry Levinson, December 21, 2007.
17. Michael Flamm, *Law and Order: Street Crime, Civil Unrest, and the Crisis of Liberalism in the 1960s* (New York: Columbia University Press, 2005), p. l46.
18. Author interview, Joseph Califano Jr., September 19, 2007.
19. Interview, Levinson.
20. *New York Times*, March 3, 1968, p. SM34.
21. Joseph A. Califano Jr., *The Triumph and Tragedy of Lyndon Johnson: The White House Years* (New York: Simon & Schuster, 1991), p. 279.
22. Flamm, *Law and Order*, p. 146.
23. Interview, Califano.
24. Harry Jaffe and Tom Sherwood, *Dream City: Race, Power, and the Decline of Washington, D.C.* (New York: Simon & Schuster, 1994), p. 80.
25. Gilbert, *Ten Blocks from the White House*, p. 102.
26. Secret Service Command Post Report, 4:00 A.M., April 6, 1968, Box 20, Equality of the Races, White House Confidential Files, Lyndon Johnson Library and Museum.
27. Details about Vance and Detroit from interview with Roger Wilkins, July 31, 2007.
28. Joseph A. Califano Jr., *The Triumph and Tragedy of Lyndon Johnson: The White House Years* (New York: Simon & Schuster, 1991), p. 279.

10.   "There Are No Ghettos in Chicago"

1.   *New York Times*, April 6, 1968, p. 1.
2.   Ibid., p. 22.
3.   J. Anthony Lukas, *Common Ground: A Turbulent Decade in the Lives of Three American Families* (New York: Vintage, 1986), pp. 32–35.
4.   Arthur M. Schlesinger Jr., *Robert Kennedy and His Times* (New York: Houghton Mifflin, 1978), p. 916.
5.   Remarks of Senator Robert F. Kennedy to the Cleveland City Club, Cleveland, Ohio, April 5, 1968. http://www.jfklibrary.org/Historical+Resources/Archives/Reference+Desk/Speeches/RFK/138RFK3SEN21SPEECHES_68APR05.htm. Retrieved March 31, 2008.

6. Vincent Cannato, *The Ungovernable City: John Lindsay and His Struggle to Save New York* (New York: Basic Books, 2001), pp. 210–214.

7. Ibid. Also, Gloria Steinem and Lloyd Weaver, "Special Report: The City on the Eve of Destruction," *New York*, April 22, 1968, p. 32E.

8. Transcript, "Anonymous A" oral history interview, April 26, 1968, by James Mosby, Moreland-Spingarn Library Archives, Howard University, pp. 16–17.

9. Mike Royko, *Boss: Richard J. Daley of Chicago* (New York: Plume, 1988), pp. 36–37.

10. Arnold R. Hirsch, *Making the Second Ghetto: Race & Housing in Chicago 1940–1960* (Chicago: University of Chicago Press, 1998), p. xv.

11. Nicholas Lemann, *The Promised Land: The Great Black Migration and How It Changed America* (New York: Alfred A. Knopf, 1991), p. 75.

12. Ibid.

13. Royko, *Boss*, pp. 167–170.

14. Ibid., p. 166.

15. Ibid., p. 134.

16. Adam Cohen and Elizabeth Taylor, *American Pharaoh: Mayor Richard J. Daley: His Battle for Chicago and the Nation* (Boston: Little, Brown, 2000), p. 441.

17. Ibid., p. 452.

18. Chicago Riot Study Committee, "Report of the Chicago Riot Study Committee to the Hon. Richard J. Daley" (1968), pp. 5–6.

19. Ibid., p. 24.

20. Committee, "Report of the Chicago Riot Study Committee to the Hon. Richard J. Daley," p. 11.

21. *Chicago Tribune*, April 6, 1968. p. 6.

22. Ibid., p. 1.

23. Committee, "Report of the Chicago Riot Study Committee to the Hon. Richard J. Daley," p. 53.

24. *Chicago Tribune*, April 6, 1968, p. 5.

25. *Chicago Daily Defender*, April 8, 1968, p. 14.

26. Committee, "Report of the Chicago Riot Study Committee to the Hon. Richard J. Daley," pp. 35–36.

27. Ibid., p. 36.

28. *Chicago Daily Defender*, April 9, 1968, p. 1.

29. Committee, "Report of the Chicago Riot Study Committee to the Hon. Richard J. Daley," p. 29.

30. Cohen and Taylor, *American Pharaoh*, p. 453.

31. Author interview, Harry McPherson, November 7, 2007.

32. *Chicago Tribune*, April 6, 1968, p. 1.

11. Roadblocks

1. "Army Operations Center Report on the Events of April 4–17, 1968," Box 1, Entry 415, Record Group 319, National Archives.

2. Ben W. Gilbert, *Ten Blocks from the White House: Anatomy of the Washington Riots of 1968* (New York: Frederick A. Praeger, 1968), p. 98.

3. Ibid., p. 102.

4. Secret Service Command Post report, 4 A.M., April 6, 1968. Box 20, HU2, Equality of the Races, White House Confidential Files, Lyndon Johnson Library and Museum.

5. Secret Service Command Post report, 12:00 P.M., April 6, 1968. Box 20, Equality of the Races, White House Confidential Files, Lyndon Johnson Library and Museum.

6. "Army Operations Center Report on the Events of April 4–17, 1968."

7. *Washington Post*, April 7, 1968, p. A1.

8. Joseph A. Califano Jr., *The Triumph and Tragedy of Lyndon Johnson: The White House Years* (New York: Simon & Schuster, 1991), p. 278.

9. Memo, Barefoot Sanders to Lyndon Johnson, April 5, 1968, Box 95, Appointment Files Diary Backup, Johnson Archives, Austin, Texas,

10. Memo, George Reedy to Lyndon Johnson, April 6, 1968, Box 7, HU 2, Equality of the Races, White House Confidential Files, Johnson Museum and Archives.

11. Memo, Jim Wirth to Lyndon Johnson, April 6, 1968, Box 7, HU 2, Equality of the Races, White House Confidential Files, Johnson Museum and Archives.

12. Memo, Arthur Krim to Horace Busby, April 5, 1968, Box 7, HU 2, Equality of the Races, White House Confidential Files, Johnson Museum and Archives.

13. Doris Kearns Goodwin, *Lyndon Johnson and the American Dream* (New York: Harper & Row, 1976), p. 4.

14. Harry McPherson, *A Political Education: A Washington Memoir* (Boston: Houghton Mifflin, 1988), p. 367.

15. Goodwin, *Lyndon Johnson and the American Dream*, p. 4.

16. McPherson, *A Political Education*, p. 367.

17. Author interview, Harry McPherson, November 7, 2007.

18. See *Washington Post*, April 7, 1968, p. A2.

19. See *Washington Evening Star*, April 7, 1968, p. A1.

20. *Wall Street Journal*, April 8, 1968, p. 1.

21. Memo from Barefoot Sanders to Joseph Califano, April 6, 1968, Box 96, Appointment Files Diary Backup, Lyndon Johnson Library and Museum.

22. Memo from Lou Schwartz to Walt Rostow, April 6, 1968, Box 96, Appointment Files Diary Backup, Lyndon Johnson Library and Museum.

23. Author interview, Joseph Califano, September 19, 2007.

24. Randall Wood, *LBJ: Architect of American Ambition* (New York: Free Press, 2007), p. 839.

25. Presidential Daily Diary, April 6, 1968. Lyndon Johnson Library and Museum. http://www.lbjlib.utexas.edu/johnson/archives.hom/diary/1968/680406.asp. Accessed April 4, 2008.

26. "Telegram from Acting Governor Shapiro to White House," April 6, 1968, Box 26, HU 2, Equality of the Races, White House Confidential Files, Lyndon Johnson Library and Museum.

27. Author interview, Bob Walton, March 28, 2008.

28. *Chicago Tribune*, April 7, 1968, p. 3.

29. Ibid., p. 9.

30. "Report Concerning the Civil Disorder in Chicago, April 6–April 11, 1968," Box 14, Warren Christopher Papers, Lyndon Johnson Library and Museum.

31. The thirty-six-square-mile Joliet Army Ammunition Plant, a primary source of TNT during the Vietnam War. As a personal aside, the author's father was based there as an Army ordnance engineer during the riots and recalled being ordered into battle dress uniform and distributed live ammunition as a precaution against a guerrilla assault on the facility.

32. Warren Christopher, *Chances of a Lifetime: A Memoir* (New York: Scribner, 2001), p. 59.

33. Califano, *The Triumph and Tragedy of Lyndon Johnson*, p. 280.

34. "Riot Data Review," prepared by the Lemberg Center for the Study of Violence, Brandeis University, Box 35, JL 3, White House Central Files, Lyndon Johnson Library and Museum.

35. "Report from USA Gus Diamond," April 6, 1968, 9:10 P.M. Box 72, Personal Papers of Ramsey Clark, Lyndon Johnson Library and Museum.

12. An Eruption in Baltimore

1. George H. Callcott, *Maryland and America 1940 to 1980* (Baltimore: Johns Hopkins University Press, 1985), p. 153.

2. Ibid., pp. 149–156.

3. While Brown's speech followed on an equally incendiary rally by the racist National States' Rights Party, he was quickly blamed for the violence and arrested.

4. Kenneth D. Durr, *Behind the Backlash: White Working-Class Politics in Baltimore, 1940–1980* (Chapel Hill: University of North Carolina Press, 2003), pp. 37–52.

5. Tom Carney oral history, December 5, 2006, by Alison Carney and Shannon Chorba, Langsdale Library Special Collections, University of Baltimore. http://archives.ubalt.edu/bsr/Tom%20Carney.pdf, accessed February 20, 2008.

6. Durr, *Behind the Backlash*, p. 91.

7. Ibid., p. 130.

8. Dan T. Carter, *The Politics of Rage: George Wallace, the Origins of the New Conservatism, and the Transformation of American Politics* (Baton Rouge: Louisiana, State University Press, 1995), p. 11.

9. Ibid., p. 215.

10. Jules Witcover, *White Knight: The Rise of Spiro Agnew* (New York: Random House, 1972), p. 4.

11. "Statement at Civil Rights Dinner at Pikesville Armory," May 4, 1964. Subseries 1.2, Spiro Agnew Papers, Special Collections, University of Maryland Libraries.

12. "Speech to Baltimore County Human Rights Commission," November 26, 1963. Subseries 1.2, Spiro Agnew Papers, Special Collections, University of Maryland Libraries.

13. "Statement to WTOP-TV," June 6, 1966. Subseries 1.2, Spiro Agnew Papers, Special Collections, University of Maryland Libraries.

14. *Baltimore Afro-American*, August 3, 1968.

15. *Baltimore North American*, May 11, 1968, p. 3-A.

16. Garry Wills, *Nixon Agonistes: The Crisis of the Self-Made Man* (Boston: Houghton Mifflin, 1970), p. 278.

17. Durr, *Behind the Backlash*, p. 68.

18. Rafael Cortada, "Baltimore's Ethnic Revival," in Laurence Krause, Lenora Heilig Nast, and R. C. Monk, eds., *Baltimore: A Living Renaissance* (Baltimore: Historic Baltimore Society, 1982), p. 64.

19. Cited in "Dorothy Pula Strohecker, "Tommys Two: The D'Alesandros," in ibid., p. 232.

20. Ibid.

21. Peter A. Jay, "Political History," in ibid., p. 147.

22. Durr, *Behind the Backlash*, p. 139.

23. D'Alesandro Oral History, Fraser Smith, May 2007, Langsdale Library Special Collections, University of Baltimore. http://archives.ubalt.edu/bsr/Mayor%20 Thomas%20D%27%20Alesandro%20III.pdf. Accessed April 10, 2008.

24. "Action Reports, Baltimore Police Department, from 0600 Hours, Friday, April 5, 1968, to 0600 Hours, Friday, April 12, 1968," University of Baltimore Online Archives, http://archives.ubalt.edu/bsr/archival.htm. Accessed April 10, 2008.

25. Ibid.

26. "Army Operations Center Report on Events of April 4–17," Box 1, Entry 415, Record Group 319, National Archives.

27. Mike Royko, *Boss: Richard J. Daley of Chicago* (New York: Plume, 1988), p. 167.

28. *Chicago Tribune*, April 8, 1968, p. 1.

29. Royko, *Boss*, p. 168.

30. *Chicago Tribune*, April 16, 1968, p. 1.

31. Royko, *Boss*, pp. 168–169.

32. Ibid., p. 164.

33. *Chicago Tribune*, April 18, 1968, p. 2.

34. Ibid., p.1

35. *Chicago Tribune*, April 7, 1968, p. 28.

36. *Chicago Tribune*, April 11, 1968, p. 20.

37. *Chicago Tribune* April 17, 1968, p. 1.

38. Box 68 and Box 72, Ramsey Clark Personal Papers, Lyndon Johnson Library and Museum.

13. Palm Sunday

1. Author interview, Peter Edelman, January 30, 2008.

2. David Maraniss, *First in His Class: A Biography of Bill Clinton* (New York: Simon & Schuster, 1995), pp. 108–109.

3. *Washington Evening Star*, April 7, 1968, p. A1.

4. *Washington Star*, April 8, 1968, p. B4.

5. Jean Stein and George Plimpton, eds., *American Journey: The Times of Robert Kennedy* (New York: Harcourt Brace Jovanovich, 1970), p. 261.

6. Jules Witcover, *The Year the Dream Died: Revisiting 1968 in America* (New York: Warner Books, 1997), p. 158.

7. For route, see Sixth Armored Calvary Regiment Field Report, April 7, Box 22, Entry 415, Record Group 319, National Archives.

8. President's Daily Diary, April 7, 1968. http://www.lbjlib.utexas.edu/johnson/archives.hom/diary/1968/680407.asp.

9. *Washington Star*, April 8, 1968, p. B4.

10. Ibid.

11. "Parafield," April 7, 1968, Box 22, Entry 415, Record Group 319, National Archives.

12. "Statement by General William Westmoreland, April 7, 1968," Box 95, Appointment Files Diary Backup, Lyndon Johnson Library and Museum.

13. President's Daily Diary.

14. *New York Times*, April 8, 1968, p. 38.

15. Paul J. Scheips, *The Role of Federal Military Forces in Domestic Disorders, 1945–1992* (Washington, D.C.: Center of Military History, 2005), pp. 320–321.

16. John Darlington oral history, Langsdale Library Special Collections, University of Baltimore. http://archives.ubalt.edu/bsr/darlington.pdf. Accessed April 7, 2008.

17. Garry Wills, *The Second Civil War: Arming for Armageddon* (New York: New American Library, 1968), p. 39.

18. Quoted in ibid.

19. James W. Button, *Black Violence: Political Impact of the 1960s Riots* (Princeton, N.J.: Princeton University Press, 1978), p. 129.

20. "Timeline by Sgt. Bobby Brown, Southern District." Retrieved from http://mysite.verizon.net/vzesdp09/baltimorepolicehistorybywmhackley2/id76.html. Accessed April 28, 2008.

21. John Darlington oral history.

22. Gerard Gassinger oral history, Langsdale Library Special Collections, University of Baltimore. http://archives.ubalt.edu/bsr/gassinger.pdf. Accessed April 7, 2008.

23. Kenneth D. Durr, *Behind the Backlash: White Working-Class Politics in Baltimore, 1940–1980* (Chapel Hill: University of North Carolina Press, 2003), p. 141.

24. Jack Bowden oral history, Langsdale Library Special Collections, University of Baltimore. http://archives.ubalt.edu/bsr/bowden-white.pdf. Accessed April 7, 2008.

25. Frank Bressler oral history, Langsdale Library Special Collections, University of Baltimore. http://archives.ubalt.edu/bsr/frank%20bressler.pdf. Accessed April 7, 2008.

26. "Baltimore Police After-Action Report," Langsdale Library Special Collections, University of Baltimore. http://archives.ubalt.edu/bsr/baltimore%20police%20reports.pdf. Accessed April 28, 2008.

27. "After-Action Report, Baltimore, by Major General Melvin Zais," Box 3, Entry 319, Record Group 415, National Archives.

28. Scheips, *The Role of Federal Military Forces*, pp. 320–321.

29. Ibid., pp. 325–326.

30. Joseph A. Califano Jr., *The Triumph and Tragedy of Lyndon Johnson: The White House Years* (New York: Simon & Schuster, 1991), p. 281.

14. Bluff City on Edge

1. *Chicago Tribune*, April 11, 1968, p. 24.

2. Ibid.

3. "Army Operations Center Report on Events of April 4–17," Box 1, Entry 415, Record Group 319, National Archives.

4. *Chicago Tribune*, April 8, 1968, p. 1.

5. Ibid., p. 11.

6. *Chicago Tribune*, April 7, 1968, p. 6.

7. *Chicago Tribune*, April 8, 1968, p. 1.

8. John J. Peterson, *Into the Cauldron* (Clinton, Md.: Clavier House, 1973), pp. 139–140.

9. Paul J. Scheips, *The Role of Federal Military Forces in Domestic Disorders, 1945–1992* (Washington, D.C.: Center of Military History, 2005), pp. 320–332.

10. Transcript of press conference, Fred Vinson, April 8, 1968, 8:20 P.M., Box 26, HU 2, Equality of the Races, White House Confidential Files, Lyndon Johnson Library and Museum.

11. Scheips, *The Role of Federal Military Forces*, p. 329.

12. Ibid.

13. Cited in ibid., p. 333.

14. *New York Times*, April 5, 1968, p. 1.

15. *New York Times*, April 7, 1968, p. 3.

16. Cited in Michael K. Honey, *Going Down Jericho Road: The Memphis Strike, Martin Luther King's Last Campaign* (New York: W. W. Norton, 2007), p. 439.

17. "After-Action Report, Personal Liaison of the Chief of Staff, Memphis, 7–9 April," Box 3, Entry 415, Record Group 319, National Archives.

18. Honey, *Going Down Jericho Road*, p. 443.

19. Ibid., p. 444.

20. *Washington Star*, April 6, 1968, p A2.

21. Honey, *Going Down Jericho Road*, p. 462.

22. *Washington Star*, April 4, 1968, p. A5.

23. Honey, *Going Down Jericho Road*, p. 476.

24. *New York Times*, April 7, 1968, p. 65.

25. Author interview, Steven Ober, April 23, 2008.

26. Honey, *Going Down Jericho Road*, p. 480.

27. *New York Times*, April 9, 1968, p. 34.

28. *Washington Evening Star*, April 7, 1968, p. A1.

29. *Washington Post*, April 9, 1968, p. A1.

30. Harry McPherson, *A Political Education: A Washington Memoir* (Boston: Houghton Mifflin, 1988), p. 369.

31. Nick Kotz, *Judgment Days: Lyndon Baines Johnson, Martin Luther King Jr., and the Laws That Changed America* (New York: Mariner Books, 2006), p. 418.

32. See *New York Times*, April 12, 1968, p. 1.

33. Author interview, Jim Gaither, December 10, 2007.

34. Lyndon Baines Johnson, *The Vantage Point: Perspectives of the Presidency 1963–1969* (New York: Holt, Rinehart, & Winston, 1971), p. 178.

35. *New York Times*, April 5, 1968, p. A2.

36. *New York Times*, April 6, 1968, p. 25.

37. *Washington Star*, April 9, 1968, p. A22.

38. *Chicago Tribune*, April 7, 1968, p. 7.

39. Lewis Gould, *1968: The Election That Changed America* (New York: Ivan R. Dee, 1993), p. 64.

40. Kotz, *Judgment Days*, p. 419.

41. *New York Times*, April 9, 1968., p. 38.

42. Secret Service Command Post report, April 8, 1968, Box 95, Appointment Files Diary Backup, Lyndon Johnson Library and Museum.

43. SR Report, April 8, 1968, 11:00 P.M., Box 8, HU 2, Equality of the Races, White House Confidential Files. Lyndon Johnson Library and Museum.

44. Memo from Intelligence Unit, April 8, 1968, Box 72, Ramsey Clark Papers, Lyndon Johnson Library and Museum.

45. "Army Operations Center Report on Events of April 4–17," Box 1, Entry 415, Record Group 319, National Archives.

46. Memo to Marvin Watson, April 8, 1968, 9:20 P.M., Box 22, HU 2, Equality of the Races, White House Confidential Files. Lyndon Johnson Library and Museum.

47. Transcript of phone call, April 9, 1968, Box 14, Warren Christopher Papers, Lyndon Johnson Library and Museum.

15.   A Country Rent Asunder

1. *New York Times*, April 10, 1968, p. 35.

2. Ibid., p. 1.

3. Ibid.

4. *Chicago Tribune*, April 9, 1968, p. A5.

5. Ibid., p. 1.

6. *New York Times*, April 10, 1968, p. 10.

7. Roger Wilkins, *A Man's Life: An Autobiography* (New York: Simon & Schuster, 1982), p. 214.

8. *New York Times*, April 9, 1968, p. 1.

9. Author interview, Roger Wilkins, July 31, 2008.

10. Ibid.

11. Lyndon Baines Johnson, *The Vantage Point: Perspectives of the Presidency 1963–1969* (New York: Holt, Rinehart, & Winston, 1971), p. 176.

12. Wilkins, *A Man's Life*, p. 215.

13. *New York Times*, April 10, 1968, p. 33.

14. FBI Carmichael Papers, Series 100-446080, FBI Archives.

15. *New York Times*, April 10, 1968, p. 33.

16. Ibid.

17. Ibid., p. 34.

18. Wilkins, *A Man's Life*, p. 213.

19. *Chicago Tribune*, April 10, 1968, p. 1.

20. Thurston Clarke, *The Last Campaign: Robert F. Kennedy and 82 Days that Inspired America* (New York: Henry Holt, 2008), p. 131.

21. Arthur M. Schlesinger Jr., *Robert Kennedy and His Times* (New York: Houghton Mifflin, 1978), p. 917.

22. *New York Times*, April 10, 1968, p. 1.

23. Charles Gorman, "Ilus Davis: Exemplar of 'The Greatest Generation,'" delivered as the Charles N. Kimball Lecture at the Western Historical Manuscript Collection,

Kansas City, April 24, 2000. www.umkc.edu/whmckc/PUBLICATIONS/ KIMBALL/CNKPDF/Gorman-04-24-2000.pdf. Accessed February 24, 2008.

24. Department of Justice Interdivision Information Unit Weekly Report, Kansas City, Missouri, April 18, 1968, by William Kitchen, Box 60, Ramsey Clark Personal Papers, Lyndon Johnson Library and Museum.

25. Ibid.

26. *Chicago Tribune*, April 11, 1968, p. N1.

27. *New York Times*, April 11, 1968, p. A1.

28. *Washington Post*, April 10, 1968, p. A1.

29. Doris Kearns Goodwin, *Lyndon Johnson and the American Dream* (New York: Harper & Row, 1976), p. 340.

30. Memo from Califano to Johnson, April 10, 1968, Box 56, HU 2, Equality of the Races, White House Confidential File, Lyndon Johnson Library and Museum.

31. Goodwin, *Lyndon Johnson and the American Dream*, p. 305.

16. Two Speeches

1. Transcript of "The Brookings Institution Seminar on District of Columbia Riot," May 20, 1968, Brookings Institution Archives.

2. Lady Bird Johnson, *A White House Diary* (New York: Holt, Rinehart, & Winston, 1970).

3. "April 10 Visit of Klaus," Folder, Box 95, Appointment Files Diary Backup, Lyndon Johnson Library and Museum.

4. *Washington Post*, April 11, 1968, p. F1.

5. Secret Service Command Post report, April 8, 1968, Box 20, HU 2, Equality of the Races, White House Confidential Files, Lyndon Johnson Library and Museum.

6. "News Release from the Office of Gov. Spiro T. Agnew," April 6, 1968, Box 3, Series 2.3, Spiro Agnew Papers, Special Collections, University of Maryland Libraries.

7. "News Release from the Office of Gov. Spiro T. Agnew," July 31, 1967, Box 2, Series 2.3, Spiro Agnew Papers, Special Collections, University of Maryland Libraries.

8. "News Release from the Office of Gov. Spiro T. Agnew," April 6, 1968, Box 3, Series 2.3, Spiro Agnew Papers, Special Collections, University of Maryland Libraries.

9. Garry Wills, *Nixon Agonistes: The Crisis of the Self-Made Man* (Boston: Houghton Mifflin, 1970), p. 282.

10. Jules Witcover, *The Year the Dream Died: Revisiting 1968 in America* (New York: Warner Books, 1997), p. 163.

11. Jules Witcover, *White Knight: The Rise of Spiro Agnew* (New York: Random House, 1972), pp. 10–14. In *Nixon Agonistes*, Wills notes that Agnew was so personally involved with the Bowie State affair that even his special assistant for education and his sole black aide did not know about it, p. 287.

12. Transcript, Thomas D'Alesandro III oral history, Fraser Smith, May 2007, Langsdale Library Special Collections, University of Baltimore. http://archives.

ubalt.edu/bsr/Mayor%20Thomas%20D%27%20Alesandro%20III.pdf. Accessed April 10, 2008.

13. Wills, *Nixon Agonistes*, pp. 288–289.

14. Witcover, *The Year the Dream Died*, p. 164.

15. Witcover, *White Knight*, p. 28.

16. Carmichael was indeed in Baltimore that day, but it is not clear that he met with anyone. George Collins, editor of the *Baltimore Afro-American*, told the *Sun* that Carmichael had spent the afternoon with a friend and at his newspaper's offices before returning to Washington that evening. *Baltimore Sun*, April 12, 1968, p. 1.

17. Wills, *Nixon Agonistes*, p. 291.

18. *Baltimore Sun*, April 12, 1968. No page number given. Copy can be found in Box 3, Series 2.1, Spiro Agnew Papers, Special Collections, University of Maryland Libraries.

19. *Bethesda-Chevy Chase Tribune*, April 19, 1968, p. 4.

20. *Catoctin Enterprise*, April 19, 1968. No page number given. Copy can be found in Box 3, Series 2.1, Spiro Agnew Papers, Special Collections, University of Maryland Libraries.

21. *Suburban Record*, April 19, 1968, p. 4. Copy can be found in Box 3, Series 2.1, Spiro Agnew Papers, Special Collections, University of Maryland Libraries.

22. *Baltimore Sun*, April 12, 1968, p. A1.

23. *Washington Post*, May 1, 1968, p. B4.

24. *Washington Star*, April 25, 1968, p. A13.

25. For details of passage and signing, see *Washington Post*, April 11, 1968, p. A1. For text of speech and other details, see *New York Times*, April 12, 1968, p. 18.

17. A Summer Postscript

1. All data from Permanent Subcommittee on Investigations of the Committee on Government Operations, *Aftermath of Riots, Washington, D.C., and Newark, N.J.*, 91st Cong., May 27, 1969, p. 3162.

2. Ibid.

3. Ibid., Testimony of Deputy Mayor Thomas Fletcher, p. 3236. That morning Sam Starobin, the District's director of the Department of General Services, read Fletcher's testimony because the deputy mayor had lost his voice.

4. Report of City Council Public Hearings on the Rebuilding and Recovery of Washington, D.C., from the Civil Disturbances of April 1968, p. 8, Washington Historical Society.

5. Harry Jaffe and Tom Sherwood, *Dream City: Race, Power, and the Decline of Washington, D.C.* (New York: Simon & Schuster, 1994). p. 86.

6. Ibid., p. 7.

7. Committee on the District of Columbia, *Civil Disturbances in Washington*, 90th Cong., 2nd sess., May 15 and May 16, 1968, p. 75.

8. Ibid., p. 70.

9. Bettye K. Eidson, "White Public Opinion in an Age of Disorder," in David Boesel and Peter Rossi, eds., *Cities under Siege: An Anatomy of the Ghetto Riots, 1964–1968* (New York: Basic Books, 1971), p. 389.

10. James W. Button, *Black Violence: Political Impact of the 1960s Riots* (Princeton, N.J.: Princeton University Press, 1978), p. 134.
11. *Washington Post*, May 24, 1968, p. B4.
12. *Washington Post*, June 6, 1968, p. D23.
13. *New York Times*, April 30, 1968, p. 35.
14. *New York Times*, April 15, 1968, p. 63.
15. *Chain Store Age*, May 1968, pp. 40–41.
16. *Modern Manufacturing*, June 1968, pp. 88–93.
17. Author interview, Ramsey Clark, September 19, 2007.
18. "Army Civil Disturbance Intelligence Activities," January 23, 1971, Box 27, Record Group 319, Entry 415, National Archives. The report adds regarding Justice's intelligence unit, "Each time the idea of intelligence comes up, the thought is to continue to get as much information as possible so that there will be an early warning system; Justice is handed the ball to coordinate the intelligence effort. In each case the ball is fumbled by Justice and the Army goes merrily on improving its capabilities. . . . The Inter-Divisional Informational Unit, as I mentioned earlier, was a laugh. It was headed by a man named Jim Devine, who was neither smart nor efficient."
19. Memo from Lieutenant Colonel Ross Goddard to Army Chief of Plans Division, August 23, 1968, Box 9, Record Group 319, Entry 415, National Archives. While recognizing the illegal nature of wiretapping, Goddard wrote that because the police would conduct any actual arrests, "There would therefore be no need to disclose the results of monitoring to anyone outside the army."
20. *New York Times*, January 18, 1971, p. 1.
21. Minutes from civil disorder meeting, April 18, 1968, Box 4, Record Group 319, Entry 415, National Archives.
22. Memo from George Mather to Army Vice Chief of Staff office, June 22, 1968, Box 1, Record Group 319, Entry 415, National Archives.
23. "Army Civil Disturbance Intelligence Activities," January 23, 1971, Box 27, Record Group 319, Entry 415, National Archives.
24. Army internal memo, February 19, 1968, Box 1, Record Group 319, Entry 415, National Archives.
25. Memo from General Ralph Yarbrough to Army Chief of Staff office, March 8, 1968, Box 1, Record Group 319, Entry 415, National Archives.
26. Jonathan Simon, *Governing through Crime: How the War on Crime Transformed American Democracy and Created a Culture of Fear* (Oxford: Oxford University Press, 2007), p. 8.
27. *Time*, May 31, 1968, pp. 14–15.
28. Author interview, Adrienne Israel, February 1, 2007.
29. Republican National Committee press release, July 24, 1967, Box 14, Campaign 1968 Research Files, Richard Nixon Library and Birthplace Foundation.
30. Televised address, March 7, 1968, Box 1, Campaign Literature, Richard Nixon Library and Birthplace Foundation.
31. *Time*, May 3, 1968, p. 21.
32. Ibid.
33. *U.S. News & World Report*, May 13, 1968, pp. 52–53.

34. *U.S. News & World Report*, June 3, 1968, pp. 52–53.

35. Lewis Gould, *1968: The Election That Changed America* (Chicago: Ivan R. Dee, 1993), p. 140.

36. Nomination acceptance speech at the Republican National Convention, August 8, 1968, Box 95, Speeches, Richard Nixon Library and Birthplace Foundation.

37. Matthew Lassiter, *The Silent Majority: Conservative Politics in the Sunbelt South* (Princeton, N.J.: Princeton University Press, 2005), p. 304.

38. "Speech to the American Society for Industrial Security," May 9, 1968, Box 4, Series 2.3, Spiro Agnew Papers, Special Collections, Library of the University of Maryland-College Park.

39. Jules Witcover, *White Knight: The Rise of Spiro Agnew* (New York: Random House, 1972), p. 214.

40. Theodore H. White, *The Making of the President 1968* (New York: Atheneum, 1969), p. 433.

41. *Time*, August 23, 1968, p. 7.

42. Witcover, *White Knight*, p. 282.

18. 1969 and After

1. *Chicago Daily Defender*, January 21, 1969, p. 4. *New York Times*, January 21, 1969, p. 23.

2. *Chicago Tribune*, January 21, 1969, p. 6.

3. *Washington Post*, February 1, 1969, p. A1.

4. Permanent Subcommittee on Investigations of the Committee on Government Operations, *Aftermath of Riots, Washington, D.C., and Newark, N.J.*, 91st Cong., May 27, 1969, p. 3240.

5. *U.S. News & World Report*, May 6, 1968, p. 10.

6. Permanent Subcommittee, *Aftermath of Riots*, p. 3231.

7. *Washington Post*, June 18, 1995, p. A1.

8. http://www.bea.gov/newsreleases/regional/spi/2008/pdf/spi0308.pdf. Accessed April 1, 2008.

9. For HIV/AIDS rates see *Washington Post*, August 10, 2005, p. B5. For unemployment, refer to March 2007 Bureau of Labor Statistics unemployment report. For poverty rate, see "D.C.'s Two Economies: Many Residents Are Falling Behind," D.C. Fiscal Policy Report, October 24, 2007. http://dcfpi.org/?p=120. Accessed April 22, 2008.

10. "Planning for Quality Schools: Meeting the Needs of District Families," March 2008. p. 4. http://www.21csf.org/csf-home/publications/planningquali tyschools2008/QualitySchoolsPhaseOneReportMarch2008.pdf. Accessed April 25, 2008.

11. *Chicago Tribune*, March 30, 1969, p. 3.

12. *New Republic*, June 11, 1966, p. 15.

13. *New Republic*, May 4, 1968, pp. 10–11.

14. Letter from Gerard "Jerry" Gassinger to his children, no date. University of Baltimore Special Collections, University of Baltimore. http://archives.ubalt .edu/bsr/gassinger.pdf. Accessed April 22, 2008.

15. Frank Bressler oral history, Langsdale Library Special Collections, University of Baltimore. http://archives.ubalt.edu/bsr/frank%20bressler.pdf. Accessed April 7, 2008.

16. Kevin M. Kruse, *White Flight: Atlanta and the Making of Modern Conservatism* (Princeton, N.J.: Princeton University Press, 2005), p. 235.

17. Norman Mailer, *Miami and the Siege of Chicago* (New York: Signet, 1968), p. 51.

18. *U.S. News & World Report*, April 22, 1968, p. 71.

19. James W. Button, *Black Violence: Political Impact of the 1960s Riots* (Princeton, N.J.: Princeton University Press, 1978), pp. 52 and 101.

20. Sar Levitan, Garth L. Magnum, and Robert Taggart III, *Economic Opportunity in the Ghetto: The Partnership of Government and Business* (Baltimore: Johns Hopkins University Press, 1970), p. 74.

21. Kruse, *White Flight*, pp. 256–257.

22. James R. Gardner, "The Civil Disturbance Mission of the Department of the Army, 1963–1973: An Analysis of Perceptions, Policies, and Programs" (dissertation, Princeton University, 1977), pp. 221–222.

23. John T. Elliff, *Crime, Dissent, and the Attorney General* (Beverly Hills, Calif: Sage, 1971), p. 127.

24. Ibid., p. 152.

25. See, for example, Karl E. Campbell, *Senator Sam Ervin, Last of the Founding Fathers* (Chapel Hill: University of North Carolina Press, 2007). Also see Sanford J. Ungar, *FBI: An Uncensored Look Behind the Walls* (Boston: Little, Brown, 1976) and David Wise, *The American Police State* (New York: Random House, 1976).

26. Gardner, "The Civil Disturbance Mission of the Department of the Army," p. 227.

27. Campbell, *Senator Sam Ervin*, p. 250.

28. *New York Times*, March 10, 1971, p. 1.

Index